"This comprehensive guide transforms how we think about talent in circular supply chains, offering practical frameworks for the skills that organizations need to thrive in this new paradigm. The capability assessment tools provide an invaluable roadmap for building the workforce that will lead tomorrow's regenerative economy."
David Watson, Managing Director, RL People

"A groundbreaking exploration of how technology enables circular transformation of supply chains, with real-world examples that bridge theory and practice. The maturity models for digital enablement provide technical leaders with clear pathways to support circular innovation while delivering measurable business value."
Gerald Jackson, Vice President Supply Chain Product Strategy, Oracle

"This essential guide brings the community dimension of circular supply chains to life through practical frameworks and actionable insights. By mapping capabilities across people, process, and technology, it provides the roadmap organizations need to create circular systems that benefit both business and society."
John Holm, Convening Partner, Circular Supply Chain Coalition, and Visiting Faculty, Sustainability MBA Program, Bard College

"Bridges academic theory with real-world application, making it an essential read for anyone interested in circular supply chain management. With the capability framework, the book addresses the critical challenges of circular supply chains and provides a common language for advancing circular operations."
Dr. Dennis A. Vegter, Researcher and Lecturer, NHL Stenden University

"An essential resource for industry and retail executives exploring the future of the circular economy. It provides clear insights that connect every part of the industrial ecosystem. By breaking down the specific skills, processes, and technologies required, Deborah Dull accelerates every reader's ability to generate significant value from rapidly emerging circular value chains."
Scot Case, retail sustainability and circularity strategist

"Brilliantly expands our understanding of reverse logistics by mapping the full spectrum of capabilities needed for truly circular supply chains. The maturity models offer organizations clear pathways to transform their operations while creating value through every stage of the product lifecycle."
Rich Bulger, author of *Going Circular*

"A landmark contribution that aligns with ASCM's work on circular supply chain standards. By mapping the capabilities across people, process, technology, metrics, and governance for orchestrating alignment, this book provides practitioners with exactly what they need to implement and scale circular operations."
Douglas Kent, Executive Vice President of Corporate and Strategic Alliances, ASCM

"A groundbreaking work that elevates standards from technical footnotes to strategic enablers of circular transformation. The capability frameworks provide organizations with clear pathways to implement standardized approaches that build trust while accelerating material flows across industry boundaries."
Vivian Tai, Director of Innovation, GS1 US

"An invaluable resource that bridges academic insights with practical implementation, providing exactly what regions need to develop circular manufacturing capabilities. The structured maturity models offer educational institutions and industry partners a shared framework for building the skills and systems that power local circular economies."
Ian McClure, Executive Director, GAME Change

"Deborah Dull brings fun and reality to circular supply chain learning. The real-life examples with practical approaches to achieving industrial circularity transform abstract concepts into concrete capabilities."
Brijesh Krishnan, Circular Economy Leader, Cummins

"A timely analysis of how platforms can boost circular supply chains at scale, supported by capability frameworks that organizations can implement today. The practical assessment tools make this an indispensable guide for anyone seeking to build the collaborative systems we need to power circular economies."
Peter Evans, Circular Tech Advisor and Co-Chair, MIT Platform Strategy Summit

Circular Supply Chains
*How to Build the Future
of Sustainable Operations*

Deborah Dull

KoganPage

Publisher's note
Every possible effort has been made to ensure that the information contained in this book is accurate at the time of going to press, and the publishers and author cannot accept responsibility for any errors or omissions, however caused. No responsibility for loss or damage occasioned to any person acting, or refraining from action, as a result of the material in this publication can be accepted by the editor, the publisher or the author.

First published in Great Britain and the United States in 2025 by Kogan Page Limited

All rights reserved. No part of this publication may be reproduced, stored or transmitted by any means without prior written permission from Kogan Page, except as permitted under applicable copyright laws.

Kogan Page
Kogan Page Ltd, 2nd Floor, 45 Gee Street, London EC1V 3RS, United Kingdom
Kogan Page Inc, 8 W 38th Street, Suite 902, New York, NY 10018, USA
www.koganpage.com

EU Representative (GPSR)
Authorised Rep Compliance Ltd, Ground Floor, 71 Baggot Street Lower, Dublin D02 P593, Ireland
www.arccompliance.com

Kogan Page books are printed on paper from sustainable forests.

© Deborah Dull, 2025

The moral rights of the author have been asserted in accordance with the Copyright, Designs and Patents Act 1988.

ISBNs
Hardback   978 1 3986 2068 1
Paperback   978 1 3986 2067 4
Ebook   978 1 3986 2069 8

British Library Cataloguing-in-Publication Data
A CIP record for this book is available from the British Library.

Library of Congress Control Number
2025009766

Typeset by Integra Software Services, Pondicherry
Print production managed by Jellyfish
Printed and bound by CPI Group (UK) Ltd, Croydon CR0 4YY

CONTENTS

About the author xi

PART ONE
Forming Circular Supply Chains from Key Concepts 1

Introduction 3

01 **Events Leading to Today's Economy** 5
The Origin Story of the Linear Economy 5
From Depression to Obsession 6
The War Machine and the Consumer Dream 7
The Mad Men Era 7
The Oil Crisis 8
Reaganomics and Thatcherism 9
The Rise of Global Trade 10
The Digital Revolution 10
The Great Recession 11
The Smartphone 11
The Pandemic 12
The Circular Economy: A New Hope 12
Notes 13

02 **The Pioneers of Circular Thinking** 17
Walter Stahel 17
McDonough and Braungart 18
Ellen MacArthur 19
Kate Raworth 20
Janine Benyus 20
Gunter Pauli 21
The Power of Many Minds 22
Patagonia 22
Interface 23

Renault 23
Philips 24
The Road Ahead 24
Notes 25

03 **Where Circular Economy Meets Supply Chain** 27
Business Models 28
Materials 30
Operations 32
Market Dynamics 34
Strategy 36
Connections into Predictions 37
Notes 37

04 **Building Tomorrow's Circular Supply Chain** 39
The Path to the Future 39
Defining the Path 41
People and Culture Capabilities 42
Process Capabilities 45
Technology Capabilities 48
Industry Standards Capabilities 51
Governance Capabilities 54

PART TWO
The Capability to Repair at Scale 57

Fictional Example: The Repair Revolution 57

05 **People and Culture Capabilities: Repairing at Scale** 61
Circular Leadership to Repair at Scale 61
New Circular Supply Chain Roles to Repair at Scale 67
Continuous Learning Culture to Repair at Scale 72

06 **Process Capabilities: Orchestrating Circular Flows to Repair at Scale** 79
The Circular Value Stream to Repair at Scale 79
Smart Recovery Protocols to Repair at Scale 84
Resource Optimization to Repair at Scale 90

07   Technology Capabilities: Digital Enablement to Repair at Scale 96

Digital Product Memory to Repair at Scale 96
Predictive Recovery Intelligence to Repair at Scale 102
Network Optimization Platform to Repair at Scale 107

08   Industry Standards Capabilities: Common Language for Circularity to Repair at Scale 113

Multi-Life Performance Metrics to Repair at Scale 113
Digital Interoperability to Repair at Scale 119
Ecosystem Collaboration Protocols to Repair at Scale 124

09   Governance Capabilities: Ensuring Circular Success to Repair at Scale 130

Value-Sharing Mechanisms to Repair at Scale 131
Quality Assurance Through Multiple Lives to Repair at Scale 136
Continuous Evolution to Repair at Scale 142

PART THREE
The Capability to Manufacture In-Market 149

Fictional Example: Global to Local 149

10   People and Culture Capabilities: Manufacturing In-Market 153

Circular Leadership to Manufacture In-Market 153
New Circular Supply Chain Roles to Manufacture
    In-Market 159
Continuous Learning Culture to Manufacture
    In-Market 164

11   Process Capabilities: Orchestrating Circular Flows to Manufacture In-Market 170

The Circular Value Stream to Manufacture In-Market 170
Smart Recovery Protocols to Manufacture In-Market 176
Resource Optimization to Manufacture In-Market 181

12 **Technology Capabilities: Digital Enablement to Manufacture In-Market** 187

Digital Product Memory to Manufacture In-Market 187
Predictive Recovery Intelligence to Manufacture
In-Market 192
Network Orchestration Platform to Manufacture
In-Market 197

13 **Standards Capabilities: Common Language for Circularity to Manufacture In-Market** 203

Multi-Life Performance Metrics to Manufacture
In-Market 203
Digital Interoperability to Manufacture In-Market 208
Ecosystem Collaboration Protocols to Manufacture
In-Market 214

14 **Governance Capabilities: Ensuring Circular Success to Manufacture In-Market** 220

Value-Sharing Mechanisms to Manufacture In-Market 220
Quality Assurance Through Multiple Lives to Manufacture
In-Market 225
Continuous Evolution to Manufacture In-Market 231

PART FOUR
The Capability to Circulate Locally 237

Fictional Example: The Urban Mining Revolution 237

15 **People and Culture Capabilities: Circulating Locally** 239

Circular Leadership to Circulate Locally 239
New Circular Supply Chain Roles to Circulate Locally 244
Continuous Learning Culture to Circulate Locally 249

16 **Process Capabilities: Orchestrating Circular Flows to Circulate Locally** 255

The Circular Value Stream to Circulate Locally 255
Smart Recovery Protocols to Circulate Locally 260
Resource Optimization to Circulate Locally 265

17   Technology Capabilities: Digital Enablement
       to Circulate Locally 271

       Digital Product Memory to Circulate Locally 271
       Predictive Recovery Intelligence to Circulate Locally 276
       Network Orchestration Platform to Circulate Locally 281

18   Standards Capabilities: Common Language for Circularity
       to Circulate Locally 287

       Multi-Life Performance Metrics to Circulate Locally 287
       Digital Interoperability to Circulate Locally 292
       Ecosystem Collaboration Protocols to Circulate Locally 297

19   Governance Capabilities: Ensuring Circular Success
       to Circulate Locally 303

       Value-Sharing Mechanisms to Circulate Locally 303
       Quality Assurance Through Multiple Lives to Circulate Locally 309
       Continuous Evolution to Circulate Locally 314

       PART FIVE
       The Capability to Collaborate Transparently 321

       Fictional Example: The Transparency Revolution 321

20   People and Culture Capabilities: Collaborating
       Transparently 325

       Circular Leadership to Collaborate Transparently 325
       New Circular Supply Chain Roles to Collaborate Transparently 331
       Continuous Learning Culture to Collaborate Transparently 336

21   Process Capabilities: Orchestrating Circular Flows
       to Collaborate Transparently 341

       The Circular Value Stream to Collaborate Transparently 341
       Smart Recovery Protocols to Collaborate Transparently 346
       Resource Optimization to Collaborate Transparently 351
       Notes 357

22   **Technology Capabilities: Digital Enablement to Collaborate Transparently** 358

Digital Product Memory to Collaborate Transparently 358
Predictive Recovery Intelligence to Collaborate Transparently 363
Network Orchestration Platform to Collaborate Transparently 368

23   **Standards Capabilities: Common Language for Circularity to Collaborate Transparently** 374

Multi-Life Performance Metrics to Collaborate Transparently 374
Digital Interoperability to Collaborate Transparently 379
Ecosystem Collaboration Protocols to Collaborate Transparently 383

24   **Governance Capabilities: Ensuring Circular Success to Collaborate Transparently** 389

Value-Sharing Mechanisms to Collaborate Transparently 389
Quality Assurance Through Multiple Lives to Collaborate
    Transparently 394
Continuous Evolution to Collaborate Transparently 399

PART SIX
Conclusion 405

25   **Next Steps** 407

Getting Started: Where Are You Today? 407
Building Your Core Team 411
Cost-Effective Starting Points 416
Common Pitfalls and How to Avoid Them 418
Creating Your Roadmap 420
Next Steps Checklist 422
Your First Year 423
The Journey Begins 423
Notes 424

Index 425

ABOUT THE AUTHOR

Deborah Dull is a leading voice in sustainable supply chain transformation and circular economy advocacy. As the founder of the Circular Supply Chain Network, she builds bridges between supply chain practitioners and circular economy initiatives globally. With experiences across multiple industries and continents, Deborah has held strategic roles at organizations including Genpact, Zero100, GE Digital, the Bill & Melinda Gates Foundation, and Microsoft, where she has driven innovation in digital supply chains, sustainability, and industrial operations.

A curious and high-energy thought leader, Deborah has authored multiple books, alongside peer-reviewed articles in leading journals. She is at the forefront of applying advanced computing and generative AI to accelerate sustainable operations and enable circular, localized repair networks. Her expertise spans product development, consumer goods, retail, digital transformation, and supply chain operations in frontier markets.

Deborah regularly shares insights at global industry forums from Seoul to Amsterdam, and academic institutions from Stanford to Strathmore University, focusing on the intersection of circular economy principles, supply chain operations, and advanced technologies. Currently pursuing a doctorate, she combines academic rigor with practical industry experience to advance sustainable supply chain practices. She serves on the GAME Change advisory board and actively contributes to developing supply chain capabilities around the world.

PART ONE

Forming Circular Supply Chains from Key Concepts

Introduction

Here's a familiar experience: You're walking down the street, enjoying your morning coffee. You're drinking from a cup created for convenience. In about 10 minutes—maybe 30 minutes if you're really enjoying the coffee—that cup will end up in the garbage. As a consumer, you've probably thought about this short-lived coffee cup before and maybe even seen art installations created from these single-use items. But as a supply chain professional, have you ever looked at a single-use item and seen the effort it takes just to get that item created in the first place? Let's take the coffee cup as an example.

The paper cup? Once a tree, now bleached, printed, and formed. The plastic lid? Started from an oil field, processed in a refinery, shaped in a factory. And the coffee itself? Grown (likely) in a faraway place with ideal growing conditions to make a delicious coffee, then picked, processed, shipped across oceans, roasted, ground, and finally brewed for you. And thanks to the marvels of today's supply chains, you can enjoy a wide geographical variety of coffee nearly anywhere in the world.

Each part of your morning coffee-on-the-go has traveled thousands of miles, changed hands many times, and used resources as inputs at every step. The scale of the impact comes when we consider the billions of cups consumed around the world. And as we apply that to items beyond coffee, we can start to realize the materials it takes to fuel our supply chains, especially as convenience continues to guide processes from consumer coffees to medical kits to industrial filters in heavy manufacturing.

It wasn't always like this, of course. We created this world of convenience and disposability. Well, our operational forefathers did.

Disposable coffee cups are just one example. Our entire economy is built on this model of extraction, production, consumption, and disposal. Think back to the port congestions during the COVID-19 pandemic. That was a clue that our global supply chains are more complex—and geographically longer—than we may have realized. For example, adding up all the value streams for all the components of a single pair of jeans, it comes to about 40,000 miles. And we know that any time an item is in motion, it's disruptable. This means the 40,000 miles for a pair of jeans, across multiple borders, introduces risk into those supply chain operations. A pair of jeans might have six or seven tiers or nodes—stops from the planet to the user. A more complicated product like a car has closer to 20 tiers. And each of these tiers uses resources from the planet as inputs and introduces risk into our supply chain operations.

These long supply chains were created through a series of economic specializations that countries developed. For example, Japan specializes in zipper production through the YKK Group. This specialization grew out of Japan's post-WWII industrial policy focusing on precision manufacturing. Impressively, YKK even produce zippers for some of their competitors. These investments into specialization came alongside a drive for cost savings. In response, supply chains began to spread their production between different regions, connected by the affordable option of ocean freight. This approach has become the foundation of our current economic model.

Looking ahead, we can see the problems this creates. The economic model we've built over the last 100 years is starting to break down. We're using resources faster than the planet can create them. We're making more waste than our technology can handle or reuse. These problems mean we need to rethink how our supply chains find their inputs.

The key change starts with seeing that items we throw away, like that coffee cup, still have value. Instead of thinking about supply chains as one-way streets that move materials from nature to garbage, we can build them as circles where materials and products keep creating value over and over.

This brings us to circular supply chains—an alternative way to think about how we make, remake, and reuse everything. It means seeing that coffee cup not as trash, but as a resource with ongoing value.

This introduction offers a foundation to the future-facing concepts we'll explore in this book, looking at the events that led to a circular economy and the pioneers in circular practices.

01

Events Leading to Today's Economy

The Origin Story of the Linear Economy

Picture a chilly winter evening in 1925. In a dimly lit room off a side street in Geneva, a group of businessmen from the world's leading light bulb manufacturers are huddled around a table, their faces illuminated by the very product they're discussing. Little do they know that this event will set the stage for a century of consumerism.

Welcome to the birth of planned obsolescence, courtesy of the Phoebus cartel, established in January 1925.

You may be wondering how light bulbs could have an impact on today's economy. As you'll read, these gentlemen were about to change the course of industrial history.

At the time, light bulbs were a newer product on the market and, while popular, weren't popular enough to keep these businesses afloat. Faced with bankruptcy, the businessman brainstormed options to stay in business. They looked at the product quality. At the time, light bulbs lasted 2,500 hours. The Phoebus cartel decided this was their angle. The light bulbs lasted too long to drive enough sales to stay in business. Their solution? Reduce the life of the light bulbs so that they burned out after 1,000 hours.[1] They could raise prices at the same time, coordinating with each other, and leave their customers with a single choice: More expensive, shorter-life light bulbs.

This event led to the first written record of the concept of "planned obsolescence" a few years later in 1932.[2] The takeaway is that they deliberately made their product worse. This event, and the use of planned obsolescence as a business growth strategy, kicked off a series of further events, which contributed to today's consumption-driven, linear economy.

This event was not unique. Similar industry agreements emerged globally. In Germany, the Verkaufsstelle Vereinigter Glühlampenfabriken (roughly translates to "sales office of united light bulb factories") coordinated with Phoebus to control European markets. Japanese manufacturers formed the Tokyo Electric alliance, adopting similar practices, thanks in part to the existing relationship with General Electric. These coordinated efforts created a template for using planned obsolescence as a growth strategy that grew globally.

These events marked the beginning of our throwaway culture. It's when we started designing products to fail, so we could sell more of those products to the same consumers. It may sound far-fetched, but it worked. And not just for light bulbs. This idea caught on across many industries.

From Depression to Obsession

The 1929 stock market crash is a notable event for many reasons. Considering the origin story of the linear economy, it is notable because it rewired how Americans thought about consumption. During this event, interest rates were near zero and unemployment was stubbornly over 10 percent,[3] so Roosevelt's administration faced the challenge of increasing consumer spending and created the New Deal programs of 1933.

The New Deal created jobs and increased consumer confidence. This economic booster is one demonstration of a concept called the state income multiplier effect, as studied by University of Arizona researchers Price V. Fishback and Valentina Kachanovskaya. Their research[4] showed that each dollar of federal grants to states during the events of the New Deal generated approximately one additional dollar in personal income. The multiplier effect showed that government spending in communities could create a cycle of ongoing economic activity, teaching policymakers that encouraging consumer spending was an effective way to grow the economy. It was a lesson that helped shape today's consumer- and consumption-focused economy.

While the United States rebuilt its economy through the New Deal, parallel events occurred globally. Britain's post-war reconstruction introduced the Beveridge Report's welfare state, fundamentally changing consumer behavior through comprehensive welfare programs, including national health services, unemployment benefits, and family allowances.[5] This encouraged citizens to participate more fully in the consumer economy by feeling an increased financial security. Japan's post-war economic growth came from similar government-led industrial policy, particularly the Ministry of International Trade and Industry's focus on specific industries such as electronics and automotive. They did this through targeted loans, technology-sharing programs, and coordinated research and development efforts. This is also an example of investment into economic specializations. These concurrent events around the world created the foundation for modern global consumer culture.

The War Machine and the Consumer Dream

When World War II began, the US rationing systems and victory gardens tested the newly created economic and infrastructure systems. This historic event also changed US manufacturing. Between 1939 and 1944, US gross national product grew by 52 percent as industrial output tripled to support war efforts.[6] The Ford Willow Run factory is a showcase of this, as it switched from making cars to B-24 Liberator bombers. In doing so, it became one of the world's largest factories.

Coming out of the war in 1945, factories needed new purposes as wartime production ramped down. During this time, manufacturing and distribution adapted. Supply chains that moved military equipment now moved household appliances and consumer goods but continued to use the more efficient production approaches that were developed during wartime.

The combination of more advanced manufacturing practices, lower labor costs, and improved efficiency allowed for more affordable pricing on everyday items for average Americans, encouraging consumption.

Consumer credit events, like the introduction of installment plans and store credit cards, meant that Americans could now purchase items without having the full amount upfront. This new way of buying through payment plans accelerated consumer spending.

The Mad Men Era

The increase in consumer spending needed a focus, and the 1950s and '60s marked the rise of modern advertising. Economic growth was apparent. In the late 1940s, Americans bought 21.4 million cars, 5.5 million stoves, and 20 million refrigerators.[7] Television ownership jumped from 10 percent to 90 percent of households during the 1950s.[8]

The first official television advertisement appeared on July 1, 1941, when the Federal Communications Commission (FCC) allowed commercial broadcasting in the United States. The Bulova watch advertisement aired during a baseball game between the Brooklyn Dodgers and Philadelphia Phillies, was 10 seconds long, and the tagline was "America runs on Bulova time."[9]

Of course, these events weren't limited to the United States. Japan's Dentsu explored new advertising approaches that blended traditional culture with modern consumerism. For example, their 1953 campaign for Morinaga Milk Caramel used traditional woodblock print styles in magazine advertisements.[10] In Europe, agencies like Paris-based Publicis focused on luxury brand marketing. For example, their 1960s work with L'Oréal created the now-famous slogan "Because I'm worth it."[11] Britain's Saatchi & Saatchi led the way on political advertising. Their 1979 "Labour Isn't Working" campaign for Margaret Thatcher[12] changed how political messages were communicated. Each region developed approaches to drive consumption, and all contributed to the growing global consumer culture.

Supply chains also developed and changed based on these events. Regular consumer demand made mass production more efficient, as manufacturers could plan ahead and create larger volumes. Larger volumes often meant reduced costs through economies of scale. These supply chains could also plan production schedules based on advertising campaigns, which meant they could coordinate between operations and sales and marketing. Distribution networks expanded to meet the needs of suburban shoppers, which required new storage and inventory systems to handle a steadier flow of consumer goods.

These events all show the development of consumer behavior that continues today. Advertising agencies created predictable demand, allowing companies to build more sophisticated supply chains that could respond to changes in demand more quickly. The combination of mass marketing and efficient distribution created a self-reinforcing cycle: Advertising drove demand, which supported better production systems, which created the budgets for more advertising.

While advertising created an increase in consumption, this expansion relied on the assumption of unlimited access to cheap energy. But the oil crisis would soon challenge this assumption.

The Oil Crisis

In October 1973, Egypt and Syria attacked Israel to regain territory lost in the 1967 war.[13] Previous diplomatic attempts had failed. The Soviet Union supported Egypt and Syria with military advisers and equipment, while the United States backed Israel with military aid. In retaliation for the US support, OPEC's Arab members cut oil exports to the US and other Israel-supporting nations,[14] using oil as a political weapon.

This led to an oil crisis. The OPEC oil embargo quadrupled prices from $3 to $12 per barrel.[15] Gas stations ran out of oil, and US factories faced energy shortages. These events disrupted decades of cheap energy and stable supply chains.

Different regions took different paths through the crisis. Japan's government launched its "Moonlight Project" in 1978.[16] The goal was to improve industrial energy efficiency through capabilities such as waste heat recovery, more efficient industrial furnaces, and energy management systems. The Moonlight Project helped shape industrial practices around the world. European countries, particularly France, accelerated nuclear power development, while Germany invested in renewable energy research.

Manufacturing practices shifted to mitigate these events. Companies developed energy monitoring systems. Factory layouts changed to reduce power use. Warehouses adopted new insulation and lighting standards.

The events of this period contributed key features of today's economy: Global supply chains vulnerable to disruption, energy efficiency as a business priority, and consumer sensitivity to fuel costs. The crisis could have prompted a shift away from planned obsolescence and fossil fuels. Instead, it reinforced the drive for cheaper production through global value chains.

Reaganomics and Thatcherism

The 1980s brought major economic changes under Reagan and Thatcher. Their policies promoted deregulation, free markets, and global trade. For example, the US corporate tax rate dropped from 70 percent to 28 percent.[17] Trade barriers were removed as the US signed 14 free trade agreements between 1985 and 1989.[18]

These events meant supply chains became even more extensive. One implication is that companies moved production to countries with lower wages and fewer regulations. For example, by 1982, 86 percent of Nike shoes were produced in South Korea and Taiwan.[19] This trend continued and by 1989, production continued to move to even lower-cost countries like Indonesia and China.

Another event is innovation in supply chain technology. Walmart used computer-tracked inventory and automated warehouses and connected barcode scanning at the point of sale (POS) to their inventory system. In their warehouses in 1987 they created the largest private satellite communication system in the United States, which connected areas of the supply chain with two-way voice and data messages.[20] This meant supply chains could respond to changes in demand even faster, as sales data automatically triggered inventory updates and reordering processes across the entire network.

In the early 1980s, Just-in-Time manufacturing developed in Japan was shared with other countries.[21] The JIT system, part of the Toyota Production System, was created to increase efficiency by reducing process waste.

The Rise of Global Trade

China's 2001 entry into the World Trade Organization[22] expanded this shift further, especially as Chinese manufacturing wages averaged 58 cents per hour[23] compared to $16 in the United States.[24]

Unsurprisingly, supply chains expanded. Port volume more than doubled in the 1990s.[25] Companies built factories where labor costs were lowest.[26] Economic specialization meant that products often moved between countries for an additional manufacturing step.

New capabilities in logistics and transportation technology during the 1990s drastically reduced costs, making global shipping the norm. The result ended up with somewhat illogical facts. For example, it became cheaper to ship a shirt from Vietnam to California than to truck it from Los Angeles to Denver, thanks to the efficiency of container shipping and improvements in global supply chains.

The Digital Revolution

As the events of globalization took us into the late 1990s and early 2000s, the internet rewired how society interacts with commerce. While the Sears catalog had pioneered remote shopping in 1893, reaching millions of US households, the internet created an entirely new experience of instant gratification and growing choice.

Amazon launched in 1995 as an online bookstore. It seemed modest at the time, but it signaled the beginning of a shift in how we shop. Walmart's development of Retail Link became a watershed event, allowing suppliers to monitor stock levels in real-time and automatically trigger replenishment—a capability that would have seemed like science fiction just a decade earlier.

Asian markets, particularly South Korea and Japan, led in digital capabilities. South Korea's early investment in broadband infrastructure made it the world's first country where online shopping outpaced retail. Japanese companies led in mobile commerce through services like DoCoMo's i-mode, reaching millions of users years before the iPhone came to market.

The Great Recession

Just as the digital transformation reached full swing, the 2008 financial crisis brought in a big spotlight on how fragile global supply networks had become. When credit markets froze, the long chains of global trade began to come apart. Companies struggled to find capital to fund inventory and operations, and global trade volumes experienced their steepest decline since World War II, declining by 12 percent in 2009.[27]

One impact of the events of the recession was industry consolidation. Larger suppliers absorbed smaller ones. This helped to reduce some of the supply chain complexity but created an increased concentration risk. The focus continued to be on cost reduction rather than systemic reform, missing another opportunity to fundamentally rethink the linear supply chain model.

The Smartphone

As we came out of the Great Recession, a new product category emerged that showcased both the marvel and madness of modern supply chains: The smartphone. A single iPhone contains components from hundreds of suppliers across dozens of countries, each precision-engineered and transported across oceans to arrive at assembly plants precisely when needed.

The smartphone shaped the global manufacturing landscape. But beneath the successes of technology innovation was increasing complexity and environmental costs. For example, the rare earth minerals required for screens and batteries left empty mines from Inner Mongolia to the Congo.[28] Semiconductor chips, essential for modern electronics, cross more than 70 borders during their production,[29] highlighting the far-reaching nature of global supply chains. E-waste grew to over 53 million metric tons annually by 2019,[30] with only a fraction reused or even properly recycled. The ongoing cycle of new models, planned obsolescence, and marketing-driven upgrades created even more consumption.

The Pandemic

Just as the smartphone era brought about a globally connected economy, an invisible virus brought that economy to its knees. The events around the COVID-19 pandemic exposed weaknesses in global supply chains that efficiency experts had either ignored or accepted as normal. The initial outbreak was in Wuhan, a manufacturing-heavy region producing a wide range of products like LCD screens and active pharmaceutical ingredients. Impacts to manufacturing created disruptions that supply chain professionals aimed to mitigate.

Different regions showed varying resilience. In South Korea, already the global leader in industrial robot density, the use of industrial robots increased dramatically as human workers stayed home. Companies like Hyundai Robotics showcased sophisticated "cobots" (collaborative robots) that could communicate with each other through interconnected systems and be managed remotely, enabling production to continue with minimal human presence.

Meanwhile, e-commerce experienced a decade of projected growth in just three months as lockdowns forced consumers online.

As the world scrambled to continue to operate through these events, the pandemic temporarily reversed sustainability progress.[31] For example, single-use plastic consumption increased as safety concerns drove buying behaviors.

The Circular Economy: A New Hope

The linear economy's limitations have become impossible to ignore. A system designed around take-make-waste now faces fundamental constraints: Resource constraints, environmental degradation causing material insecurity, and mounting waste that represents escaped value. The circular supply chain offers an alternative path, and challenges the strategies created back in the events of the Phoebus cartel.

This new model is more than simply recycling. As we'll explore together in this book, the circular supply chain is a fundamental redesign of how we source, make, move, and use the items around us in our homes and industries.

The shift extends beyond individual companies to entire regions. The European Union's Circular Economy Action Plan[32] sets targets for waste reduction and material reuse. China's circular economy development[33] leverages the idea of industrial symbiosis—industrial parks where a co-located factory's waste becomes another's raw material. These policy frameworks create the economic conditions necessary for circular systems to thrive.

The journey from the Phoebus cartel to today demonstrates humanity's capacity to reshape economic systems. The linear economy wasn't inevitable; it was designed. The same creative force that built global supply chains can reimagine them now.

Early adopters are already showing the way. Interface, the world's largest commercial carpet manufacturer, has achieved its Mission Zero goals, which decouple its environmental impact from profitability. Dutch company Fairphone produces modular smartphones designed for repair and upgrade rather than replacement. These pioneers prove that circular principles work in practice, not just theory.

The transition means we need to redefine how we measure success. GDP and quarterly profits provide incomplete metrics of a healthy economy designed for the long term. New indicators like utilization, product and component reuse, and supply chain resilience provide a better way to capture true value creation. Some companies such as Unilever have already integrated these metrics into their strategic planning.

Supply chain professionals are at the center of this shift. The skills that optimized global logistics networks can now redesign them for circularity. The expertise that created just-in-time manufacturing can develop closed-loop product flows. The innovation that enabled global track-and-trace can now capture products and materials to retain their highest value.

The pandemic, climate change, and resource constraints have exposed the limitations of linear supply chains. These challenges come alongside technological capabilities and growing awareness of the need for change. The tools, knowledge, and urgency for transformation have aligned. The question isn't whether supply chains will become circular, but how quickly we can make the transition.

Notes

1   Krajewski, M. (2014) The Great Lightbulb Conspiracy, IEEE Spectrum, https:// spectrum.ieee.org/the-great-lightbulb-conspiracy (archived at https://perma.cc/ N63K-YXTH)

2   The University of Auckland (2024) A short history of planned obsolescence, www.auckland.ac.nz/en/news/2024/07/15/short-history-of-planned-obsolescence. html (archived at https://perma.cc/CYL3-7NUE)

3 Bureau of Labor Statistics (n.d.) Bureau of Labor Statistics Data, https://data.bls. gov/timeseries/LFU21000100&series_id=LFU22000100&from_year=1929&to_ year=1939&periods_option=specific_periods&periods=Annual+Data (archived at https://perma.cc/KWX2-AV9N)

4 Fishback, P. and Kachanovskaya, V. (2015) The multiplier for federal spending in the States during the Great Depression, *The Journal of Economic History*, 75(1), pp.125–62, doi:https://doi.org/10.1017/s0022050715000054 (archived at https://perma.cc/B35P-RWZZ)

5 UK Parliament (n.d.) 1942 Beveridge Report, www.parliament.uk/about/ living-heritage/transformingsociety/livinglearning/coll-9-health1/coll-9-health/ (archived at https://perma.cc/84JT-NYCU)

6 Eggli, J. (2024). U.S. Economic Productivity 1941–1944, San Jose State University, https://sjsu.edu/faculty/watkins/eggli.htm (archived at https://perma. cc/FTE5-MPJY)

7 PBS (2019) The rise of American consumerism, American Experience, PBS, www.pbs.org/wgbh/americanexperience/features/tupperware-consumer/ (archived at https://perma.cc/EQ4L-EASA)

8 Wiegand, S. (2016) The impact of the television in 1950s America, dummies, www.dummies.com/article/academics-the-arts/history/american/the-impact-of-the-television-in-1950s-america-151457/ (archived at https://perma.cc/ SM8E-BBKP)

9 Reisinger, D. (2016) The first "legal" TV commercial aired 75 years ago today, Fortune, https://fortune.com/2016/07/01/bulova-tv-commercial/ (archived at https://perma.cc/SA4R-H4X5)

10 Watanabe, R. (2023) Morinaga Milk Caramel advertisement, People's Graphic Design Archive, https://peoplesgdarchive.org/item/9405/morinaga-milk-caramel-advertisementandnbsp (archived at https://perma.cc/UKB8-CNQ8)

11 L'Oréal Paris (n.d.). L'Oréal Paris celebrates 50th anniversary of "Because You're Worth It" slogan, www.lorealparisusa.com/beauty-magazine/makeup/ makeup-trends/loreal-paris-because-youre-worth-it-anniversary (archived at https://perma.cc/YZY7-XVEY)

12 Fallon, I. (2007) Saatchi & Saatchi: The agency that made Tory history, *The Independent*, www.independent.co.uk/news/media/saatchi-saatchi-the-agency-that-made-tory-history-744791.html (archived at https://perma.cc/ Z2GQ-YG9L)

13 Hassenstab, N. (2023) 50 years on: Explaining the Yom Kippur War, American University, www.american.edu/sis/news/20231006-50-years-on-explaining-the-yom-kippur-war.cfm (archived at https://perma.cc/9XLU-MLSM)

14 Office of the Historian (2023) Milestones: 1969–1976, https://history.state.gov/ milestones/1969-1976/oil-embargo (archived at https://perma.cc/6DN2-9HJ4)

15 Corbett, M. (2013) Oil Shock of 1973–74, Federal Reserve History, www.
federalreservehistory.org/essays/oil-shock-of-1973-74 (archived at https://
perma.cc/3QEU-DXA6)

16 Minoru, S. (2009) A half century of Japan's industrial science and technology
policy and the Agency of Industrial Science and Technology, REITI, www.rieti.
go.jp/en/columns/a01_0265.html (archived at https://perma.cc/82L8-HBM5)

17 Robinson, S. (2024) Historical tax rates: The rhetoric and reality of taxing the
rich, The Concord Coalition, www.concordcoalition.org/issue-brief/historical-
tax-rates-the-rhetoric-and-reality-of-taxing-the-rich/ (archived at https://perma.
cc/5GZX-SWWZ)

18 Office of the United States Trade Representative (n.d.) List of trade agreements,
https://ustr.gov/archive/assets/Document_Library/Reports_Publications/2002/2002_
Trade_Policy_Agenda/asset_upload_file556_6351.pdf (archived at https://perma.
cc/8A6B-BKVT)

19 Harvard Business School (1994) International sourcing in athletic footwear:
NIKE and Reebok, www.hbs.edu/faculty/Pages/item.aspx?num=12974
(archived at https://perma.cc/5EDX-CR3V)

20 Wailgum, T. (2007) 45 years of Wal-Mart history: A technology time line, CIO,
www.cio.com/article/274537/infrastructure-45-years-of-wal-mart-history-a-
technology-time-line.html (archived at https://perma.cc/7AUT-VH65)

21 Schonberger, R. (1982) The transfer of Japanese manufacturing approaches to
US industry, University of Nebraska, https://digitalcommons.unl.edu/cgi/
viewcontent.cgi?article=1186&context=managementfacpub (archived at
https://perma.cc/Q9HB-NS9V)

22 Wakasugi, R. (2015) How did China's W.T.O. entry affect its companies?
World Economic Forum, www.weforum.org/stories/2015/06/how-did-chinas-
wto-entry-affect-its-companies (archived at https://perma.cc/G4BG-Z4ZM)

23 Ezrati, M. (2023) The East-West wage gap not nearly as compelling as it once
was, Forbes, www.forbes.com/sites/miltonezrati/2023/01/30/the-east-west-
wage-gap-not-nearly-as-compelling-as-it-once-was/ (archived at https://perma.
cc/QUB9-AURZ)

24 US Department of Labor (2002) National compensation survey: Occupational
wages in the United States, www.bls.gov/ocs/publications/pdf/united-states-
july-2001.pdf (archived at https://perma.cc/C7JN-9E5C)

25 Nightingale, L. (2022) One hundred ports: The numbers tell the story, Lloyd's
List, www.lloydslist.com/LL1141949/One-Hundred-Ports-The-numbers-tell-
the-story (archived at https://perma.cc/DUY8-BHBQ)

26 Crafts, N. (2004) The world economy in the 1990s: A long run perspective,
www.lse.ac.uk/Economic-History/Assets/Documents/WorkingPapers/
Economic-History/2004/WP8704.pdf (archived at https://perma.cc/24M8-
QS6D)

27 World Trade Organization (2010) 2010 Press Releases—Trade to expand by
9.5% in 2010 after a dismal 2009, www.wto.org/english/news_e/pres10_e/
pr598_e.htm (archived at https://perma.cc/UCT3-VHHB)

28 Maughan, T. (2015) The dystopian lake filled by the world's tech lust, BBC.
com, www.bbc.com/future/article/20150402-the-worst-place-on-earth
(archived at https://perma.cc/M4X9-YQXN)

29 Harris, M. (2022) These 5 charts help demystify the global chip shortage, IEEE
Spectrum, https://spectrum.ieee.org/global-chip-shortage-charts (archived at
https://perma.cc/X9R6-C7Y8)

30 unitar (2020) The Global E-waste Monitor 2020 – Quantities, flows, and the
circular economy potential, https://ewastemonitor.info/gem-2020/ (archived at
https://perma.cc/VM2X-4JQ9)

31 Yuan, H. et al. (2023) Progress towards the Sustainable Development Goals
has been slowed by indirect effects of the COVID-19 pandemic, *Nature*, 4(1),
doi:https://doi.org/10.1038/s43247-023-00846-x (archived at https://perma.cc/
YPV9-QTJV)

32 European Commission (2020). Circular Economy Action Plan, https://
environment.ec.europa.eu/strategy/circular-economy-action-plan_en (archived
at https://perma.cc/4REG-GN55)

33 Mathews, J. A., Tan, H., and Hu, M.-C. (2018). Moving to a circular economy
in China: Transforming industrial parks into eco-industrial parks, *California
Management Review*, 60 (3), pp.157–81, doi:https://doi.org/10.1177/
0008125617752692 (archived at https://perma.cc/UX8W-MD27)

02

The Pioneers of Circular Thinking

The transition from linear to circular supply chains didn't happen by accident. Like the light bulb and planned obsolescence that helped create our consumption-driven economy, the movement toward circularity has its own cast of characters, and these pioneers sought to create value through preservation rather than obsolescence.

Each of these pioneers approach the challenge from a different angle. From an economist questioning product lifecycles, to a sailor understanding resource limitations, to a biologist studying nature's perfect cycles—each pioneer has added crucial pieces to our understanding of how circular supply chains can function.

Their collective work shows us that circular supply chains aren't just ideas. These pioneers have demonstrated practical approaches to transforming how we produce, consume, and reuse materials. Their work helps us understand why we need to change our supply systems, and how we can make that change happen.

As we examine their contributions, we'll see how their different perspectives combine to create a foundation for circular supply chain development. The purpose of showcasing these pioneers is so you are familiar with the leading ideators of the circular economy and can recognize their work as you create a more circular supply chain for your own team, supply chain, or region.

Walter Stahel: Performance Economy

In 1976, when global manufacturing was racing toward increasingly linear production models, Swiss economist Walter Stahel introduced a paradigm shift in how we think about industrial systems. While companies were optimizing supply chains for speed and single-use efficiency, Stahel challenged the fundamental assumption that economic growth required perpetual resource extraction and disposal.

His groundbreaking report, "Jobs for Tomorrow: The Potential for Substituting Manpower for Energy," co-authored with Genevieve Reday-Mulvey,[1] introduced the concept of a "closed-loop" economy. Through detailed economic analysis, Stahel demonstrated how extending product lifecycles could transform traditional supply chain relationships. He showed that remanufacturing operations could maintain product quality while using only 10 percent of the energy needed for new production. It was a revelation that challenged the industrial approach at the time, and still does today.

His research into strategies to extend the life of products helped companies reconceptualize how their supply chains work. Rather than optimizing for one-way flow from production to disposal, Stahel showed how companies could create value through multiple product lifecycles.

Perhaps most significantly, Stahel demonstrated how circular systems could create skilled employment while reducing resource dependence. His analysis showed that extending product life through repair, reuse, and remanufacturing could generate more local jobs than traditional manufacturing. This finding continues to influence how companies balance automation with human skills in circular operations and is increasingly relevant in today's retiring labor market where reskilling is needed across supply chain roles.

McDonough and Braungart: Redesigning Industrial Systems

The late 1990s marked another pioneering moment in the evolution of circular thinking. William McDonough, an architect, and Michael Braungart, a chemist, challenged the fundamental design principles that had shaped industrial supply chains since World War II. Their 2002 publication, "Cradle to Cradle: Remaking the Way We Make Things,"[2] proposed a radical reimagining of how products enter and move through supply chains.

The Cradle to Cradle certification system they developed has reshaped how companies evaluate materials and design products. Unlike traditional supply chain certifications focused on process compliance, their system examines material health, material reuse, renewable energy use, water stewardship, and social fairness. Companies like Herman Miller and Shaw Industries have redesigned their products and supply chains to meet these comprehensive standards.

One notable example from these pioneers applying the Cradle to Cradle certification is Shaw Industries through their EcoWorx carpet tile system, which separated materials into the biological and technical cycles. More importantly, they pioneered what they called a 'reverse supply chain protocol' that fundamentally changed how materials flowed through their manufacturing systems. Rather than optimizing for one-way movement from production to disposal, Shaw created a circular logistics network with collection points, specialized processing centers, and sophisticated tracking systems. They developed new inventory management approaches that balanced virgin and reused materials, while implementing a materials passport system to maintain quality through multiple lifecycles. Their success proved that companies could create value by managing both biological and technical materials through multiple product lifecycles, establishing a model that has become central to modern circular supply chains.

Ellen MacArthur: From Sailing the World to Saving It

Ellen MacArthur's journey to circular economy leadership began in remarkable circumstances. A sailing pioneer, she broke records in 2005 for solo circumnavigation, as she sailed for 71 days and 14 hours.[3] This experience provided a unique perspective on resource management—when you're alone at sea, every material on board must be carefully considered, used, and reused. For MacArthur, this created a profound understanding of the phrase "finite resources" that would shape her future work.

The Ellen MacArthur Foundation, established in 2010, has transformed these insights into actionable frameworks for businesses and governments. The Foundation has worked across its community to build the economic case for circular systems, demonstrating through detailed analysis how circular supply chains can deliver both environmental and economic benefits. Their 2012 report, "Towards the Circular Economy,"[4] quantified for the first time the economic opportunity of circular systems.

The Foundation's work has recently focused on supply chain. Their research has highlighted how current linear supply chains, optimized for efficiency rather than resilience, create systemic vulnerabilities. Their recent white paper, "Building the Circular Supply Chain,"[5] provides an introductory framework for transitioning from linear to circular operations, addressing key operational changes needed across industries.

Kate Raworth: Redefining Economic Success Metrics

Kate Raworth's "Doughnut Economics" model, introduced in 2012 and expanded in her 2017 book,[6] pioneers how we measure and manage economic systems, including supply chains. While traditional economics focused on optimizing supply chains for continuous growth and efficiency, Raworth's framework introduces a more nuanced approach that considers both social and environmental boundaries.

The model's structure is conceptually straightforward but operationally transformative. The inner ring of the doughnut represents social foundations, or the essential resources and services that supply chains must deliver to meet basic human needs. The outer ring of the doughnut shows the ecological ceilings, or the environmental limits that supply chain operations must use to maintain planetary health. Between these boundaries lies what Raworth terms the "safe and just space for humanity."

This framework has significant implications for supply chain design and measurement. Traditional supply chain metrics focused primarily on cost reduction and delivery speed must expand to include both social and environmental impacts. For example, when Amsterdam adopted the Doughnut model in 2020,[7] it required companies to evaluate their supply chains against both social criteria (like fair labor practices and living wages) and environmental impacts (such as carbon emissions and material consumption).

The Doughnut model also addresses a crucial gap in circular economy thinking by providing clear boundaries for supply chain operations. While circular principles focus on material flows and waste elimination, Raworth's framework adds crucial context about the ultimate purpose of these systems—meeting human needs while preserving ecological systems.

Janine Benyus: Learning from Nature's Supply Chains

Janine Benyus is a pioneer in the study of biomimicry for business. In 1997, she offered a new perspective on industrial system design.[8] While traditional supply chains were engineered for linear efficiency, Benyus's perspective is to observe how nature's 3.8 billion years of evolution had already developed sophisticated operations systems that could inform the design of modern operations.

Her work reveals how biological supply chains—from nutrient cycles in forests to material flows in coral reefs—achieve remarkable efficiency without generating persistent waste. These natural systems demonstrate perfect circularity: Every output becomes an input, every "waste" product serves as a resource for another process. This insight has profound implications for industrial supply chain design.

Benyus's frameworks have influenced how companies approach material innovation and process design. For example, studying spider silk's production process—which creates strong, flexible fiber at ambient temperature using only water as a solvent—has led to innovations in manufacturing processes that reduce energy use and eliminate toxic chemicals. The Shinkansen bullet train's nose design, inspired by kingfisher beaks, demonstrates how biomimicry can improve operational efficiency while reducing resource consumption.

Gunter Pauli: Cascading Value Through Supply Networks

Gunter Pauli's work through the Zero Emissions Research and Initiatives (ZERI) network has fundamentally challenged how we think about waste in supply chains. While traditional operations viewed waste management as a cost center, Pauli demonstrated how integrated supply networks could transform waste streams into value streams, creating what he termed the "Blue Economy."

His approach envisions cascading supply chains where outputs from one process become inputs for another. The ZERI framework, developed in the 1990s,[9] showed how interconnected manufacturing processes could eliminate waste while creating additional revenue streams. For example, Pauli's work with coffee processors demonstrated how spent coffee grounds could support mushroom cultivation, with the remaining substrate becoming high-protein animal feed—transforming what was once waste into two valuable product streams.

Through the Blue Economy initiative, Pauli has documented over 100 innovations that demonstrate how supply chains can be redesigned to mimic natural systems. His work with breweries showed how spent grain could feed cattle, while the cattle's waste could generate biogas for power generation—creating closed-loop systems that increase resource productivity while reducing environmental impact.

The Power of Many Minds

Much like our modern supply chains, the development of circular economy thinking demonstrates the power of interconnected ideas. While each pioneer has brought distinct insights—Stahel's product lifecycles, MacArthur's resource limitations, Raworth's economic boundaries, Benyus's natural systems, McDonough and Braungart's material flows, and Pauli's waste-to-value innovations—their collective work creates something greater than the sum of its parts.

These pioneers continue to evolve ideas through new research, practical applications, and emerging technologies. Each successful showcase of circular principles in today's supply chains builds upon their foundational insights while adding new understanding.

Now let's explore more examples of supply chains putting these concepts into action. While it's true that most corporations today still operate within an extractive economic model, there are pioneering brands that are using their resources and influence to challenge the status quo.

Patagonia: The Outdoor Giant That's All In

Patagonia has long been a pioneer for sustainable business practices, and their commitment to circularity goes beyond just sourcing recycled materials. They're rethinking their entire supply chain and how they interact with customers to reclaim products.

Patagonia has implemented a radical transparency initiative. They've mapped out their entire supply chain, from the farms where their cotton is grown to the factories where their products are assembled.[10] This transparency allows them to identify areas for improvement and ensure ethical practices throughout their supply network.

One of Patagonia's most innovative circular initiatives is their Worn Wear program, supported by repair centers and facilitating the resale of used garments. Patagonia has established a central repair facility in Reno, Nevada, and augments this with mobile repair vans and various store locations. Since 2005, they have repaired nearly half a million items, with the repair center mending up to 50,000 garments annually.[11] The focus on repair necessitates a shift in how they design and manufacture their products, ensuring that everything is made with repair in mind, influencing decisions from the design phase to material selection.

Interface: Turning the Carpet Industry on Its Head

Interface, a global commercial flooring pioneer, proves that even traditional manufacturing businesses can embrace circularity. Their journey offers valuable insights into how companies can transform their operations and supply chains.

Interface has made remarkable strides in using recycled and bio-based materials in their products. Their Net-Works program is a prime example of innovative sourcing. They collect discarded fishing nets from coastal communities in the Philippines, Cameroon, and Indonesia, which are then recycled into nylon for carpet tiles.[12] This program sources recycled materials, addresses ocean plastic pollution, and provides income to vulnerable coastal communities. It's a perfect example of how circular thinking can create multiple benefits across the supply chain.

Interface's ReEntry program takes back old carpet tiles, not just their own but competitors' products too. They've developed a special process to separate the yarn and backing components of carpets, allowing these materials to be recycled into new carpets.

This program required Interface to rethink their entire manufacturing process. They had to design products that could be easily disassembled and develop new technologies to process reclaimed materials. It's a prime example of how embracing circularity often requires reimagining the entire production process. Their journey is documented in the movie *Beyond Zero*, which highlights their pioneering spirit, having set the goal in 1994 to have a neutral environment impact by 2020.[13]

Renault: Driving Circularity in the Automotive Industry

The automotive industry is traditionally resource-intensive, but Renault is showing that even car manufacturers can adopt circular practices.

Renault has been operating a remanufacturing plant in Choisy-le-Roi, France, since 1949.[14] This facility takes used parts—engines, gearboxes, turbochargers, and more—and restores them to original specifications. These remanufactured parts are then sold at a lower price than new parts, with the same quality guarantee. They win because their margins are better on these remanufactured parts, and their customers win because they save money on their parts purchase.

Renault has also implemented closed-loop recycling for several materials. For example, they recycle copper from electrical harnesses and platinum group metals from catalytic converters. These materials are then fed back into their supply chain to produce new parts.

To make this work, Renault had to collaborate closely with their suppliers and develop new processes for dismantling and recycling. It's a great example of how circular practices often require involving entire supply networks.

Philips: Lighting the Way to Circularity

Philips, especially its lighting division (now Signify), has been a pioneer of circular economy practices in the electronics industry.

Philips introduced a "pay-per-lux" model in 2016,[15] where they retain ownership of the lighting equipment and customers pay for the light service. This shift from selling products to selling services has profound implications for their operations.

Under this model, Philips is incentivized to create long-lasting, energy-efficient products that are easy to maintain and upgrade. This has led to changes in their product design, manufacturing processes, and supply chain management. They've had to develop new capabilities in areas like predictive maintenance and efficient collection and refurbishment of used equipment.

The Road Ahead: Lessons from the Pioneers

As we look at these examples, a few key themes emerge:

1 Design for circularity: All these companies have had to rethink their product—and supply chain—design to enable repair, reuse, and recycling.

2 Reverse logistics: Implementing circular practices requires setting up mature networks to reclaim and prepare used products and components.

3 Business model innovation: Many of these circular initiatives require rethinking not just how products are made, but how they're sold and used. This leads to impacts on the supply chain and operations.

4 Transparency and traceability: To truly close the loop, companies need to have a clear understanding of their entire supply chain, but not their

traditional linear supply chain—their new, repair-focused supply chain which should be shorter and more regional.

5 Collaboration is key: Whether it's working with fishing communities to source reclaimed nylon or partnering with reuse firms to close material loops, circularity often requires close collaboration with a wide range of stakeholders.

While no pioneer has all the answers, the efforts explored in this introduction show us that circular practices are not just theoretical—they can be implemented at scale in real-world business operations.

Notes

1 Stahel, W. and Ready-Mulvey, G. (1981) Jobs for tomorrow: The potential for substituting manpower for energy, ResearchGate, www.researchgate.net/publication/40935606_Jobs_for_tomorrow_the_potential_for_substituting_manpower_for_energy (archived at https://perma.cc/8AFZ-VTXR)

2 McDonough, W. (2002) *Cradle to Cradle: Remaking the way we make things*, https://mcdonough.com/writings/cradle-cradle-remaking-way-make-things/ (archived at https://perma.cc/MF58-9TDP)

3 MacArthur, E. (2016) Adventurers of the Year 2005, *National Geographic*, www.nationalgeographic.com/adventure/article/ellen-macarthur-2005 (archived at https://perma.cc/N6TD-LGHR)

4 Ellen MacArthur Foundation (2012) Towards the Circular Economy: Economic and business rationale for an accelerated transition, Green Policy Platform, www.greenpolicyplatform.org/research/towards-circular-economy-economic-and-business-rationale-accelerated-transition (archived at https://perma.cc/4KWW-Z3AY)

5 Ellen MacArthur Foundation (2023) Circular supply chains, www.ellenmacarthurfoundation.org/circular-supply-chains (archived at https://perma.cc/EW9N-CVJL)

6 Raworth, K. (2013) www.kateraworth.com/ (archived at https://perma.cc/Z5KQ-ZJAK)

7 Peters, A. (2020) Amsterdam is now using the "doughnut" model of economics: What does that mean? Fast Company, www.fastcompany.com/90497442/amsterdam-is-now-using-the-doughnut-model-of-economics-what-does-that-mean (archived at https://perma.cc/SZJ7-YVQC)

8 Benyus, J. (1997) *Biomimicry: Innovation inspired by nature*, Harper Perennial

9 Zeri (n.d.) www.zeri.org/index.html (archived at https://perma.cc/PLF6-JLZD)

10 Patagonia (n.d.) Material traceability, www.patagonia.com/our-footprint/
material-traceability.html (archived at https://perma.cc/Z3FY-WRMT)

11 Knowledge Hub (2020) Patagonia Worn Wear—Repair program for clothes,
https://knowledge-hub.circle-economy.com/article/3780?n=Patagonia-Worn-
Wear---Repair-program-for-clothes (archived at https://perma.cc/TG2V-QCUN)

12 Interface (2015) Net-Works: The world's first inclusive business model to
recycle discarded fishing nets made in the Philippines and now primed to go
global, https://investors.interface.com/news/press-release-details/2015/
Net-Works-The-worlds-first-inclusive-business-model-to-recycle-discarded-
fishing-nets-Made-in-the-Philippines-and-now-primed-to-go-global/default.
aspx (archived at https://perma.cc/4YMK-WLLL)

13 United Nations Climate Change (2022) From mission zero to climate take
back: How Interface is transforming its business to have zero negative impact,
https://unfccc.int/climate-action/momentum-for-change/climate-neutral-now/
interface (archived at https://perma.cc/H94F-69EW)

14 Ellen MacArthur Foundation (2021) Europe's first circular economy factory
for vehicles: Renault, www.ellenmacarthurfoundation.org/circular-examples/
groupe-renault (archived at https://perma.cc/3HRV-BF75)

15 Ellen MacArthur Foundation (2022) Why buy light bulbs when you can buy
light? Signify, www.ellenmacarthurfoundation.org/circular-examples/why-buy-
light-bulbs-when-you-can-buy-light-signify (archived at https://perma.cc/
Y3HU-YWBH)

03

Where Circular Economy Meets Supply Chain

The circular economy is connected by three principles. These principles are meant to be taken in order, and can be applied to business models, materials and products, and to our supply chains and operations:

1 "Use Less" means designing out waste from the start. One example of this is moving production or remanufacturing closer to the point of use, removing the wasted transportation miles and extra inventory needed to hedge against changes in demand, especially in a long supply chain. Helen of Troy, owner of Hydro Flask, announced mid-2023 their plan to start shifting production from China to the Western Hemisphere, helped along by automation investments. Often driven by a "China plus one" or geopolitical risk mitigation, the added benefit is a shorter supply chain.

2 "Use Better" focuses on keeping products and materials in use. One example is how Caterpillar's remanufacturing program takes back used components, remanufactures them to original specifications, and sells them with the same warranty as new parts—while charging customers less than for new components.

3 "Use Forever" aims to regenerate natural systems. Examples include planted facility roofs, returning more water to the watershed than drawn, or investing in local communities. Seventh Generation have designed their operations so that the water they use in their manufacturing processes is cleaner when it is returned to the watershed than when it was extracted. The goal in regeneration is to have more to use in our supply chains tomorrow than we have to use today.

As we explore the following framework, you'll see how these elements interconnect and reinforce each other. Business model innovations enable new approaches to material and product innovation, which then create opportunities for operational improvements. Market dynamics influence strategy choices, which shape supply chain decisions. Understanding these relationships is helpful for anyone looking to lead the transition to a circular supply chain, so you are aware of the differences and overlap of each of these connections.

Remember that coffee cup we started with? In a circular economy, it might be a durable cup you return for cleaning and reuse. Or perhaps it's made from agricultural waste that can be composted to grow more crops. Or maybe the whole concept of "to-go" coffee evolves into something entirely different. The possibilities are endless when we start thinking in circles rather than lines.

Business Models: The Foundation for Change

Let's think about a light bulb for a moment. Not just any light bulb, but specifically the ones discussed at that fateful meeting in Geneva in 1924, where the Phoebus cartel deliberately reduced their products' lifespan from 2,500 to 1,000 hours. As we have explored, this moment marks more than just a business decision—it represents the birth of planned obsolescence, a strategy that would shape the next century of commerce. Today, as we predict both resource scarcity and also growing waste, this 1924 meeting can be a cautionary tale, and a starting point, for understanding how dramatically business models need to change, and the connection to supply chains.

The traditional business model is straightforward: Design products to fail or become obsolete, sell as many as possible, and repeat. This approach worked remarkably well in an era of abundant resources and minimal environmental concern. However, as we've seen with everything from smartphones that slow down just before new models release to printers that stop working after a predetermined number of pages, this model is increasingly at odds with both environmental sustainability and customer interests.

Enter circular business models. These approaches fundamentally reimagine how companies create, deliver, and capture value. Rather than profiting from selling more products, circular business models thrive on keeping products in use longer and maintaining—or increasing—their value over time.

Let's explore three approaches that are reshaping industries.

Rethinking Ownership Through Service Models

The transformation of business models toward service-based offerings is a shift in how companies create and deliver value to their customers. Consider Uber's approach to transportation. Competing with car ownership that results in cars that sit idle 95 percent of the time,[1] Uber created a platform that increases vehicle utilization rates—a key metric first identified by circular economy pioneer Walter Stahel. By enabling multiple riders to share the same vehicle throughout the day, Uber's model reduces the total number of cars needed (showcasing the first principle of the circular economy to "use less"), and also changes the supply chain dynamics.

One connection to supply chain is that instead of managing complex global supply chains to produce millions of new vehicles annually, the focus shifts to maintaining and optimizing existing assets within local markets.

This shift to service-based models has connections throughout the supply chain. When companies retain ownership of their assets, they are incentivized to get the most out of that asset for as long as possible. The focus moves from producing high volumes of goods, to optimizing operations so that those goods last longer and perform better.

Supply chain managers in this transition will find themselves focusing more on maintenance networks and spare parts logistics than on raw material sourcing and primary manufacturing. This transformation has spread across industries, from Michelin offering "tires-as-a-service" to commercial fleets to Rolls-Royce's "power-by-the-hour" model for jet engines. Each example demonstrates how servitization can align business success with environmental stewardship while simplifying supply chain complexity.

The Sharing Economy and Asset Utilization

Remember that statistic about cars sitting idle 95 percent of the time? The sharing economy addresses this inefficiency directly. Companies like Zipcar recognized that many urban dwellers need occasional access to vehicles but not constant ownership. Their model transforms personal transportation from a product to purchase into a service to access.

The sharing economy builds upon these service-based models by focusing explicitly on maximizing asset utilization. Companies like WeWork have transformed how businesses think about office space, creating flexible environments that can be used by multiple organizations throughout the day. Tool libraries enable occasional DIYers to access professional equipment without needing to purchase and store their own tools. Fashion rental services like Rent the Runway make designer clothing accessible while reducing waste and inventory requirements.

The connection to supply chain is that these sharing models require different approaches to logistics and inventory management. Instead of managing one-way flows of goods from manufacturer to consumer, supply chain professionals must design and operate service networks that facilitate continuous movement of assets between users. This includes the capability to take back or recapture products, clean and refurbish them, and manage assets and inventory that are distributed rather than centralized.

Reusable Packaging: Rethinking "Disposable"

TerraCycle's Loop platform offers a focus on one of the more popular topics of the circular economy: Packaging. While it may seem to some like an afterthought, supply chain professionals are well aware of the importance of packaging throughout our operations. TerraCycle worked with brands like Häagen-Dazs, Crest, and Tide to replace disposable packaging with durable packaging that is collected, cleaned, and reused. They have reimagined the customer experience and the connection to supply chain is the need to have a convenient way to capture those durable packages back into a value chain to prepare them for the next user. Packaging examples also exist outside of consumer goods. One example is CHEP, the international pallet and container company, which has built a successful business around reusable shipping materials. Their blue pallets circle the globe in a carefully managed system that reduces both costs and environmental impact. As a member of the Ellen MacArthur Foundation and advocate for circular operations, they have a unique combination of both a circular business model and also a connection to supply chains.

Materials: Rethinking Resources

In the circular economy, materials aren't just consumed—they're borrowed from the Earth and meant to be returned in useful forms. This mindset fundamentally changes how we think about resources, moving us from a linear take-make-waste model to a circular system where materials maintain their value through multiple lifecycles.

The Hierarchy of Material Use

Think of materials like water in a fountain: The higher up we can keep them circulating, the more value we preserve. This creates a natural hierarchy of material use strategies. The less we need to do to a product, component, or material before returning it to a value chain, the better. This is because it will take less time, fewer materials, and less capital, which delivers on the promise of the business case for circular operations.

Reuse represents the highest form of circularity. When Interface, the world's largest commercial carpet manufacturer, takes back used carpet tiles, they often find that many are still perfectly serviceable. By cleaning and redistributing these tiles, they preserve not just raw materials but all the energy and effort that went into manufacturing them.

Refurbishment comes next. Consider how Apple's refurbishment program takes used iPhones, replaces necessary components, and resells them with full warranties. This process uses far fewer resources than manufacturing new phones while maintaining high product quality and consumer confidence.

Recycling, while better than disposal, actually sits at the bottom of our circular hierarchy. When we recycle a plastic bottle, we have to use additional energy to break it down and reform it—and often, the resulting material is of lower quality than the original. This is why companies like Loop are moving beyond recycling to reusable packaging systems that preserve material integrity through multiple use cycles.

Material Innovation: Nature as Teacher

As we learned from Janine Benyus, nature offers lessons in material circularity. Consider how a fallen tree in a forest becomes food for fungi, which in turn nourish new plant growth. This inspired companies to explore material science and innovations. For example, Ecovative, which grows packaging materials from mushroom mycelium and agriculture by-product. Their products protect items during shipping just as well as synthetic foam but can be composted after use, becoming nutrients for new growth.

Biofacturing represents another frontier in circular materials. Modern Meadow, for example, grows leather-like materials in laboratories using cell cultures. This approach eliminates the environmental impact of traditional leather production while creating materials that can be precisely engineered for specific applications.

The success of circular materials often depends on operational capabilities. For example, Renault's remanufacturing success relies on sophisticated reverse logistics systems and advanced testing capabilities. These operational elements are designed to recover materials and prepare them to meet quality standards while keeping costs competitive.

How do we know if we're succeeding with circular materials? Traditional metrics like recycling rates tell only part of the story. Forward-thinking organizations are adopting more sophisticated measures, such as product and material circularity indicators to track how long materials stay in productive use.

As we move into examining operations, remember that material choices shape operational possibilities. The decisions we make about materials today determine what kinds of circular systems we can build tomorrow.

Operations: The Engine of Circularity

You've probably been to a factory before. The value stream means inputs enter one end, outputs exit the other; waste streams mean that waste flows steadily to disposal sites. Now imagine instead a facility where "waste" from one process feeds another, where energy cascades from high-grade to low-grade uses, and where materials flow in cycles rather than straight lines. This redesign from linear to circular operations represents one of our greatest challenges—and opportunities—in building a circular economy.

Operations sit at the intersection of supply chain design and material flows. While business models might dictate what we aim to achieve, and material choices determine what's possible, operations are where theory meets practice. This is where circular supply chains either flourish or falter.

Consider the case of BMW's Leipzig plant. Here, the plant uses four wind turbines to supply renewable energy. They are also integrated into an energy management system that matches production schedules to power availability. The plant's paint shop, traditionally an energy-intensive operation, uses excess heat from other processes, reducing both energy consumption and costs. This operational design required rethinking the facility and had connections across the entire supply chain network, including energy suppliers, material flows, and production scheduling.

Industrial Symbiosis: Waste as Resource

The concept of industrial symbiosis offers a hyper-local example of circular operations in action. The most famous example is from Kalundborg, Denmark. What began as a partnership among factories to share scarce fresh water for production processes has evolved into a complex web of resource sharing.

The Asnæs Power Station in Kalundborg demonstrates how "waste" becomes valuable in a circular system. The power station's steam heats approximately 3,500 local homes[2] and businesses (a form of the third principle of the circular economy of regeneration, through contributing to local communities) while also supplying steam to Novo Nordisk, a major pharmaceutical and enzyme manufacturer, creating an efficient district heating network. The gypsum produced as a by-product of the power station's desulfurization process becomes a key raw material for Gyproc's wallboard manufacturing, eliminating their need to import natural gypsum and reducing the carbon footprint of their production process.

The facility's interconnections extend even further through water and energy sharing—the nearby Statoil refinery (now part of Equinor) provides treated effluent water to the power plant, while also supplying excess gas to Gyproc for drying plasterboard. The power station's salt cooling water supports a local aquaculture operation producing trout and turbot, and the resulting fish farm sludge, along with biological materials from Novo Nordisk, provides nutrient-rich fertilizer for local farms, completing several circular material loops within the community.

This a blueprint for how circular supply chains can create value through operational integration. Each partnership reduces costs for both parties while minimizing environmental impact but also dramatically increases material security, since operations are physically connected through pipes. The key lies in seeing beyond individual facility boundaries to identify opportunities across the broader supply network.

Resource Circulation in Practice

Let's examine three critical operational resources and how circular thinking transforms their use:

- Water: Traditional operations treat water as a one-time-use resource. Circular operations implement cascading water use systems, where high-quality water is used first for sensitive processes, then cascades to less demanding applications before being treated and recirculated. Toyota's plant in Georgetown, Kentucky, is designed to reduce water usage by 1.5 million gallons annually.[3]

- Steam and heat: Energy typically follows a one-way path in linear operations. Circular operations capture and reuse heat through multiple cycles. Interface's factory in the Netherlands captures waste heat from one process to power another, creating a cascade of energy use that significantly reduces overall consumption.

- Oils and lubricants: Instead of disposing of used industrial oils, circular operations use filtration and reconditioning systems. Mobile Oil's closed-loop lubricant program helps customers extend oil life while ensuring proper treatment and reuse, transforming a waste stream into a valuable resource.

The transition to circular operations depends on the connection to supply chain capabilities and new ways to measure success. Apple's recycling robot Daisy demonstrates this—while it can disassemble 200 iPhones per hour,[4] its effectiveness relies entirely on supply chain networks that both deliver phones to the facility and ensure recovered materials find new purposes. This capability expands traditional metrics like efficiency and productivity to include new measures that capture circular performance, from resource productivity to system-wide optimization across partner networks. While this transition requires significant coordination across supply chains which goes against the way most were designed, the benefits of reduced costs and increased resilience make it increasingly compelling.

Market Dynamics: Where Business Models Meet Materials

The marketplace represents a critical intersection in our circular framework—the connection between business models and materials. In this space, theoretical possibilities encounter real-world constraints, and supply chains play a crucial mediating role in determining what succeeds and what fails.

Market Barriers and Supply Chain Solutions

Barriers to participating in secondary material markets include availability of materials, infrastructure gaps, and network capabilities. While these appear as market failures, they are also supply chain challenges. For example, secondary materials often exist in sufficient quantities, but supply chains lack the networks to efficiently capture, process, and redistribute them.

The textile industry illustrates this challenge. Less than 1 percent of clothing is recycled into new fibers, despite sufficient material volume existing in the market.[5] The barrier isn't technology—chemical recycling can now produce fibers of equal quality to virgin materials. Instead, the challenge lies in supply chain infrastructure: Collection networks aren't dense enough to gather sufficient volume, sorting facilities can't efficiently separate fiber types, and processing facilities are too far from either collection points or manufacturers to be economical.

The automotive glass market faces similar network challenges. Windshields contain high-quality laminated glass that could be recycled, but most end up in landfills because supply chains lack the specialized collection and processing infrastructure. When windshields are replaced at service centers, the existing (forward) supply chain isn't set up to handle reverse flows. Processing facilities exist but are too scattered to make collection economical. This network gap prevents a viable secondary market from forming, despite the clear demand for recycled glass from manufacturers.

Making Secondary Markets Work

As discussed, the economics of secondary markets depend on three key supply chain factors: Collection density, processing scale, and transportation distance. Each handling step adds cost that must be offset by material value. The most successful companies tackle these factors systematically.

Saint-Gobain's gypsum wallboard operations demonstrate this approach. They've made recycled gypsum cost-competitive with virgin material by placing collection points strategically, near demolition sites, the source of this material. They establish facilities to process the material that are close to both the collection points and to manufacturing plants. By doing this, their supply chain network design minimizes transport distances while maximizing processing efficiency. By collecting close to the point of use, they are also able to capture more material, which supports sufficient scale to justify automated sorting technology.

Building lasting secondary markets requires creating scalable infrastructure to support the growth anticipated in the near future. The lead acid battery industry offers an example of one approach. Through years of supply chain and market development, they have created a network that can recover over 99 percent of used lead acid batteries.[6] Key to this success was systematic and intentional investment in collection points, standardized handling processes, and strategically located recycling facilities. Most importantly, they developed clear quality standards and testing protocols that gave buyers confidence in recycled materials.

These examples highlight a crucial lesson: Successful secondary markets don't just happen—they're built through deliberate supply chain development and market-level collaboration. Companies must invest in physical infrastructure, develop supplier capabilities, and create systems to verify material quality. Only when these supply chain fundamentals are in place can secondary markets achieve significant scale.

Strategy: Making Circular Supply Chains Work at Scale

When companies announce circular economy goals, they often underestimate the fundamental supply chain transformations required. Traditional supply chain strategies optimize for cost, quality, and delivery speed in one direction. Circular supply chains must optimize these same metrics while simultaneously managing reverse flows, maintaining material quality through multiple lifecycles, and coordinating complex networks of partners.

The semiconductor manufacturing industry illustrates both the challenges and significant achievements possible in circular supply chain strategy. One example comes from ASML, a Dutch company that creates photolithography machines, which are a key step of the semiconductor supply chain.

REAL-WORLD EXAMPLE
ASML

ASML aimed to use captured and remanufactured parts in new machines, but encountered challenges. For example, their supplier contracts required updates for reverse logistics, and their inventory systems needed modification to track components through multiple lifecycles.

However, ASML's systematic approach to these challenges has delivered remarkable results. Their 2023 performance shows that 95 percent of all systems sold in the past 30 years[7] are still active in the field, and they achieve an 87 percent reuse rate for parts returned from field and factory operations.[8] One specific success story is their work with supplier Lamers (part of Aalberts Advanced Mechatronics) on the external interface module for their TWINSCAN XT and NXT systems.[9] Through careful supply chain coordination, they proved rebuilt modules could achieve as-new quality standards, with each reused module saving 200kg of waste and €40–50k in costs.[10]

ASML is now scaling these successes through dedicated infrastructure. They're establishing global reuse centers near their manufacturing sites in Linkou (Taiwan), Veldhoven (Netherlands), and the United States (Wilton and San Diego). This strategic expansion of their supply chain network supported savings of €781 million from reusing service parts in 2022, up from €686 million in 2021, demonstrating how circular strategies can deliver both environmental and business benefits in even the most demanding technical environments.

Supply chain strategy for circular systems requires fundamentally different approaches to risk management. Companies must consider new risks like material quality degradation over multiple lifecycles, supply variability in reverse flows, and partner reliability in collection networks. The most successful companies build these considerations into their core strategy rather than treating them as add-on sustainability initiatives.

Connections into Predictions

The connections between business models, materials, operations and markets form the foundation for circular supply chains. When business models create demand for circular products, supply chains need new capabilities to source materials, optimize operations, and develop markets. These capabilities build upon each other—operational excellence enables more ambitious business models, which drive material innovation, which creates new market opportunities. Understanding these connections helps supply chain professionals identify where to focus their efforts in building circular capabilities.

Notes

1   Eckdish Knack, R. (2005) Pay As You Park, American Planning Association, http://shoup.bol.ucla.edu/PayAsYouPark.htm (archived at https://perma.cc/7KC5-YCU2)

2   Tech Briefs (2024) My opinion: Industrial symbiosis is good for the environment and for the pocketbook, www.techbriefs.com/component/content/article/52266-my-opinion-industrial-symbiosis-is-good-for-the-environment-and-for-the-pocketbook (archived at https://perma.cc/794Y-A3C7)

3   Staley, C. (2024) Gov. Beshear Announces Largest Dollar Investment of 2024: Toyota Investing $922 Million To Build Advanced Paint Facility in Georgetown, State of Kentucky

4   Peters, A. (2019) Apple's iPhone recycling robot can take apart 200 iPhones an hour—can it dismantle the company's footprint? Fast Company, www.fastcompany.com/90413038/apples-iphone-recycling-robot-can-take-apart-200-iphones-an-hour-can-it-dismantle-the-companys-footprint (archived at https://perma.cc/JGU6-3HPW)

5   平子 (2024) Why fashion's 'recycling' is not saving the planet, *The Japan News*, https://japannews.yomiuri.co.jp/science-nature/environment/20240214-168819/ (archived at https://perma.cc/666Q-EPJ2)

6   Battery Council International (2023) New study confirms U.S.' most recycled consumer product—lead batteries—maintains remarkable milestone: 99% recycling rate, https://batterycouncil.org/news/press-release/new-study-confirms-lead-batteries-maintain-remarkable-99-recycling-rate/ (archived at https://perma.cc/8S5T-93EK)

7   ASML (2023) 2023 Annual Report, www.asml.com/en/investors/annual-report/2023 (archived at https://perma.cc/U74D-LR8D)

8   ASML (2022) Highlights—Annual Report 2022, www.asml.com/en/investors/annual-report/2022/highlights (archived at https://perma.cc/E86X-97MX)

9   ASML (2023) Seven ways that ASML is making re-use an everyday mantra, www.asml.com/en/news/stories/2023/seven-ways-reuse-everyday (archived at https://perma.cc/G5DD-WANV)

10 ASML (2023) Seven ways that ASML is making re-use an everyday mantra, www.asml.com/en/news/stories/2023/seven-ways-reuse-everyday (archived at https://perma.cc/BUV8-U7YN)

04

Building Tomorrow's Circular Supply Chain

The Path to the Future: Core Capabilities

The journey from our current linear supply chains to this circular future requires deliberate evolution across five core capabilities: Digital infrastructure, physical networks, workforce development, technology enablement, and performance measurement.

Digital Infrastructure: The Foundation

Just as the internet revolutionized information flow, digital product passports are transforming how we track and trace products through multiple lifecycles. Every product and component requires a digital identity that travels with it through repair, reuse, and eventual material reclamation. Early adopters are already implementing these systems, creating the data backbone needed for circular decisions. These systems enable real-time decisions about repair locations, component harvesting, and value preservation opportunities.

Physical Networks: From Centralized to Distributed

Today's centralized repair facilities must evolve into networks of local repair hubs, mobile maintenance units, and community workshops. Companies like Fairphone and iFixit have proven the viability of distributed repair networks, while firms like Philips are creating regional refurbishment centers. The challenge lies not in the technology itself, but in building these capabilities close to where products are used. This transformation requires rethinking not just repair locations, but the entire approach to maintaining product value within communities.

Workforce Evolution: New Skills, New Roles

The workforce transformation may be the most profound change. Supply chain professionals of the future will need capabilities that blend technical expertise with local knowledge. Circular Value Preservers will optimize product life extension through local repair networks. Network Developers will build repair capabilities within communities, while Component Harvest Specialists will ensure parts maintain their highest value through multiple use cycles. Digital Twin Orchestrators will maintain virtual product histories that inform repair decisions, and Repair Network Coordinators will optimize maintenance operations across local hubs.

Technology Enablers: Beyond Automation

The technology foundations are rapidly maturing into a connected ecosystem of solutions. Artificial intelligence drives predictive maintenance and repair optimization, while augmented reality enables remote expert guidance for local technicians. IoT sensors monitor product condition in real-time, feeding data to digital passports that track complete product histories. Mobile repair platforms bring maintenance capabilities directly to products, while automated diagnostic systems speed up local repairs. These technologies work together to maximize product life while minimizing transportation.

Measuring Success: New Metrics for Circularity

Traditional supply chain metrics focused on cost and speed must expand to encompass the full scope of circular value preservation. Average distance to repair becomes a critical metric, alongside product life extension rates and component reuse percentages. Local repair success rates demonstrate community capability development, while value retention metrics show how effectively we're keeping products at their highest utility. Transportation avoided through local repair highlights both environmental and economic benefits of distributed networks.

The Implementation Journey

The roadmap to 2035 requires systematic capability building across three phases. The Foundation Phase, from 2024 to 2027, focuses on establishing digital passports, basic repair networks, and component tracking systems. The Expansion Phase, running through 2031, sees the deployment of predictive maintenance, mobile repair units, and community repair hubs. The final Integration Phase brings autonomous optimization, real-time value preservation, and seamless local-to-global coordination.

The Business Case for Change

The economics of this transformation are compelling. Companies pioneering local repair models are discovering significant benefits beyond just cost reduction. Transportation expenses drop as repairs move closer to product locations. New revenue streams emerge from repair services, while customer loyalty grows through local presence. Component value retention improves through better tracking and optimal reuse. Perhaps most importantly, product reliability increases as repair data feeds back into design improvements.

The Path Forward

The supply chain profession stands at the forefront of this revolution. The capabilities we develop today will determine how quickly we can realize the circular future. Success requires more than just technology—it demands a fundamental rethinking of how we preserve value locally. Looking ahead to 2035, one thing is clear: The circular supply chain isn't just an environmental imperative—it's a business necessity. The companies that master these capabilities first will define the next era of supply chain excellence.

The question isn't whether supply chains will become circular, but how quickly we can build the local capabilities to make it happen. The journey to 2035 begins in our communities, with every decision we make about repair, reuse, and value preservation shaping the future of global supply chains.

Defining the Path: Building Circular Capabilities

When supply chain teams tackle circular operations, they discover that it takes new capabilities. Their people need different mindsets and skills. Their processes need to handle complex flows of materials moving in multiple directions. Their technology systems, designed for linear efficiency, can't track products and components through multiple lifecycles. Their quality standards, perfect for new production, struggle to evaluate recovered materials. Their governance structures, built for traditional supplier relationships, can't coordinate complex networks of circular value creation. These experiences reveal a hint about circular transformation: It requires building new capabilities across every dimension of operations.

The transition from linear to circular supply chains represents one of the most significant transformations in industrial history. Organizations can reimagine how they produce and distribute products, and how they create and capture value across multiple product lifecycles. This transformation will need new capabilities that span from shop floor to executive suite, from individual facilities to global networks, from immediate operations to long-term strategy.

This challenges five critical areas of capabilities. First, organizations can develop the people and culture capabilities that create the foundation for circular operations, transforming mindsets while building new types of expertise. Second, they need sophisticated process capabilities that can handle the complexity of circular material flows and value creation. Third, they can build technology infrastructure that can track and optimize products and materials through multiple lifecycles. Fourth, they need to develop standards that make sure there is consistent quality and enable effective collaboration across networks. Finally, they can create governance frameworks that coordinate complex webs of partners while ensuring fair value distribution.

As we explore circular supply chains, we'll see how leading organizations are building the capabilities that make circular operations possible and advantageous. This section acts as a preview to the rest of this book. We'll start to explore the capabilities needed to build and run a circular supply chain, across people, process, technology, standards, and governance, and dive in more to these in the coming chapters.

People and Culture Capabilities: Enabling the Circular Mindset

When Grundfos, providing pump and water solutions, began their journey toward circular operations, they expected the biggest challenges to be in technology and process design. Instead, they discovered that the transformation needs to happen in the mindsets and capabilities of their people. For example, engineers who had spent their careers perfecting new product manufacturing now need to reimagine their roles as stewards of materials through multiple lifecycles. Managers trained in linear efficiency metrics now need to develop new ways of measuring success. The company's experience revealed a capability about circular supply chains: While technology and processes enable circularity, it's the people who drive the transformation.

People capabilities include three critical dimensions. First, organizations can nurture a shift in mindset from "use and dispose" to "preserve and extend"—a change that touches every level from shop floor to executive suite. Second, they need to develop new types of expertise, creating roles that may not have existed in traditional supply chains while transforming existing positions to embrace circular principles. Finally, they can reimagine how teams work together, breaking down silos that could be perhaps tolerated in linear operations, but become barriers to circular success.

Circular Leadership: A New Lens for Operations

When Continental's tire division team first explored circular manufacturing, they found an unexpected challenge. Their quality teams, trained to judge products against pristine, new-production standards, struggled to evaluate refurbished tires. "Perfect" had always meant "new." The idea that a recovered and restored tire could be equally valuable—or even superior due to upgraded materials and processes—required a new way of thinking.

This challenge shows the cultural capability at the heart of circular supply chains. Traditional manufacturing mindsets treat products as having a single, linear lifecycle: Raw materials in, finished goods out, and eventual disposal. Success meant optimizing this one-way flow. And in circular operations, every "endpoint" becomes a potential beginning. Every product returning from the field brings opportunities for value creation, rather than disposal challenges.

This touches every level of the organization. At Xerox, where printing solutions undergo multiple lifecycles, the training for shop floor technicians expanded from assembly specialists to create product lifecycle managers. They developed expertise in evaluating returned equipment, making complex decisions about repair versus upgrade paths, and identifying opportunities for component recovery. Middle managers now learn to balance traditional efficiency metrics with circular economy objectives, developing new frameworks for measuring success that are still reasonable enough for boardroom discussions. Senior leaders face perhaps the biggest shift—working within quarterly productivity targets to include the concepts and new measurements around circular value streams.

New Circular Supply Chain Roles: The Evolution of Experience

When Philips Healthcare launched their circular program for medical imaging equipment, they discovered their traditional roles needed rescoping. Their analysts, trained to forecast new equipment sales, found themselves facing new questions. For example: How can I predict when a hospital will buy new equipment, and when they might be ready to upgrade? How can I forecast the future value of components that haven't yet been recovered? Their set of traditional supply chain tools weren't set up to support these types of scenarios.

This evolution of roles reflects how circular supply chains operate. Where traditional supply chain professionals focus on optimizing one-way flows of new products, circular supply chain professionals focus on managing complex networks of materials moving in multiple directions. This creates new roles and also adjusts existing ones.

ASML's semiconductor equipment program shows how technical roles have expanded. Their field service engineers increase their capabilities from being known as maintenance specialists to now also becoming lifecycle optimization experts. While they repair equipment, they are also helping their customers plan strategic upgrades, optimize service timelines, and make sure their equipment can last as long as possible. Their capabilities span traditional mechanical and electrical systems while also using new skills in predictive analytics and circular economy principles.

Continuous Learning Culture: Building Circular Teams

When Fairphone first attempted to create truly repairable smartphones, they discovered that traditional team structures stood in their way. Design teams, accustomed to optimizing for sleek aesthetics and minimal production costs, worked separately from repair technicians who would eventually need to service these devices. The manufacturing teams focus on assembly efficiency but didn't consider how components might later be separated and recovered. Overall, the company realized that creating circular products takes more than new designs—it also required different ways of organizing their teams.

This challenge reveals another capability for circular operations: Traditional organizational boundaries often become barriers to circular success. Where linear supply chains could operate effectively with specialized teams focused on their individual functions, circular operations take intentional collaboration and integration. This requires organizations to reimagine what their teams do, and how they work together.

GE Healthcare's medical equipment program demonstrates this in practice. Their training programs have expanded beyond a focus on individual technical skills to also include cross-functional learning experiences. In these, service technicians work alongside design engineers, and manufacturing specialists collaborate with material recovery experts. These interactions build technical capabilities—they create shared understanding of how decisions in one area affect the entire circular system. Engineers learn firsthand how their design choices impact repair complexity, while service teams provide crucial feedback that influences future product development. We know that "going to Gemba" is a powerful tool, and the team at GE Healthcare saw it in action.

Process Capabilities: Orchestrating Circular Flows

When supply chains start their circular journey, they often find that their existing processes are like one-way streets in a city that needs complex transit networks. Their carefully optimized processes developed for moving new products one way from factory to customer can't handle the reverse: Products flowing backwards from customers to repair centers, or components moving sideways between recovery facilities.

The shift from linear to circular operations requires more than adding reverse logistics capabilities to existing supply chains. Supply chains need to also develop new capabilities that can handle multiple streams of materials moving backwards and sideways, through networks of recapturing and revaluing.

This includes three capabilities. First, organizations can reimagine their value streams, creating processes that can track and optimize materials flowing through multiple states of transformation. Second, they need to develop smart recovery operations that go beyond traditional repair to combine advanced diagnostics with decision-making about highest-level value recovery. Finally, they can master network orchestration to coordinate the web of material flows, knowledge sharing, and resource optimization across networks.

The Circular Value Stream: Redefining Value and Waste

When Ericsson first mapped their Network Equipment Recovery program, what emerged looked less like a traditional supply chain and more like a complex transit system. Equipment flowed from manufacturing to customers, and between repair centers, through upgrade facilities, into component harvesting operations, and back into production. The journey of a single telecommunications rack might return from a network upgrade, provide components for three different repair operations, and still yield valuable materials for recycling. The team felt they were redefining value streams beyond what they had previously managed.

This complexity shows how materials and products flow through circular supply chains. Traditional value streams resembled rivers, with materials flowing in one direction from source to sea. Circular value streams function more like water cycles—materials flow continuously through different states, each transformation creating new opportunities for value retention and creation.

Nokia's move toward circular operations for their telecommunications equipment operations reveals how organizations learn to manage these complex flows. Their system tracks items moving through the network and monitor the potential value in each possible scenario. When equipment arrives at a facility, for example, circular-focused algorithms help determine optimal recovery approaches to guide materials to their highest value. They now balance questions such as: Should this unit be repaired and returned to service? Could its components provide more value in upgrading other systems? Might certain materials be more valuable if recovered for use in new production? Each decision point represents an opportunity to maximize both economic and environmental value.

Smart Recovery Protocols: Optimizing for the Highest Value

When Hitachi Construction Machinery first established their component rebuilding centers, they discovered that traditional repair approaches fell short. Their technicians, skilled at diagnosing individual component failures, now faced entire hydraulic systems that had operated for years in environments ranging from arctic mining sites to equatorial forests. Each system contained dozens of interconnected components, each aging differently based on its operating history. The company realized that successful recovery takes more than fixing what is broken—it requires an understanding of how entire systems evolve over time.

This challenge shows how recovery operations in circular supply chains go beyond the capabilities of traditional repair and maintenance. Where conventional repair focuses on restoring broken items to working condition, circular recovery operations create multiple pathways for value creation. This capability combines advanced diagnostics, predictive analytics, and deep material science knowledge to maximize value across entire product systems.

John Deere shows an example of this capability in its Reman operations. The facilities can scale up and down with seasonal equipment returns, and they have developed systems that adapt recovery strategies based on predicted agricultural cycles. For example, when a combine harvester arrives for remanufacturing during the off-season, their teams assess its current condition. In this assessment, they analyze wear patterns from its operating history, predict which components might fail in the next season, and proactively upgrade systems to prevent future downtime. This predictive approach expands their recovery operations from reactive repair to proactive value creation.

Resource Optimization Equipping and Resourcing for Circularity

When Volvo first attempted to scale their remanufacturing operations globally, they encountered a challenge that highlights the complexity of circular networks. A repair facility in Sweden discovered an innovative way to restore a critical engine component, potentially saving thousands of units from premature recycling. And how could they quickly share this knowledge with facilities in Asia and North America? The company realized that success in circular operations requires even more than excellent local facilities – it also takes orchestration of the knowledge and resources across their entire network.

This shows a capability for circular supply chains: The value created through circular operations depends heavily on how effectively organizations coordinate across their networks. Where traditional supply chains could often succeed through hub-and-spoke coordination, circular operations require orchestrating across material flows, knowledge sharing, and resource optimization.

The power of network orchestration becomes particularly clear in Cummins' engine remanufacturing operations. Their facilities operate as interconnected nodes in a global value creation network. For example, when one facility faces capacity constraints, capacity can be dynamically rebalanced with other nearby locations. Recovered components are assessed and redirected to the repair center where they can add the most value. Most importantly, innovations in recovery techniques spread rapidly across the network, driving continuous improvement in operations worldwide.

Technology Capabilities: Digital Enablement

When supply chain teams sit down to explore how to manage products through multiple lifecycles, they often start with looking at technology. They usually find that their existing internal approach to technology isn't able to support life-over-life tracking. Their systems, designed for traditional linear tracking, can't handle the complexity of monitoring thousands of components through multiple lives, predicting performance across different operating conditions, and optimizing recovery decisions across multiple networks. The transition to circular operations needs new technologies capable of managing complexity at unprecedented scales.

The shift from linear to circular operations requires technology systems that can see, understand, and optimize complex networks of material flows and value creation opportunities. Traditional systems focused on tracking linear processes can evolve into platforms that can manage products through multiple lifecycles, guide recovery operations, and orchestrate resource flows across global networks. This isn't about adding new features to existing systems—it is about reimagining how technology enables circular operations from the ground up.

This capability includes three dimensions. First, organizations can develop digital product lifecycle management systems that create digital threads following products through multiple lives. Second, they need intelligent recovery systems that combine artificial intelligence, machine learning, and advanced analytics to optimize value recovery at scale. Finally, they can implement network intelligence platforms that can orchestrate complex material flows and resource optimization across global circular ecosystems.

Digital Product Memory: Following the Lifecycles

When Rolls-Royce revolutionized aircraft engine services with their "Power by the Hour" program, they faced a challenge in product lifecycle management. Their engineers needed to track basic maintenance records, and the detailed performance history of thousands of components operating in unique conditions across global flight networks. Each engine told a complex story through its data: The thermal stresses of takeoffs in Dubai's heat, the moisture exposure of Asian monsoon seasons, the vibration patterns of trans-Atlantic routes. The company realized that successful circular operations required creating sophisticated digital systems that could capture, analyze, and act on these intricate product lifecycles.

This challenge shows how digital product lifecycle management in circular supply chains expands on traditional asset tracking capabilities. Where conventional systems focused on basic location and maintenance records, circular operations require creating comprehensive digital threads that follow products through multiple transformations. These systems become the memory and nervous system of circular operations, enabling decisions about maintenance, recovery, and value creation.

The capabilities of these systems are showcased in HPE's Technology Renewal Centers. Their digital lifecycle management platforms track individual units, and can manage the interdependencies between components, software versions, and upgrade paths. When enterprise computing equipment arrives for assessment, the system can provide a complete picture: The original configuration, upgrade history, performance trends, and compatibility with current technology standards. This context helps teams make decisions about recovery strategies, balancing immediate restoration needs against long-term value creation opportunities.

Predictive Recovery: Beyond Human Scale

When Vestas first attempted to scale their wind turbine blade repair operations globally, they found a challenge that pushed the limits of human expertise. Their technicians faced an ever-growing variety of damage patterns: Stress fractures from arctic wind conditions, erosion from coastal salt spray, impact damage from desert sandstorms. Each blade told a unique story of environmental wear, and even their most experienced engineers struggled to consistently determine optimal repair strategies across thousands of cases. The company realized that maintaining quality at scale required moving beyond individual human judgment to intelligent systems that could process vast amounts of repair data and guide complex decisions.

This challenge highlights the role of intelligent recovery systems in transforming circular operations. Where traditional repair relies primarily on human expertise and standard procedures, modern recovery operations leverage artificial intelligence, machine learning, and advanced analytics to process complexity at scale. These systems don't replace human expertise—they amplify it by enabling consistent, data-driven decisions.

The role of augmented reality in intelligent recovery becomes particularly powerful in circular operations. Caterpillar's remanufacturing facilities use AR systems that guide technicians through sophisticated repair procedures. These systems display instructions, and then they adapt based on real-time component conditions, helping make sure that quality is consistent across all operations. When a technician encounters an unusual damage pattern, for example, the system can connect them with relevant repair histories and expert guidance.

Network Orchestration: A Platform For the Circular Ecosystem

When Lenovo first attempted to optimize their global asset recovery network, they discovered that local efficiency often came at the cost of network-wide performance. A decision to refurbish laptops in Singapore might seem optimal when viewed in isolation, but could deprive a repair center in Mexico of crucial components, or miss an opportunity to upgrade devices for a growing market in Eastern Europe. The company realized that true optimization required intelligence systems that could see and analyze patterns across their entire global network, making decisions that maximized value creation that optimizes for keeping products and components as local as possible.

This challenge shows how network intelligence can enable circular operations. Where traditional systems optimized individual facilities or regional clusters, modern circular networks require intelligence platforms that can process huge amounts of data to coordinate operations. These systems track materials and orchestrate important balancing acts between repair operations, component recovery, material flows, and market opportunities.

Toyota's evolution in managing their remanufacturing operations demonstrates the power of network intelligence. Their systems share repair procedures between facilities to create dynamic knowledge networks that support operations. For example, when a facility in Brazil discovers a more efficient way to remanufacture a transmission component, the system doesn't just document the procedure—it analyzes how this innovation could benefit other operations and can adjust work routing and component recovery strategies across the network to maximize the value of this new capability.

Industry Standards Capabilities: Common Language for Circularity

When SKF first attempted to scale their bearing remanufacturing operations globally, they discovered that the standards designed for linear manufacturing created unexpected barriers to circular operations. They asked themselves questions such as: How could they verify that a refurbished bearing would perform as well as a new one? How should they measure and communicate the condition of recovered components? How could they ensure consistent quality across a network of recovery partners? The company's experience highlighted a capability: The transition to circular operations requires a new set of industry standards. This means new ways of measuring performance, managing information, and enabling collaboration.

The shift from linear to circular operations often takes more than just adapting existing standards. Organizations can develop new frameworks that can evaluate performance across multiple product lifecycles and must have shared language for the value to be realized. In doing so, they can enable sharing of complex product histories and guide effective collaboration between partner organizations. Traditional standards focused on new production will expand to support circular material flows and value creation.

Industry standards include three dimensions. First, organizations can develop performance standards that can effectively measure and ensure quality across multiple product lifecycles. Second, they need data and digital standards that create common understanding across complex networks of recovery and reuse. Finally, they can establish industry collaboration standards that enable diverse organizations to work together effectively in circular operations.

Multi-Life Performance: Measuring Success Again and Again

When 3M's adhesive products division first attempted to create standards for recovered materials, they found an interesting challenge. Their traditional quality metrics, designed for virgin materials, couldn't capture the nuanced performance characteristics of adhesives that had gone through separation and recovery processes. A recovered adhesive might actually perform better in some applications due to molecular changes during its first lifecycle, yet existing standards would classify it as inferior. The company realized they needed to reimagine how they defined and measured performance in a circular context.

This challenge shows how performance standards in circular supply chains expand on and change traditional quality metrics. Where conventional standards focused on measuring products against new production specifications, circular operations require different frameworks that can evaluate performance across multiple lifecycles. These standards can balance immediate performance requirements with long-term circularity objectives, creating new ways to define and measure success.

Innovation in performance standards often emerges from understanding how products evolve through use. For example, when Bosch developed standards for their remanufactured automotive components, they discovered that traditional pass-fail criteria missed crucial performance insights. Their new standards incorporate wear pattern analysis, looking at whether a component meets specifications today, and how it's likely to perform through its next lifecycle. This predictive element goes beyond point-in-time measurement to now include a forward-looking evaluation.

Digital Interoperability: Creating the Common Language of Circularity

When SAP began developing digital systems to support circular operations across multiple manufacturers, they discovered a challenge. Each company tracks product lifecycle data differently—one manufacturer's "refurbished" was another's "remanufactured," while component condition descriptions ranged from simple numeric grades to complex technical assessments. Without standardized ways to describe product states, material conditions, and recovery processes, even the most sophisticated digital systems struggled to enable effective collaboration across circular networks.

This challenge showcases that data and digital standards form the foundation for circular operations. Where traditional supply chains could often function with basic data exchanges, circular systems require shared standards that create common understanding across partners engaging in recovery, refurbishment, and reuse. These standards enable clear communication about everything from material compositions to recovery procedures to performance histories.

The impact extends beyond operational efficiency to enabling new forms of collaboration. When Microsoft developed standards for their circular IT programs, they created frameworks that enabled closer cooperation with recovery partners. For example, their standardized data structures and digital interfaces track products by creating a common understanding that networks of partners work together more effectively, maximizing value recovery across the circular ecosystem.

Ecosystem Collaboration Protocols: Accelerating Industry Sharing

When Michelin first expanded their tire retreading operations beyond their own facilities to include partner networks, they found a challenge that highlights the complexity of circular collaboration. Their recovery processes, which worked seamlessly in their own facilities, proved difficult for partners to replicate consistently. They discovered this was due to different interpretations of quality standards, varying approaches to process documentation, and inconsistent methods of sharing technical knowledge. The company realized that successful scaling of circular operations requires more that sharing technical specifications—it takes frameworks for collaboration that could ensure consistency while accommodating partner diversity.

This challenge shows that industry collaboration standards enable circular operations. Where traditional supply chains could often function with basic supplier requirements, circular systems need comprehensive frameworks that enable multiple organizations to work together. These standards can balance the need for consistency with the flexibility to accommodate different organizational capabilities and local conditions.

Whirlpool's evolution in their appliance recycling program shows the need for collaboration standards. Their frameworks specify material recovery requirements by creating detailed protocols for how partners should assess, process, and document appliance recycling operations. For example, when a recycling partner receives end-of-life appliances, the standardized procedures guide outlines everything from initial assessment to material separation to quality verification. These standards make sure recovery operations are consistent while enabling partners to integrate circular practices into their existing operations.

Governance Capabilities: Ensuring Circular Success

When Philips Healthcare began transitioning their medical imaging business toward circular operations, they discovered that traditional governance models were not sufficient. This was because their existing frameworks were designed for linear supply chains. They struggled to address the new questions that the team faced, such as: How should value be shared when multiple partners contribute to extending a product's life? How could quality be ensured across multiple recovery cycles? How should complex networks of partners be coordinated to maximize circular value creation? The company's experience showcases a capability required: The transition to circular operations takes different approaches to governance.

The shift from linear to circular operations requires more than new processes and technologies—it also takes new governance frameworks that can coordinate complex networks of partners while ensuring consistent quality and fair value distribution. Circular efforts have failed in the past due to a lack of shared leadership across organizations.

This capability includes three areas. First, supply chains will develop frameworks for creating and sharing value across complex partner networks, ensuring that circular operations create sustainable benefits for all partners. Second, approaches to quality and compliance that can maintain consistent standards across multiple product lifecycles. Finally, a new approach to network management, coordinating diverse partners in ways that optimize circular performance while encouraging continuous improvement.

Value Sharing Mechanisms: Aligning Incentives Across Networks

When Philips Healthcare first established their circular program for medical imaging equipment, the governance challenge went beyond traditional supplier relationships. A recovered CT scanner might involve value creation at multiple points: The original manufacturer's expertise in assessment, a local partner's skill in repair, another facility's innovation in component recovery, and a logistics provider's efficiency in managing complex material flows. The company realized that sustainable circular operations required new governance approaches for recognizing and sharing value across networks of contributors.

This challenge reveals how governance of value creation changes in circular supply chains. Where traditional models could rely on straightforward value-add calculations, circular operations require new frameworks that recognize and reward multiple forms of value creation across complex networks. These governance structures can balance immediate operational efficiency with long-term circular objectives while ensuring fair distribution of both responsibilities and rewards.

Rolls-Royce's "Power by the Hour" program shows one example of circular value governance. Their framework measures traditional metrics like repair quality and turnaround time, but also includes an approach for evaluating how different partners contribute to equipment longevity and performance optimization. When a maintenance partner develops an innovative repair technique that extends component life, the governance structure ensures they share in the long-term value created through reduced material consumption and improved asset performance.

Quality Assurance: Ensuring Trust Through Multiple Lifecycles

When Siemens Healthcare first expanded their medical imaging equipment recovery program, they found a quality governance challenge that tested traditional approaches. Their quality systems, designed for new production, struggled to address questions unique to circular operations: How do you verify that a refurbished MRI scanner will perform as reliably as a new one? How do you ensure compliance with evolving medical regulations across multiple product lifecycles? How do you maintain consistent quality standards across a network of recovery partners? The company realized that circular operations required different approaches to quality governance.

This challenge reveals how quality and compliance governance transforms in circular supply chains. Where traditional systems focus on controlling new production quality, circular operations require governance capabilities that can focus on reliability and compliance across multiple product lives. These governance structures can maintain quality standards while adapting to the unique challenges of recovered and refurbished products.

Innovation in quality governance often emerges from the need to validate new recovery processes. For example, when Stryker developed their medical device remanufacturing program, they created governance capabilities for qualifying and validating new recovery techniques. Their approach can verify final product quality, and they do this by establishing rigorous governance for the new recovery methods that produce safe, effective results. When a team develops an innovative way to restore a complex component, governance structures create a way to do thorough validation before implementation.

Continuous Evolution: Creating Ecosystems for Industry Collaboration

When HP launched their global printer cartridge recycling program, they encountered a network governance challenge. Their existing supplier management systems, designed for linear production networks, couldn't handle the complexity of coordinating hundreds of collection points, dozens of recovery facilities, and multiple material processors across different regions. Each node in the network needs different levels of oversight, different types of support, and different performance metrics. The company realized that successful circular operations require new approaches to network governance.

This challenge highlights that network management enables circular supply chains. Where traditional governance focused on managing linear supplier relationships, circular operations require capabilities that can coordinate across partners. These governance structures can balance network-wide optimization with local autonomy while ensuring consistent performance across diverse operations.

The impact extends beyond operational efficiency to enable network-wide innovation. When Apple implemented their recycling and recovery program, they created governance structures that encouraged continuous improvement across the network. Their systems manage current operations while also creating governance frameworks for identifying and scaling innovations that enhance circular performance. This capability helps make sure that the network continuously evolves and improves its capabilities.

PART TWO

The Capability
to Repair at Scale

FICTIONAL EXAMPLE
The Repair Revolution

Maya stood at the window of her office in the converted warehouse space in Hackney Wick, London, watching the early morning light reflect off the canal. A year ago, this building had been another empty industrial relic. Now it hummed with activity as repair technicians prepared for the day ahead.

The journey had started during a supply chain crisis—a dock workers' strike at Felixstowe had left containers stranded. Her team had been scrambling to source replacement parts for critical equipment, some as simple as seals and bearings that could be made locally.

"We've got five factories within 50 miles of London," she had told her skeptical executive board, "and every time something breaks, we're waiting weeks for parts from halfway around the world. We need repair sovereignty."

The phrase had caught their attention. Her proposal was radical in its simplicity: Start with one facility serving as both a community repair café and an industrial maintenance hub. Use emerging technologies like AR glasses for repair guidance, small-scale manufacturing for parts creation, and digital tools for knowledge sharing.

The old warehouse had been transformed into distinct zones: A bright, open space for community repairs, an industrial area for heavy equipment, and a small manufacturing cell for creating replacement parts. The setup wasn't perfect yet, but it was proving that local repair at scale was possible.

The coffee shop owner, James, arrived with a commercial-grade coffee grinder. "I've been quoted 12 weeks for parts," he explained, frustration evident in his voice. "My backup grinder's nowhere near as good."

The repair station looked more like a high-tech medical bay than a traditional repair shop, with an overhead camera system, tablets displaying repair procedures, and AR glasses ready to guide the process. The AI software compared images to their growing database of repair cases. Within minutes, they had a match: Worn burrs and a failing motor coupling.

"Here's the interesting part," Maya told James. "We can make these parts right here." Their hybrid manufacturing system was already crafting replacement parts. "We've actually improved on the original design. The ones we make last about 30 percent longer because we use a more wear-resistant alloy."

Three months later, their success was creating new challenges. What started as four repair stations had grown to 12. The manufacturing cell had doubled. Most notably, patterns emerged across seemingly unrelated repairs—a bearing design that worked well in food processing equipment found applications in medical devices.

Their apprenticeship program brought 20 students from local technical colleges to learn repair skills using AR guidance systems. Each successful repair was documented, creating new procedures in their growing knowledge base. This wasn't only about fixing products—they were building systematic knowledge of how to improve what they repaired.

Six months in, manufacturers began noticing. One major appliance maker proposed a breakthrough partnership: Complete repair specifications for their entire product line, shared through Maya's network. In return, they wanted access to the repair data to improve their designs.

Maya looked around their newest facility in Stratford. The space felt different—more like a technology center than a traditional repair shop. Stations were equipped with advanced diagnostic systems. The manufacturing cell included capabilities for complex electronic components. Most significantly, a large screen displayed real-time repair data flowing between their network and the manufacturer's design team.

Their latest impact report showed the transformation's scale:

- 60 percent reduction in repair response times
- 40 percent decrease in transportation emissions

- 200+ new technical jobs created
- 30 percent increase in average product lifespan
- 50,000+ successful repairs completed
- £15 million in estimated savings for local businesses

Maya watched the mix of experienced technicians, apprentices, and automated systems working together. The future they'd imagined—where repair was local, accessible, and normal—was becoming reality. And with inquiries coming in from Manchester, Birmingham, and Glasgow, the repair revolution was just beginning.

05

People and Culture Capabilities

Repairing at Scale

The transition to repair-based supply chains begins with people. Success comes from developing new mindsets, evolving technical skills, and fostering collaboration across traditional boundaries. While technology enables repair at scale, it's the human capabilities—from technicians using AR glasses to apprentices learning new skills—that bring these systems to life. Leading organizations recognize that investing in these three core human capabilities creates the foundation for lasting change: Circular leadership, new circular supply chain roles, and continuous learning culture.

Circular Leadership to Repair at Scale

Developing leaders who understand value exists beyond single-use lifecycles. This encompasses training supply chain professionals to identify opportunities for material reuse, repair, and reintegration.

In Chapter 4, we explored how traditional supply chains were built on planned obsolescence, highlighted by the Phoebus cartel's deliberate reduction of light bulb lifespans. This mindset has shaped the last century of industrial development, creating supply chains optimized for replacement rather than repair. However, a shift is possible. It will be one where repair becomes the default response rather than an afterthought.

The fictional example shows how this repair capability creates value across multiple stakeholders. The community repair café serves local businesses, while the industrial maintenance hub keeps factories running efficiently. This dual-purpose model shows how repair capabilities can scale from consumer products to industrial equipment. This creates jobs while reducing waste and transportation emissions.

This capability mirrors what leading organizations are already doing today. Vitsœ, the furniture manufacturer, designs products specifically for repair and upgrade, with some pieces remaining in continuous use for over 50 years. Their success shows that repair isn't just about fixing what's broken—it's about reimagining the entire product lifecycle. Similarly, Arburg's industrial machines come with detailed repair documentation and guaranteed long-term parts availability, proving this approach works in industrial settings.

Just as the fictional example network evolved from a single location in Hackney Wick to multiple specialized hubs across London, organizations can work to develop their repair capabilities. The assessment framework below will help you understand where your organization stands today and identify concrete next steps for building stronger repair capabilities.

Finding Your Level

To assess your organization, you'll need input from multiple perspectives across your value chain. Schedule focused conversations with key stakeholders with the goal of understanding both the current state of repair in your organization and the barriers to advancing this capability.

Plan to speak with representatives from five key stakeholder groups. For each group, you'll see specific questions designed to uncover how this capability is valued and implemented across your organization. Take notes during these conversations—the patterns that emerge will help you identify your organization's current level and next steps.

After gathering responses to these questions, look for patterns:

- If most answers focus on warranty obligations and cost minimization, you're likely at Level 1
- If you see basic repair services but limited integration with design, you're probably at Level 2
- If repair consistently influences decisions but isn't yet driving innovation, you're at Level 3
- If repair is actively driving innovation and strategy, you've reached Level 4

FOR CUSTOMERS

1 How important is repairability in your purchasing decisions?

2 What repair options would you like to see available?

3 What prevents you from choosing repair over replacement?

4 How do repair capabilities influence your brand loyalty?

5 What value do you place on repair services?

FOR SERVICE AND OPERATIONS

1 What percentage of service requests result in repair versus replacement?

2 How long do we maintain repair parts availability?

3 What systems support our repair operations?

4 How do we capture and share repair knowledge?

5 What barriers prevent more repairs from being completed?

FOR SUPPLY CHAIN PARTNERS

1 How do repair considerations influence our supplier selection?

2 What repair capabilities exist in our supplier network?

3 How do we collaborate on repair solutions?

4 What barriers exist to sharing repair knowledge?

5 How do we manage repair parts inventory across the network?

FOR PRODUCT DEVELOPMENT

1 How early in the design process do we consider repairability?

2 What percentage of design reviews include repair considerations?

3 How do we incorporate repair feedback into new designs?

4 What documentation standards exist for repair procedures?

5 How do we evaluate the trade-offs between initial cost and repairability?

FOR EXECUTIVE LEADERSHIP

1 How does repair capability factor into our business strategy?

2 What metrics do we use to measure repair's impact on business performance?

3 How do we balance repair investments against other priorities?

4 What role does repair play in our sustainability goals?

5 How do we evaluate the financial impact of repair versus replacement?

Level 1 (Beginning)

Organizations at this level view repair primarily as a warranty obligation or necessary evil. This is similar to how businesses in the fictional example initially approached equipment failures before the repair hub opened. Like the coffee shop owner James's original situation, waiting 12 weeks for replacement parts, these organizations default to replacement rather than repair. Product designs prioritize initial cost and ease of assembly over repairability. Service documentation focuses on warranty period requirements, and repair data isn't systematically collected or analyzed.

Key characteristics:

- Repair viewed primarily as warranty obligation
- No formal repair documentation exists beyond warranty period
- Parts availability limited to warranty period
- Repair data not systematically collected

NEXT STEPS FOR LEVEL 1

Review your assessment results with your leadership team. The goal is to create a shared understanding of your current state and align improvement priorities.

Start by building awareness of repair's strategic value. Focus first on collecting basic repair data to understand current state and opportunities. Create a pilot repair program for one product line to show potential benefits.

Consider these targeted actions based on your level:

- Start collecting basic repair data (types of failures, repair costs, customer requests)
- Identify the top three most-requested repairs
- Create a pilot repair program for one product line
- Engage with the service team to understand repair challenges

Level 2 (Developing)

Organizations at this level mirror the earliest days of the fictional example in Hackney Wick, when they were just beginning to show the value of repair. Like the first repair stations, they've started offering basic repair services and maintaining some repair capabilities but haven't fully integrated repair thinking into their operations. Similar to the initial challenges with the executive board in the fictional example, these organizations often struggle with balancing repair capabilities against traditional efficiency metrics, though they recognize repair's potential value.

Key characteristics:

- Basic repair services offered post-warranty
- Some repair documentation exists but may be incomplete
- Limited parts availability beyond warranty period
- Basic repair data collection started but not fully utilized

NEXT STEPS FOR LEVEL 2

Focus on systematically integrating repair thinking into your operations. Build connections between service teams and product development. Create formal processes for capturing and using repair data. Invest in repair training and documentation.

Consider these targeted actions based on your level:

- Develop repair metrics dashboard for tracking key performance indicators
- Include repair team representatives in all design reviews
- Create and implement repair documentation standards
- Launch comprehensive repair technician training program
- Establish a process for studying successful repairs to identify design improvements

Level 3 (Advanced)

Organizations at this level operate like the mature hub network in the fictional example, with repair fully integrated and seen as a strategic priority. Just as the network expanded into specialized locations across London, these organizations maintain repair documentation and plan for long-term parts availability. Like the system of AR-guided repairs and knowledge capture in the fictional example, they actively use repair data to influence design decisions. Repair is no longer seen as a cost center.

Key characteristics:

- Repair integrated into product design process
- Comprehensive repair documentation readily available

- Extended parts availability planned during design phase
- Repair data actively influences product development decisions

NEXT STEPS FOR LEVEL 3

Work on expanding repair influence across your organization. Create formal programs for capturing and sharing repair innovations, develop networks to scale repair capabilities and begin sharing repair knowledge beyond your organization.

Consider these targeted actions based on your level:

- Establish a repair innovation program with dedicated resources
- Create automated repair feedback loops to design team
- Develop strategy for scaling repair network
- Implement comprehensive design-for-repair guidelines
- Set organization-wide repair-based performance metrics

Level 4 (Leading)

Organizations at this level have achieved what the network in the fictional example accomplished through their manufacturer partnership to turn repair into a competitive advantage. Like the expanding network of specialized repair hubs, they've developed sophisticated systems for sharing repair knowledge and capabilities. Similar to how the success in the fictional example led manufacturers to redesign products for repairability, these organizations influence their entire industry's approach to repair and see it as fundamental to their business model and customer relationships.

Key characteristics:

- Repair drives product innovation and improvement
- Open repair documentation and procedures widely shared
- Planned parts interchangeability across product lines
- Active development of repair networks and capabilities

NEXT STEPS FOR LEVEL 4

Focus on leading industry-wide capabilities toward repair-based models. Share knowledge openly to build repair ecosystems and develop new business models based on repair capabilities.

Consider these targeted actions based on your level:

- Create an open platform for sharing repair knowledge
- Develop industry-standard repair certification programs
- Launch repair-based business models
- Establish repair innovation centers
- Lead development of industry repair standards
- Create repair-focused supplier development programs

New Circular Supply Chain Roles to Repair at Scale

Building teams that excel at coordinating across traditionally separate domains. This involves bringing together specialists from across supply chain functions to collaborate on circular solutions.

In Chapter 4, we explored how traditional supply chain roles need to change for circular operations, with professionals developing new expertise across multiple product lifecycles. Technicians must evolve to combine traditional mechanical skills with digital capabilities and predictive analytics.

Supply chains are showcasing the use of augmented reality glasses and AI-powered diagnostic systems to repair complex equipment. For example, apprenticeship programs can enable technical roles with students learning the repair procedures through advanced manufacturing systems and digital documentation tools.

Leading organizations today demonstrate similar capabilities. Siemens' Mechatronic Systems Certification Program combines hands-on mechanical training with instruction in digital twins and smart production systems, preparing technicians for Industry 4.0 manufacturing. Similarly, BMW's Automotive Service Technician Education Program equips staff with expertise in advanced workshop systems and diagnostic tools, emphasizing electrical systems and cutting-edge engine technology.

Finding Your Level

To assess your organization, you'll need input from multiple perspectives across your value chain. Schedule focused conversations with key stakeholders with the goal of understanding both the current state of repair in your organization and the barriers to advancing this capability.

Plan to speak with representatives from five key stakeholder groups. For each group, you'll see specific questions designed to uncover how this capability is valued and implemented across your organization. Take notes during these conversations—the patterns that emerge will help you identify your organization's current level and next steps.

After gathering responses to these questions, look for patterns:

- If most answers focus on traditional supply chain roles with limited evolution, you're likely at Level 1
- If you see some specialized circular roles emerging but limited integration, you're probably at Level 2
- If circular roles consistently influence operations but aren't yet driving innovation, you're at Level 3
- If specialized circular roles are actively driving business transformation, you've reached Level 4

FOR SERVICE TECHNICIANS

1 How comfortable are you with digital diagnostic tools?
2 What percentage of your work involves advanced technologies?
3 How do you share knowledge with colleagues?
4 What skills do you feel you need to develop?
5 How has your role changed in the last few years?

FOR TECHNOLOGY LEADERS

1 What new technologies are planned for deployment?
2 How do we assess technology adoption readiness?
3 What technical skills gaps exist in our workforce?
4 How do we support continuous learning?
5 What barriers exist to technology adoption?

FOR TRAINING AND DEVELOPMENT

1 What percentage of training includes digital tools and technologies?
2 How do we balance traditional and new technical skills?
3 What certification programs exist for emerging technologies?

4 How do we measure skill development effectiveness?

5 What partnerships exist with educational institutions?

FOR HR AND TALENT DEVELOPMENT

1 How are job descriptions evolving with new technical requirements?

2 What recruitment challenges exist for technical roles?

3 How do we assess technical competencies?

4 What career paths exist for technical specialists?

5 How do we retain technically skilled employees?

FOR EXECUTIVE LEADERSHIP

1 How do technical skills factor into our strategic planning?

2 What investment are we making in technical skill development?

3 How do we measure return on training investments?

4 What role do technical capabilities play in our competitive advantage?

5 How do we balance traditional and emerging skill requirements?

Level 1 (Beginning)

Organizations at this level mirror the traditional repair shops that the team in the fictional example initially encountered. They are primarily focused on mechanical skills with limited digital integration. Sometimes innovation is met with skepticism from those who rely heavily on individual expertise passed down through apprenticeships. Similar to how local businesses initially approached repairs in the fictional example, these organizations view technical skills through a traditional lens, with digital tools limited to basic tasks like work orders or inventory lookups. Training happens mainly through shadowing experienced staff, much like traditional repair shops.

Key characteristics:

- Limited use of digital tools in service operations
- Training focused on current procedures
- Minimal integration of new technologies
- Knowledge sharing primarily informal
- Traditional job descriptions and career paths

NEXT STEPS FOR LEVEL 1

Review your assessment results with your leadership team. The goal is to create a shared understanding of your current technical capabilities and align improvement priorities.

Start by identifying critical skill gaps and their impact on operations. Focus first on basic digital literacy and create structured training programs for core technologies. Develop a pilot program to show the value of enhanced technical capabilities.

Consider these targeted actions based on your level:

- Create a basic digital skills inventory and gap analysis
- Implement structured documentation for current procedures
- Develop a basic digital literacy training program
- Start tracking technology usage and adoption rates
- Create mentorship program pairing experienced and new technicians

Level 2 (Developing)

Organizations operate like the early days of the fictional example in Hackney Wick, when they first introduced AR glasses and digital diagnostics to the team. Like the initial repair stations, they've started integrating digital tools but usage remains inconsistent. Similar to the first technicians learning to use the overhead camera systems and tablets, these organizations are building basic digital literacy alongside traditional repair skills. They've begun formal training programs but still struggle with consistently blending mechanical and digital expertise.

Key characteristics:

- Digital tools used for routine operations
- Structured training program including some new technologies
- Basic knowledge-sharing systems in place
- Growing comfort with digital interfaces
- Updated job descriptions reflecting technical requirements

NEXT STEPS FOR LEVEL 2

Focus on systematically developing technical capabilities across your organization. Build comprehensive training programs that integrate traditional and digital skills. Create clear career paths for technical specialists and establish formal knowledge-sharing systems.

Consider these targeted actions based on your level:

- Expand a digital training program to cover all key technologies
- Implement a formal certification process for technical skills
- Create structured mentorship and knowledge-sharing programs
- Develop a technology adoption roadmap with clear milestones
- Establish baseline metrics for technical skill development

Level 3 (Advanced)

Organizations reflect the mature hub operations, where technicians combine traditional repair skills with advanced digital tools. Like the network as it expanded across London, they've developed comprehensive training programs that integrate AR guidance, predictive analytics, and advanced manufacturing systems. Similar to how the apprenticeship program in the fictional example evolved, these organizations have created clear career paths that value both mechanical expertise and digital capabilities, with active knowledge sharing across their network.

Key characteristics:

- Advanced digital tools routinely used across operations
- Comprehensive training program for all skill levels
- Formal knowledge-sharing platforms actively used
- Clear career development paths for technical specialists
- Strong integration between traditional and digital skills

NEXT STEPS FOR LEVEL 3

Work on expanding technical capabilities across your organization and industry. Create formal programs for technical innovation and knowledge creation. Develop networks to scale technical training and certification. Begin sharing expertise beyond your organization.

Consider these targeted actions based on your level:

- Create a technical innovation program with dedicated resources
- Develop advanced certification paths for emerging technologies
- Establish cross-training opportunities across disciplines
- Build external partnerships for skill development
- Implement predictive analysis of future skill requirements

Level 4 (Leading)

Organizations show capabilities like the network achieved in the fictional example through their manufacturer partnership. Like the team's evolution into a technical innovation hub, they're actively developing new ways to combine traditional craftsmanship with cutting-edge technology. Similar to how repair hubs in the fictional example became centers of excellence in specific technical domains, these organizations lead their industries in defining future skill requirements and creating development pathways. They've achieved what was envisioned in the fictional example—turning repair expertise into a core competitive advantage that shapes their entire industry.

Key characteristics:

- Cutting-edge technology integration across all operations
- Industry-leading training and certification programs
- Active knowledge-creation and sharing platforms
- Strong educational and research partnerships
- Predictive approach to future skill requirements

NEXT STEPS FOR LEVEL 4

Focus on leading industry-level capabilities for advanced technical capabilities. Share knowledge openly to build learning ecosystems. Develop new approaches to technical skill development and certification.

Consider these targeted actions based on your level:

- Lead industry working groups on skill development standards
- Create open platforms for technical knowledge sharing
- Develop predictive models for future skill requirements
- Build technology innovation and training centers
- Establish industry-wide certification programs
- Create technical skill development consortiums

Continuous Learning Culture to Repair at Scale

Creating an environment where teams actively share knowledge about repair techniques, material innovations, and process improvements across the circular network.

In Chapter 4, we explored how traditional organizational boundaries can become barriers to circular success. There is power in breaking down these silos, showing how diverse teams can work together, from community repair technicians to industrial specialists to apprentices.

The fictional example illustrates this through multiple examples: AR-enabled repair sessions where experienced technicians guide apprentices, cross-training between community and industrial repair teams, and knowledge sharing across different repair hubs. Knowledge is immediately documented and shared across the network, benefiting the entire ecosystem.

Leading organizations today show similar capabilities. Programs like Toyota's Share program use maintenance teams across different plants to collaborate on common challenges, while technicians can access global expertise through connected tools. Similarly, Philips Healthcare has created "innovation hubs" where teams collaborate to use technology with one focus being on product repairability and maintenance procedures.

Finding Your Level

To assess your organization, you'll need input from multiple perspectives across your value chain. Schedule focused conversations with key stakeholders with the goal of understanding both the current state of repair in your organization and the barriers to advancing this capability.

Plan to speak with representatives from five key stakeholder groups. For each group, you'll see specific questions designed to uncover how this capability is valued and implemented across your organization. Take notes during these conversations—the patterns that emerge will help you identify your organization's current level and next steps.

After gathering responses to these questions, look for patterns:

- If most answers focus on individual knowledge with minimal sharing, you're likely at Level 1
- If you see some knowledge sharing but limited systematic learning, you're probably at Level 2
- If learning consistently influences operations but isn't yet transformative, you're at Level 3
- If systematic learning actively drives network-wide improvement, you've reached Level 4

FOR TECHNICAL SPECIALISTS

1   How do you collaborate with non-technical teams?

2   What platforms enable knowledge sharing?

3   How do you balance specialist and collaborative work?

4   What barriers exist to effective collaboration?

5   How do you maintain expertise while working across functions?

FOR PROJECT TEAMS

1   How often do you work with other functions?

2   What tools support cross-functional collaboration?

3   How are decisions made across functional boundaries?

4   What challenges do you face in collaborative work?

5   How do you share knowledge across teams?

FOR PROCESS OWNERS

1   How do processes support collaboration?

2   What metrics track collaborative success?

3   How do you identify collaboration opportunities?

4   What tools enable cross-functional work?

5   How do you balance functional and collaborative goals?

FOR TRAINING AND DEVELOPMENT

1   How do we share best practices across functions?

2   How do we develop collaboration skills?

3   What collaboration training exists?

4   How do we assess collaborative capabilities?

5   What tools support collaborative learning?

FOR EXECUTIVE LEADERSHIP

1   How do we incentivize cross-functional collaboration?

2   What resources are dedicated to supporting collaboration?

3   How do we measure collaboration effectiveness?

4 What barriers to collaboration exist at the leadership level?

5 How does collaboration factor into strategic planning?

Level 1 (Beginning)

Organizations at this level experience the fragmented repair landscape initially found in the fictional example, where repair shops operated in isolation and knowledge stayed within individual businesses. These organizations maintain traditional boundaries between functions; design teams rarely interact with repair technicians, and knowledge sharing happens primarily by chance. Similar to how local businesses initially struggled to access repair expertise, these organizations lack ways for different teams to work together consistently.

Key characteristics:

- Limited structured collaboration
- Functional silos predominate
- Informal knowledge sharing
- Few collaboration tools or platforms
- Traditional organizational boundaries

NEXT STEPS FOR LEVEL 1

Review your assessment results with your leadership team. Focus on creating a shared understanding of current collaboration patterns and their impact on performance.

Consider these targeted actions based on your level:

- Map current collaboration patterns and identify gaps
- Create basic cross-functional meeting structures
- Implement simple knowledge-sharing tools
- Identify collaboration champions in each function
- Start tracking basic collaboration metrics

Level 2 (Developing)

Organizations look like the early days of the fictional example establishing the Hackney Wick hub, where they began breaking down barriers between community repairs and industrial maintenance. Like the initial repair stations, they've started creating spaces where different specialists can work together and share insights. Similar to the first experiments in the fictional example with the AR repair guidance system, they've implemented basic tools for collaboration, but teams are still learning how to work effectively across traditional boundaries. They recognize the value of collaboration but haven't yet fully changed their organizational structures to support it.

Key characteristics:

- Basic collaboration structures in place
- Some cross-functional processes defined
- Basic collaboration tools implemented
- Growing recognition of collaboration value
- Initial breakdown of functional silos

NEXT STEPS FOR LEVEL 2

Focus on strengthening collaboration capabilities across your organization. Build comprehensive support systems for cross-functional work and establish clear metrics for collaborative success.

Consider these targeted actions based on your level:

- Implement formal collaboration platforms
- Create cross-functional project teams
- Develop a collaboration skills training program
- Establish collaboration metrics
- Review and revise organizational structures

Level 3 (Advanced)

Organizations reflect the mature hub operations in the fictional example, where community repair technicians, industrial specialists, and apprentices work together. Like when teams discovered new ways to repair items and share that knowledge across the network, these organizations have developed robust systems for cross-functional collaboration. They have created structures that enable teams to maintain deep expertise while working across boundaries.

Key characteristics:

- Strong collaboration infrastructure
- Effective cross-functional processes
- Advanced collaboration tools utilized
- Clear collaboration metrics
- Supportive organizational structures

NEXT STEPS FOR LEVEL 3

Work on expanding collaboration capabilities across your ecosystem. Create formal programs for collaborative innovation and establish networks for knowledge sharing.

Consider these targeted actions based on your level:

- Create a collaboration innovation program
- Develop advanced collaboration tools
- Establish cross-organizational networks
- Build external partnerships
- Implement predictive collaboration analytics

Level 4 (Leading)

Organizations show capabilities like the network in the fictional example achieved through their manufacturer partnership. Like the team's evolution into a collaborative innovation hub that influenced product design and repair practices across industries, these organizations have changed collaboration into a core competitive advantage. Similar to how the repair hubs in the fictional example became centers of excellence that shared knowledge openly across their ecosystem, these organizations actively shape how teams work together both internally and across organizational boundaries. They've achieved what the team in the fictional example envisioned—creating collaborative networks that continuously improve repair capabilities while developing new approaches to cross-functional work.

Key characteristics:

- Industry-leading collaboration practices
- Innovative collaboration tools and methods

- Extensive knowledge-sharing networks
- Strong ecosystem partnerships
- Predictive collaboration capabilities

NEXT STEPS FOR LEVEL 4

Focus on leading industry capabilities toward enhanced collaboration. Share knowledge openly to build collaborative ecosystems and develop new approaches to cross-functional and cross-organizational work.

Consider these targeted actions based on your level:

- Lead industry collaboration initiatives
- Create open collaboration platforms
- Develop predictive collaboration models
- Build collaboration innovation centers
- Establish industry-wide networks
- Create collaboration standards

06

Process Capabilities

Orchestrating Circular Flows to Repair at Scale

The transition from traditional repair to repair at scale requires advanced process capabilities. Processes must evolve beyond simple fix-and-return operations to handle complex flows of materials, knowledge, and resources across multiple locations. Leading organizations are developing three core process capabilities that enable repair to function systematically rather than as isolated events: Circular Value Stream, Smart Recovery Protocols, and Resource Optimization.

The Circular Value Stream to Repair at Scale

Expanding traditional value stream mapping to capture circular opportunities, including repair loops, material recovery, and reintegration points.

In Chapter 4, we explored how circular value streams function more like water cycles than traditional linear flows, with materials and products moving through multiple lifecycles. The change from linear to circular value streams means that a single product might flow between community repair hubs, specialized facilities, and manufacturing centers, creating value at each step.

The fictional example illustrates this change through a few examples: How a coffee grinder repair led to improved component designs that benefited future repairs, how knowledge gained from industrial repairs informed consumer product solutions, and how the network balanced resources across multiple locations.

Leading organizations today demonstrate similar capabilities. Caterpillar's remanufacturing operations manage complex flows of components across their global network, tracking parts through multiple lifecycles while continuously optimizing value creation. Similarly, Philips Healthcare's circular operations create value streams that connect hospital equipment through multiple rounds of upgrade and refurbishment, aiming to maximize use.

Finding Your Level

To assess your organization, you'll need input from multiple perspectives across your value chain. Schedule focused conversations with key stakeholders with the goal of understanding both the current state of repair in your organization and the barriers to advancing this capability.

Plan to speak with representatives from five key stakeholder groups. For each group, you'll see specific questions designed to uncover how this capability is valued and implemented across your organization. Take notes during these conversations—the patterns that emerge will help you identify your organization's current level and next steps.

After gathering responses to these questions, look for patterns:

- If most answers focus on linear material flows with limited recovery, you're likely at Level 1
- If you see some circular material tracking but limited integration, you're probably at Level 2
- If circular value streams consistently influence operations but aren't yet driving strategy, you're at Level 3
- If circular value streams actively drive innovation and improvement, you've reached Level 4

FOR OPERATIONS MANAGERS

1 How do we coordinate flows between locations?
2 What systems track material and product movements?
3 How do we optimize network resources?
4 What barriers exist to network efficiency?
5 How do we manage network capacity?

FOR VALUE STREAM MANAGERS

1 How do we identify value creation opportunities?
2 What processes support continuous improvement?

3 How do we share best practices across locations?

4 What barriers exist to value optimization?

5 How do we measure value stream performance?

FOR PLANNING TEAMS

1 How do we forecast network capacity needs?

2 What tools support network planning?

3 How do we balance competing demands?

4 What processes guide resource allocation?

5 How do we manage network inventory?

FOR STRATEGY TEAMS

1 How do we manage circular material flows?

2 What metrics track network performance?

3 How do we coordinate with partners?

4 What tools support network visibility?

5 How do we handle network disruptions?

FOR EXECUTIVE LEADERSHIP

1 How do we measure value creation across our network?

2 What investments are we making in network optimization?

3 How do we balance local and network-wide efficiency?

4 What role does circularity play in our value streams?

5 How do we incentivize network-level performance?

Level 1 (Beginning)

Organizations operate in a disconnected repair landscape, where each shop works in isolation with little awareness of broader value creation opportunities. Like local businesses struggling individually with similar repair challenges, these organizations manage value streams as linear, one-way flows. They lack visibility into how value could be created and captured across a network of connected operations.

Key characteristics:

- Linear, disconnected value streams
- Location-centric operations
- Limited network visibility
- Basic material tracking
- Siloed performance metrics

NEXT STEPS FOR LEVEL 1

Review your assessment results with your leadership team. Focus on building understanding of network value streams and their potential impact on overall performance. Start by creating visibility into current flows and identifying opportunities for connection.

Consider these targeted actions based on your level:

- Map current value streams across locations
- Implement a basic network tracking system
- Identify potential circular flows
- Create network performance metrics
- Begin cross-location coordination meetings

Level 2 (Developing)

Organizations resemble the early network development in the fictional example, where the team began connecting community and industrial repairs; they've started seeing their operations as interconnected rather than isolated. Similar to the first experiments in the fictional example of sharing repair knowledge between locations, they're beginning to recognize opportunities for network-wide value creation but haven't fully systematized these connections.

Key characteristics:

- Basic network connectivity established
- Growing circular flow awareness
- Initial cross-location coordination
- Shared performance metrics emerging
- Network visibility improving

NEXT STEPS FOR LEVEL 2

Focus on strengthening network connections and developing more advanced coordination capabilities. Build systems that can track and optimize value creation across multiple locations and lifecycles.

Consider these targeted actions based on your level:

- Implement a network management platform
- Develop circular flow metrics
- Create network optimization processes
- Establish cross-location planning systems
- Launch network improvement programs

Level 3 (Advanced)

Organizations mirror the established network in the fictional example, where value flows seamlessly between community repair hubs and industrial operations. Like when the team discovered how insights from repairs could benefit other applications, they actively manage value creation across multiple nodes. Similar to the specialized repair hubs working in concert in the fictional example, they optimize value streams across their entire network.

Key characteristics:

- Integrated network operations
- Advanced flow tracking
- Active circular value creation
- Network-wide optimization
- Strong data integration

NEXT STEPS FOR LEVEL 3

Work on expanding network capabilities and developing more advanced optimization approaches. Create systems that can predict and respond to network dynamics while maximizing value creation opportunities.

Consider these targeted actions based on your level:

- Implement predictive network analytics
- Create value stream innovation program
- Develop advanced optimization models
- Establish network resilience metrics
- Build cross-network collaboration platforms

Level 4 (Leading)

Organizations change network value streams into a key capability. Like the fictional example team's ability to create value through multiple touchpoints such as community repairs and manufacturer design improvements, these organizations shape how networked value creation evolves. Similar to how the repair hubs in the fictional example influenced entire industry practices, these organizations lead in developing new approaches to network value optimization.

Key characteristics:

- Industry-leading network practices
- Advanced analytics deployment
- Innovative value creation approaches
- Repair optimization systems
- Predictive network capabilities

NEXT STEPS FOR LEVEL 4

Focus on leading industry capabilities toward more advanced network value streams. Share knowledge openly to build network ecosystems. Develop new approaches to value creation and optimization.

Consider these targeted actions based on your level:

- Create open network innovation platforms
- Develop industry-wide standards
- Build network innovation centers
- Lead industry working groups
- Establish network research partnerships
- Create network optimization frameworks

Smart Recovery Protocols to Repair at Scale

Standardizing how teams assess, repair, and reintegrate materials and products, ensuring consistent quality across multiple lifecycles.

In Chapter 4, we explored how traditional repair approaches often fall short when scaling to handle diverse products and complex failures. The transition to circular operations requires advanced recovery processes that combine advanced diagnostics with data-driven decision making.

The fictional example illustrates this capability through multiple touchpoints: AI-powered diagnostic systems that could identify common failure patterns, augmented reality tools guiding technicians through repairs, and automated systems for tracking repair outcomes and sharing successful procedures.

Leading organizations today show these capabilities. Siemens' gas turbine service operations use AI to enhance their diagnostic systems that analyze sensor data to predict failures before they occur, while their AR-enabled industrial procedures ensure consistent quality across global operations. Similarly, ASML's semiconductor equipment recovery program combines predictive analytics with advanced repair procedures to maintain complex systems through multiple lifecycles.

Finding Your Level

To assess your organization, you'll need input from multiple perspectives across your value chain. Schedule focused conversations with key stakeholders with the goal of understanding both the current state of repair in your organization and the barriers to advancing this capability.

Plan to speak with representatives from five key stakeholder groups. For each group, you'll see specific questions designed to uncover how this capability is valued and implemented across your organization. Take notes during these conversations—the patterns that emerge will help you identify your organization's current level and next steps.

After gathering responses to these questions, look for patterns:

- If most answers focus on individual expertise and basic repair procedures with minimal data support, you're likely at Level 1
- If you see some smart recovery tools and data collection but limited integration, you're probably at Level 2
- If data-driven recovery consistently guides decisions but isn't yet driving innovation, you're at Level 3
- If advanced recovery intelligence actively shapes industry practices, you've reached Level 4

FOR OPERATIONS TEAMS

1 What diagnostic tools and systems are currently in use?

2 How do we capture and analyze repair data?

3 What automated systems support recovery operations?

4 How do we make decisions about repair versus replace?

5 What barriers exist to implementing smarter recovery processes?

FOR TECHNICAL TEAMS

1 How do we use data in recovery operations?

2 What predictive capabilities exist in our systems?

3 How do we validate recovery procedures?

4 What tools support technical decision-making?

5 How do we integrate new technologies into recovery processes?

FOR CUSTOMER SERVICE

1 How do we manage customer expectations during recovery?

2 What feedback do we receive about recovery operations?

3 How do we communicate recovery options to customers?

4 What systems track customer satisfaction with repairs?

5 How do we handle complex recovery situations?

FOR QUALITY TEAMS

1 How do we ensure consistent recovery quality?

2 What metrics track recovery performance?

3 How do we validate new recovery procedures?

4 What role does data play in quality assurance?

5 How do we maintain standards across operations?

FOR EXECUTIVE LEADERSHIP

1 How do recovery operations factor into our business strategy?

2 What investments are we making in smart recovery capabilities?

3 How do we measure recovery operation performance?

4 What role does data analytics play in our recovery strategy?

5 How do we balance recovery costs with value creation?

Level 1 (Beginning)

Organizations resemble the repair shops initially encountered in the fictional example, relying primarily on individual technician expertise with minimal data or technology support. Often waiting weeks for parts, these organizations handle repairs reactively with basic tools and documentation. Initially diagnosing problems through trial and error, these organizations lack systematic approaches to recovery operations and depend heavily on individual knowledge rather than shared learning systems.

Key characteristics:

- Manual diagnostic processes dominate
- Limited data collection from repairs
- Individual expertise drives decisions
- Basic quality control procedures
- Minimal systematic knowledge sharing

NEXT STEPS FOR LEVEL 1

Review your assessment results with your leadership team. Focus on building awareness of smart recovery capabilities and their potential impact on operational performance.

Consider these targeted actions based on your level:

- Implement a basic repair data collection system
- Document current recovery procedures
- Identify most common failure patterns
- Create standard diagnostic checklists
- Begin tracking basic recovery metrics

Level 2 (Developing)

Organizations are beginning to introduce basic diagnostic tools and data collection and have started implementing technology to support recovery operations. Similar to the initial experiments with AR guidance in the fictional example, they're beginning to systematize their approach but haven't yet fully integrated advanced analytics or predictive capabilities into their recovery processes.

Key characteristics:

- Basic automated diagnostic tools in use
- Systematic data collection established
- Initial analytics capabilities
- Structured quality control processes
- Formal knowledge sharing beginning

NEXT STEPS FOR LEVEL 2

Focus on expanding smart recovery capabilities systematically across your operations. Build connections between different systems and develop more advanced analytics capabilities.

Consider these targeted actions based on your level:

- Implement advanced diagnostic tools
- Develop predictive analytics pilots
- Create a formal recovery procedure database
- Establish recovery performance metrics
- Launch a technician training program for smart systems

Level 3 (Advanced)

Organizations reflect the mature hub operations in the fictional example, where AI-powered diagnostics and AR guidance seamlessly support recovery operations. These organizations combine advanced technology with human expertise to optimize recovery decisions and systematically capture and apply insights to improve their operations continuously.

Key characteristics:

- Advanced diagnostic systems deployed
- Predictive analytics guide decisions
- Data-driven quality control
- Automated knowledge sharing
- Strong systems integration

NEXT STEPS FOR LEVEL 3

Work on expanding smart recovery capabilities across your network. Create formal innovation programs and establish advanced analytics capabilities.

Consider these targeted actions based on your level:

- Implement AI-powered diagnostic systems
- Create a recovery innovation program
- Develop advanced analytics capabilities
- Establish a predictive maintenance program
- Build cross-network knowledge-sharing platforms

Level 4 (Leading)

Organizations demonstrate capabilities like the network in the fictional example achieved through their manufacturer partnership. Like the team's evolution into a technical innovation center, they're actively developing new approaches to recovery operations that influence entire industries. Similar to how the repair hubs in the fictional example became centers of excellence informing product design, these organizations shape how smart recovery evolves across their sectors.

Key characteristics:

- Industry-leading recovery technologies
- Advanced AI/ML systems deployed
- Advanced quality control
- Extensive knowledge networks
- Predictive and prescriptive capabilities

NEXT STEPS FOR LEVEL 4

Focus on leading industry capabilities toward smarter recovery operations. Share knowledge openly to build recovery ecosystems. Develop new approaches to recovery operations.

Consider these targeted actions based on your level:

- Create open recovery innovation platforms
- Develop industry-wide standards
- Build recovery innovation centers
- Lead industry working groups
- Establish advanced training programs
- Create recovery research partnerships

Resource Optimization to Repair at Scale

Developing processes that maximize the use of existing materials through sharing, repair, and alternative sourcing.

In Chapter 4, we explored how circular operations require advanced coordination of resources across networks of partners and facilities. Effective resource orchestration enables repair at scale.

The fictional example illustrates this orchestration through several powerful examples, including balancing workloads between community and industrial repairs, and managing shared resources like specialized tools and AR glasses. When the medical device manufacturer needed urgent support, the system orchestrated not just the repair team but also the manufacturing of replacement parts and the sharing of expertise across the network.

Leading organizations today demonstrate similar capabilities. Toyota's global parts distribution network ensures consistent quality through standardized processes linking manufacturers, distributors, and dealers worldwide. Similarly, Volkswagen's myVW Virtual Assistant demonstrates how AI can systematize maintenance knowledge, helping owners access verified repair procedures and technical documentation on demand.

Finding Your Level

To assess your organization, you'll need input from multiple perspectives across your value chain. Schedule focused conversations with key stakeholders with the goal of understanding both the current state of repair in your organization and the barriers to advancing this capability.

Plan to speak with representatives from five key stakeholder groups. For each group, you'll see specific questions designed to uncover how this capability is valued and implemented across your organization. Take notes during these conversations—the patterns that emerge will help you identify your organization's current level and next steps.

After gathering responses to these questions, look for patterns:

- If most answers focus on local resource management with minimal coordination, you're likely at Level 1
- If you see some resource sharing but limited network optimization, you're probably at Level 2

- If resource orchestration consistently guides operations but isn't yet driving innovation, you're at Level 3
- If network-wide resource optimization actively drives performance, you've reached Level 4

FOR SERVICE DELIVERY TEAMS

1 How do we balance resource availability with demand?
2 What processes guide resource deployment?
3 How do we handle urgent resource needs?
4 What systems track resource utilization?
5 How do we ensure service quality with shared resources?

FOR TECHNICAL TEAMS

1 How do we share specialized resources?
2 What systems enable remote support?
3 How do we manage tool and equipment sharing?
4 What barriers exist to resource flexibility?
5 How do we coordinate expertise across locations?

FOR OPERATIONS MANAGERS

1 How do we coordinate resources between locations?
2 What systems support resource sharing?
3 How do we handle peak demand periods?
4 What barriers exist to effective coordination?
5 How do we manage resource conflicts?

FOR RESOURCE PLANNERS

1 How do we forecast resource needs?
2 What tools support resource allocation?
3 How do we prioritize competing demands?
4 What metrics track resource efficiency?
5 How do we manage capacity planning?

FOR EXECUTIVE LEADERSHIP

1   How do we optimize resource allocation across our network?

2   What investments are we making in coordination capabilities?

3   How do we measure resource utilization?

4   What role does technology play in resource management?

5   How do we balance efficiency with flexibility?

Level 1 (Beginning)

Organizations experience fragmented resource management. These organizations manage resources reactively with minimal coordination and lack systematic approaches to resource sharing and optimization.

Key characteristics:

- Manual resource coordination processes
- Reactive allocation approaches
- Limited visibility into resource availability
- Local control of specialized resources
- Basic tracking and measurement systems

NEXT STEPS FOR LEVEL 1

Review your assessment results with your leadership team. Focus on creating basic visibility into resource availability and utilization patterns. Start building the foundation for more coordinated resource management.

Consider these targeted actions based on your level:

- Create a network-wide resource inventory
- Implement a basic scheduling system
- Document resource-sharing procedures
- Start tracking utilization metrics
- Establish coordination meetings between locations

Level 2 (Developing)

Organizations have started implementing basic systems for resource sharing and coordination. Similar to the first attempts in the fictional example at managing specialized tools and expertise across locations, they're developing more systematic approaches but haven't yet achieved seamless orchestration.

Key characteristics:

- Basic digital coordination tools
- Growing network visibility
- Initial resource sharing processes
- Structured allocation procedures
- Improved utilization tracking

NEXT STEPS FOR LEVEL 2

Focus on strengthening coordination capabilities and implementing more advanced resource management systems. Build processes that enable smoother sharing of resources across your network.

Consider these targeted actions based on your level:

- Implement resource management platform
- Develop prioritization frameworks
- Create resource-sharing protocols
- Establish network-wide metrics
- Launch cross-location training programs

Level 3 (Advanced)

Organizations reflect the mature network operations in the fictional example, where resources flow dynamically between repair hubs based on real-time needs. Teams like these can handle multiple urgent repairs simultaneously by rebalancing resources and expertise, and can actively optimize resource deployment across their network. Similar to how the specialized hubs in the fictional example shared capabilities, they coordinate resources to maximize value creation among partners.

Key characteristics:

- Advanced coordination systems
- Real-time resource visibility
- Dynamic allocation capabilities

- Predictive need assessment
- Automated coordination tools

NEXT STEPS FOR LEVEL 3

Work on expanding orchestration capabilities and developing more advanced optimization approaches. Create systems that can predict and respond to changing resource needs while maintaining service quality.

Consider these targeted actions based on your level:

- Implement AI-powered resource optimization
- Create predictive allocation models
- Develop advanced sharing platforms
- Establish resilience metrics
- Build cross-network expertise sharing

Level 4 (Leading)

Organizations showcase capabilities like the fully evolved network in the fictional example—creating resource orchestration as a strategic advantage. Like the team's ability to dynamically deploy specialized capabilities across London, they actively shape how networked resources are managed. Similar to how the repair hubs in the fictional example became centers of excellence with shared resources and expertise, these organizations lead their industries in developing new approaches to resource optimization.

Key characteristics:

- Industry-leading orchestration practices
- Advanced AI/ML deployment
- Innovative sharing approaches
- Advanced optimization systems
- Predictive deployment capabilities

NEXT STEPS FOR LEVEL 4

Focus on leading industry capabilities toward more advanced resource orchestration. Share knowledge openly to build orchestration ecosystems. Develop new approaches to resource optimization.

Consider these targeted actions based on your level:

- Create open orchestration platforms
- Develop industry-wide standards
- Build innovation centers
- Lead working groups on resource sharing
- Establish research partnerships
- Create optimization frameworks

07

Technology Capabilities

Digital Enablement to Repair at Scale

Technology capabilities form the digital foundation that enables and accelerates repair operations to scale. The repair hub network in the fictional example shows how advanced systems support what used to be isolated repair efforts into a coordinated, intelligent ecosystem, using AI-powered diagnostics and network optimization platforms. The journey from a single location in Hackney Wick to a network of specialized hubs across London was supported by careful development of key digital capabilities.

This chapter explores three interconnected technology capabilities that organizations need to develop: Digital Product Memory, Predictive Recovery Intelligence, and Network Optimization Platform. As we examine each capability, we'll see how the network in the fictional example leverages these technologies to systematically extend product life while creating new value through each repair cycle. The progression from basic digital tools to advanced AI-driven platforms shows how technology can enable repair at scale while continuously improving operations through captured insights.

Digital Product Memory to Repair at Scale

Creating comprehensive digital records that track a product's complete history through multiple lifecycles, repairs, and material changes.

In Chapter 4, we explored how traditional tracking systems needed to evolve to manage products through multiple lifecycles. Advanced digital systems can create "product memory" that enables more effective repair and value creation throughout a product's life.

The fictional example illustrates this capability through several powerful examples: The AI-powered diagnostic system that instantly recognized patterns in James's coffee grinder from previous repairs, and the comprehensive tracking of industrial equipment performance that supported preventive maintenance. The team discovered that effective lifecycle tracking wasn't just about collecting data—it was about transforming that information into actionable insights that improved future repairs and influenced product design.

Leading organizations today show similar capabilities. Rolls-Royce's "Power by the Hour" program uses advanced digital tracking to monitor aircraft engine performance across multiple lifecycles, enabling predictive maintenance and continuous improvement. Similarly, Siemens' digital twin technology creates virtual representations of their gas turbines, tracking performance data through multiple service cycles while informing design improvements. These examples show how digital product lifecycle management has become fundamental to enabling circular operations at scale.

Finding Your Level

To assess your organization, you'll need input from multiple perspectives across your value chain. Schedule focused conversations with key stakeholders with the goal of understanding both the current state of repair in your organization and the barriers to advancing this capability.

Plan to speak with representatives from five key stakeholder groups. For each group, you'll see specific questions designed to uncover how this capability is valued and implemented across your organization. Take notes during these conversations—the patterns that emerge will help you identify your organization's current level and next steps.

After gathering responses to these questions, look for patterns:

- If most answers focus on basic maintenance records and manual tracking, you're likely at Level 1
- If you see digital tools in use but with limited integration or analytics, you're probably at Level 2
- If digital tracking consistently informs decisions but isn't yet driving innovation, you're at Level 3
- If digital product data is actively driving design and strategy, you've reached Level 4

FOR ENGINEERING TEAMS

1   How do we capture and store product performance data?

2   What digital tools support product lifecycle tracking?

3   How do we use historical product data in new designs?

4   What barriers exist to comprehensive lifecycle tracking?

5   How do we validate and maintain data quality?

FOR SERVICE OPERATIONS

1   What digital systems support maintenance and repair?

2   How do we capture repair and service histories?

3   What predictive capabilities exist in our tracking systems?

4   How do we share product data across locations?

5   What prevents better use of product lifecycle data?

FOR TECHNOLOGY TEAMS

1   What platforms manage our product lifecycle data?

2   How do we ensure data security and accessibility?

3   What analytics capabilities support product tracking?

4   How do we integrate different data sources?

5   What emerging technologies could enhance our capabilities?

FOR QUALITY TEAMS

1   How do we use lifecycle data for quality assurance?

2   What metrics track product performance over time?

3   How do we validate product history data?

4   What role does data play in failure analysis?

5   How do we maintain data consistency across operations?

FOR EXECUTIVE LEADERSHIP

1   How does product lifecycle data inform our business strategy?

2   What investments are we making in digital tracking capabilities?

3   How do we measure return on digital infrastructure investments?

4 What role does product data play in our innovation process?

5 How do we balance short-term tracking needs with long-term data capabilities?

Level 1 (Beginning)

Organizations maintain basic digital records primarily focused on warranty tracking and maintenance logs. Like the scattered repair documentation initially found in the fictional example, these systems track only basic information such as service dates and part replacements. Similar to how local repair shops kept minimal records before innovation in the fictional example, these organizations lack systematic ways to capture and use product lifecycle data. Their digital tools are limited to simple databases or spreadsheets, with little ability to analyze patterns or share insights across operations.

Key characteristics:

- Basic digital maintenance records
- Manual data collection processes
- Limited data sharing between systems
- Minimal analytics capabilities
- Focus on warranty period tracking

NEXT STEPS FOR LEVEL 1

Begin building your digital foundation by establishing basic systems for tracking product lifecycles. Focus on creating consistent data collection processes and helping teams understand the value of systematic digital tracking.

Consider these targeted actions based on your level:

- Implement a basic digital tracking system
- Create standard data collection procedures
- Establish data quality guidelines
- Begin capturing repair histories
- Start analyzing failure patterns

Level 2 (Developing)

Organizations look like the early days of the fictional example in Hackney Wick, where they began implementing basic digital tracking systems. Like the first repair stations equipped with overhead cameras and diagnostic tablets, they've started capturing more detailed product data and repair histories. They're beginning to use digital tools to share knowledge between locations, though they haven't yet developed advanced analytics capabilities or comprehensive product histories.

Key characteristics:

- Digital tracking platforms implemented
- Growing data collection automation
- Basic analytics capabilities
- Initial integration between systems
- Improved data accessibility

NEXT STEPS FOR LEVEL 2

Focus on expanding your digital capabilities while building connections between different systems and locations. Work on developing more advanced analytics capabilities that can begin informing operational decisions and improvements.

Consider these targeted actions based on your level:

- Expand digital tracking capabilities
- Develop predictive analytics pilots
- Create comprehensive data standards
- Implement knowledge-sharing platforms
- Establish data governance processes

Level 3 (Advanced)

Organizations reflect the mature hub operations in the fictional example, where comprehensive digital tracking enables predictive maintenance and knowledge sharing across the network. Like when the team used AI-powered diagnostics to identify common failure patterns, these organizations maintain detailed digital histories that inform both immediate repairs and future improvements. Similar to how the network in the fictional example tracked products through multiple repair cycles, they capture and analyze product lifecycle data to optimize both repairs and designs.

Key characteristics:

- Comprehensive digital tracking
- Strong analytics capabilities

- Predictive maintenance enabled
- Integrated data systems
- Active knowledge sharing

NEXT STEPS FOR LEVEL 3

Work on expanding product lifecycle data into a strategic asset that drives continuous improvement. Create systems that can predict and respond to product performance trends while maintaining comprehensive digital histories.

Consider these targeted actions based on your level:

- Implement AI-powered analytics
- Create a digital innovation program
- Develop advanced prediction models
- Build cross-network data sharing
- Establish digital transformation metrics

Level 4 (Leading)

Organizations show capabilities like those that the network in the fictional example achieved through their manufacturer partnerships. Like the team's ability to influence product design through accumulated repair data, they've created advanced digital platforms that track products through multiple lifecycles while continuously generating insights for improvement. Similar to how the repair hubs in the fictional example became centers of excellence informing manufacturer decisions, these organizations use digital lifecycle management to drive innovation across their entire ecosystem, transforming product data into a key competitive advantage.

Key characteristics:

- Industry-leading digital capabilities
- Advanced AI/ML deployment
- Innovation-driving analytics
- Comprehensive digital twins
- Predictive lifecycle management

NEXT STEPS FOR LEVEL 4

Focus on leading industry capabilities toward more advanced digital lifecycle management and product memory. Share knowledge openly to build digital ecosystems while developing new approaches to capturing and creating value from product lifecycle data.

Consider these targeted actions based on your level:

- Create open innovation platforms
- Develop industry-wide standards
- Build digital innovation centers
- Lead industry working groups
- Establish research partnerships

Predictive Recovery Intelligence to Repair at Scale

Using AI and analytics to determine optimal repair strategies and material reuse opportunities based on product condition and market needs.

In Chapter 4, we explored how traditional repair approaches needed to evolve beyond individual expertise to handle complexity at scale. Intelligent systems can combine AI-powered diagnostics, augmented reality guidance, and predictive analytics to optimize recovery operations across multiple locations and product types.

The fictional example illustrates this transformation through examples such as the AI system that instantly recognized patterns in James's coffee grinder from previous repairs, and the comprehensive tracking of industrial equipment that supported preventative maintenance. The team in the fictional example discovered that successful repair at scale required more than just skilled technicians—it needed intelligent systems that could process vast amounts of repair data and guide complex decisions.

Leading organizations today show similar capabilities. Vestas' wind turbine maintenance program uses AI to support diagnostics to analyze complex wear patterns from different environmental conditions, while Caterpillar's remanufacturing operations use augmented reality to guide technicians through advanced repairs. These examples show how intelligent recovery systems have become fundamental to enabling repair at scale.

Finding Your Level

To assess your organization, you'll need input from multiple perspectives across your value chain. Schedule focused conversations with key stakeholders with the goal of understanding both the current state of repair in your organization and the barriers to advancing this capability.

Plan to speak with representatives from five key stakeholder groups. For each group, you'll see specific questions designed to uncover how this capability is valued and implemented across your organization. Take notes during these conversations—the patterns that emerge will help you identify your organization's current level and next steps.

After gathering responses to these questions, look for patterns:

FOR OPERATIONS LEADERSHIP

1 How do intelligent systems support our recovery operations?
2 What investments are we making in recovery automation?
3 How do we measure intelligent system effectiveness?
4 What role does AI/ML play in recovery decisions?
5 How do we balance automation with human expertise?

FOR TECHNICAL TEAMS

1 What diagnostic tools support recovery operations?
2 How do we validate automated recovery decisions?
3 What predictive capabilities exist in our systems?
4 How do we integrate different diagnostic tools?
5 What prevents better use of intelligent systems?

FOR SERVICE TEAMS

1 How comfortable are technicians with AI-guided repairs?
2 What percentage of repairs use automated guidance?
3 How do we capture feedback on system accuracy?
4 What barriers exist to system adoption?
5 How do we maintain expertise with automation?

FOR DATA SCIENCE TEAMS

1 What ML models support recovery operations?
2 How do we validate model accuracy?

3 What data sources inform recovery decisions?

4 How do we improve model performance?

5 What limits our predictive capabilities?

FOR QUALITY TEAMS

1 How do we validate automated recovery procedures?

2 What metrics track intelligent system performance?

3 How do we ensure consistent recovery quality?

4 What role does automation play in QA?

5 How do we maintain standards with intelligent systems?

Level 1 (Beginning)

Organizations at this level rely primarily on individual technician expertise and manual diagnostic processes, similar to the traditional repair shops initially encountered in the fictional example. Like the fragmented repair shops before the network expanded, these organizations lack systematic approaches to diagnostics and recovery. Their tools are basic, with minimal automation or intelligent support for decision-making.

Key characteristics:

- Manual diagnostic processes
- Limited use of automated tools
- Reliance on individual expertise
- Basic quality control procedures
- Minimal data collection

NEXT STEPS FOR LEVEL 1

Begin building foundational capabilities in intelligent recovery by implementing basic automated diagnostic tools and data collection. Focus on creating systematic approaches to recovery while helping teams understand the value of intelligent systems.

Consider these targeted actions:

- Implement basic diagnostic tools
- Start collecting repair data

- Create standard recovery procedures
- Train teams on automated systems
- Establish baseline performance metrics

Level 2 (Developing)

Organizations look like the early days in the fictional example in Hackney Wick, when they first introduced AI diagnostics and AR guidance. Like the initial repair stations, they've begun implementing basic intelligent systems but haven't yet achieved consistent adoption or integration. Similar to the early experiments in the fictional example with overhead cameras and tablets, they're starting to collect and analyze repair data but haven't fully developed predictive capabilities.

Key characteristics:

- Basic automated diagnostics in place
- Initial AR/AI tools implemented
- Growing data collection
- Emerging predictive capabilities
- Inconsistent system adoption

NEXT STEPS FOR LEVEL 2

Focus on expanding intelligent recovery capabilities while building connections between different systems and locations. Work on developing more advanced analytics capabilities that can begin informing recovery decisions.

Consider these targeted actions:

- Expand diagnostic system capabilities
- Implement AR guidance tools
- Develop predictive analytics pilots
- Create a recovery knowledge base
- Establish system adoption metrics

Level 3 (Advanced)

Organizations reflect mature hub operations in the fictional example, where AI-powered diagnostics and AR guidance seamlessly support recovery operations. Like when the team handled complex industrial repairs, these organizations effectively combine intelligent systems with human expertise. Similar to how the network adapted in the fictional example to recovery procedures based on accumulated data, they systematically use analytics to optimize operations.

Key characteristics:

- Advanced AI/ML diagnostics
- Integrated AR guidance
- Strong predictive capabilities
- Systematic knowledge capture
- Data-driven optimization

NEXT STEPS FOR LEVEL 3

Work on transforming intelligent recovery into a strategic advantage that drives continuous improvement. Create systems that can predict and respond to recovery needs while maintaining consistent quality across operations.

Consider these targeted actions:

- Implement advanced AI/ML models
- Create an intelligent recovery program
- Develop a predictive maintenance system
- Build cross-network analytics
- Establish innovation metrics

Level 4 (Leading)

Organizations show capabilities like the network in the fictional example achieved through their manufacturer partnership. Like the team's ability to handle a range of products and equipment, they've created advanced recovery systems that combine multiple intelligent technologies. Similar to how the repair hubs in the fictional example became centers of excellence, these organizations actively shape how intelligent recovery evolves across their industries.

Key characteristics:

- Industry-leading intelligent systems
- Advanced AI/ML deployment

- Advanced AR integration
- Predictive optimization
- Continuous innovation

NEXT STEPS FOR LEVEL 4

Focus on leading industry capabilities for more advanced intelligent recovery systems. Share knowledge openly to build recovery ecosystems while developing new approaches to combining human expertise with artificial intelligence.

Consider these targeted actions:

- Create open innovation platforms
- Develop industry-wide standards
- Build intelligent recovery centers
- Lead industry working groups
- Establish research partnerships

Network Optimization Platform to Repair at Scale

Building integrated systems that coordinate material flows, repairs, and reintegration across the circular ecosystem.

In Chapter 4, we explored how traditional systems optimized individual facilities rather than entire networks, creating inefficiencies and missed opportunities. Network intelligence can be very powerful, with advanced systems coordinating operations across multiple locations while optimizing resource deployment and knowledge sharing.

The fictional example team discovered that successful scaling required more than just connecting locations—it needed intelligent systems that could see and optimize patterns across the entire network.

Leading organizations today show similar capabilities. Toyota's global manufacturing network uses advanced systems to coordinate operations across facilities, while Siemens' service operations use technology platforms to optimize resource deployment across their service network. These examples show how network intelligence has become fundamental to enabling circular operations at scale.

Finding Your Level

To assess your organization, you'll need input from multiple perspectives across your value chain. Schedule focused conversations with key stakeholders with the goal of understanding both the current state of repair in your organization and the barriers to advancing this capability.

Plan to speak with representatives from five key stakeholder groups. For each group, you'll see specific questions designed to uncover how this capability is valued and implemented across your organization. Take notes during these conversations—the patterns that emerge will help you identify your organization's current level and next steps.

After gathering responses to these questions, look for patterns:

- If most answers focus on local optimization and manual coordination, you're likely at Level 1
- If you see basic network visibility but limited optimization, you're probably at Level 2
- If network intelligence guides decisions but isn't yet driving innovation, you're at Level 3
- If AI and ML actively optimize network-wide operations, you've reached Level 4

FOR NETWORK OPERATIONS

1 How do we coordinate operations across locations?
2 What systems optimize network-wide performance?
3 How do we handle resource allocation decisions?
4 What tools provide network visibility?
5 How do we respond to network disruptions?

FOR TECHNOLOGY TEAMS

1 What platforms support network coordination?
2 How do we integrate different location systems?
3 What predictive capabilities exist network-wide?
4 How do we ensure network data quality?
5 What prevents better network optimization?

FOR PLANNING TEAMS

1   How do we forecast network capacity needs?

2   What tools support network-wide planning?

3   How do we optimize resource deployment?

4   What metrics track network performance?

5   How do we balance competing priorities?

FOR ANALYTICS TEAMS

1   What models support network optimization?

2   How do we validate network-wide patterns?

3   What data drives network decisions?

4   How do we improve prediction accuracy?

5   What limits our network visibility?

FOR LOCATION LEADERS

1   How do network systems support local operations?

2   What visibility exists across locations?

3   How are resources shared network-wide?

4   What barriers exist to network coordination?

5   How do we balance local and network needs?

Level 1 (Beginning)

Organizations operate like the disconnected repair shops initially encountered in the fictional example, with each location functioning independently.
Like the fragmented repair shops before the network developed, these
organizations lack visibility across operations and coordinate mainly
through manual communication. Their systems focus on local optimization
with minimal awareness of network-wide patterns or opportunities.

Key characteristics:

- Location-centric operations
- Manual network coordination
- Limited cross-location visibility

- Basic performance tracking
- Minimal resource sharing

NEXT STEPS FOR LEVEL 1

Begin building foundational capabilities in network coordination by implementing basic visibility tools and communication systems. Focus on creating awareness of network-wide patterns while helping teams understand the value of coordinated operations.

Consider these targeted actions:

- Implement basic network visibility tools
- Create cross-location communication channels
- Establish network performance metrics
- Map current resource flows
- Start tracking network patterns

Level 2 (Developing)

Organizations look like the early days of connecting repair hubs in the fictional example, when they first began coordinating between locations. They've implemented basic systems for network visibility and resource sharing but haven't yet achieved advanced optimization. Similar to the early challenges balancing workloads in the fictional example, they're beginning to see network-wide patterns but struggle to respond effectively.

Key characteristics:

- Basic network visibility established
- Initial resource-sharing processes
- Growing cross-location coordination
- Emerging optimization capabilities
- Inconsistent network response

Next Steps for Level 2

Focus on strengthening network connections while building more advanced coordination capabilities. Work on developing analytics that can begin optimizing operations across the entire network.

Consider these targeted actions:

- Expand network visibility systems
- Implement resource optimization tools
- Develop cross-location analytics
- Create network coordination protocols
- Establish network response metrics

Level 3 (Advanced)

Organizations look like the mature network operations in the fictional example, where intelligent systems seamlessly coordinate activities across multiple locations. These organizations effectively optimize network-wide resources and operations. Similar to how the network routed repairs to specialized hubs in the fictional example, they systematically leverage network patterns to improve performance.

Key characteristics:

- Comprehensive network visibility
- Advanced optimization capabilities
- Dynamic resource allocation
- Predictive analytics deployment
- Systematic knowledge sharing

NEXT STEPS FOR LEVEL 3

Work on transforming network intelligence into a strategic advantage that drives continuous improvement. Create systems that can predict and respond to network dynamics while maintaining optimal performance.

Consider these targeted actions:

- Implement advanced network analytics
- Create a network innovation program
- Develop predictive optimization models
- Build cross-network coordination platform
- Establish network resilience metrics

Level 4 (Leading)

Organizations show capabilities like the fully evolved network in the fictional example, where intelligent systems orchestrate operations across London while continuously improving network performance. Like the team's ability to handle multiple urgent needs at the same time, they've created advanced platforms that optimize resources and knowledge sharing. Similar to how repair hubs became an integrated ecosystem in the fictional example, these organizations actively shape how network intelligence evolves across their industries.

Key characteristics:

- Industry-leading network platforms
- Advanced AI/ML optimization
- Advanced resource orchestration
- Predictive network management
- Continuous ecosystem innovation

NEXT STEPS FOR LEVEL 4

Focus on leading industry capabilities for more advanced network intelligence. Share knowledge openly to build collaborative ecosystems while developing new approaches to network optimization.

Consider these targeted actions:

- Create open network platforms
- Develop industry-wide standards
- Build network innovation centers
- Lead industry working groups
- Establish research partnerships

08

Industry Standards Capabilities

Common Language for Circularity to Repair at Scale

Standards form the critical foundation that enables repair ecosystems to function effectively at scale. Successful repair operations require clear frameworks for evaluating performance, documenting procedures, and enabling collaboration across networks of partners. These standards transform what might be isolated repair capabilities into scalable, reliable systems that can serve both community and industrial needs.

This section explores three interconnected standards capabilities that organizations need to develop: Multi-Life Performance Metrics, Digital Interoperability, and Ecosystem Collaboration Protocols. As we examine each capability, we'll see how the network in the fictional example leverages these standards to ensure consistent quality while enabling continuous improvement and knowledge sharing.

Multi-Life Performance Metrics to Repair at Scale

Establishing clear standards for measuring product and material performance across multiple use cycles.

In Chapter 4, we explored how traditional standards focused on new production needed to evolve to evaluate performance across multiple product lifecycles. Now, the evolution to circular supply chains means that repaired equipment can meet or exceed original performance specifications through multiple use cycles.

The fictional example shows this change through James's coffee grinder repair, where the team in the fictional example restored functionality and also improved the original design with more durable burrs.

Leading organizations today show these capabilities. SKF's bearing remanufacturing program has developed standards to evaluate components for restoration, using the same processes and quality assurance as new bearing manufacturing. This approach can extend bearing service life, reduce costs, and lower environmental impact by reusing up to 90 percent less energy compared to producing new bearings.[1] SKF's remanufacturing services also provide full traceability and can even improve bearings to meet new or higher specifications for specific applications.

Finding Your Level

To assess your organization, you'll need input from multiple perspectives across your value chain. Schedule focused conversations with key stakeholders with the goal of understanding both the current state of repair in your organization and the barriers to advancing this capability.

Plan to speak with representatives from five key stakeholder groups. For each group, you'll see specific questions designed to uncover how this capability is valued and implemented across your organization. Take notes during these conversations—the patterns that emerge will help you identify your organization's current level and next steps.

After gathering responses to these questions, look for patterns:

- If most answers focus on basic quality checks against new product or material standards, you're likely at Level 1
- If you see some adapted testing for recovered products or materials but limited standardization, you're probably at Level 2
- If performance metrics consistently track multiple lifecycles but aren't yet driving innovation, you're at Level 3
- If multi-life performance data actively drives material innovation and business strategy, you've reached Level 4

FOR QUALITY TEAMS

1   How do we verify the performance of repaired/refurbished products?
2   What metrics do we use to track performance across multiple lifecycles?

3   How do our standards compare to new product specifications?

4   What documentation exists for performance verification?

5   How do we update standards based on field performance?

FOR SERVICE OPERATIONS

1   How do we measure repair quality?

2   What performance data do we collect during service?

3   How do we validate repair procedures?

4   What feedback loops exist to improve standards?

5   How do we handle performance variations across repairs?

FOR TECHNICAL EXPERTS

1   How do we establish performance criteria for repairs?

2   What testing protocols exist for repaired products?

3   How do we validate improved designs?

4   What role does data play in standards development?

5   How do we manage performance trade-offs?

FOR CUSTOMERS

1   What performance expectations do you have for repaired products?

2   How do you measure repaired product performance?

3   What documentation do you require?

4   How do you compare repaired vs new performance?

5   What concerns do you have about repaired product reliability?

FOR SUPPLY CHAIN PARTNERS

1   How do we align performance standards across partners?

2   What testing capabilities exist in the network?

3   How do we share performance data?

4   What barriers exist to standardization?

5   How do we manage quality across the network?

Level 1 (Beginning)

Organizations at this level operate like traditional repair shops, focusing mainly on getting items working again without deeper consideration of long-term performance. Their approach resembles conventional break-fix models, with basic testing limited to immediate functionality. They lack systematic ways to document repairs or track how products perform over time. Quality control is informal and largely dependent on individual technician expertise.

Key characteristics:

- Basic functionality testing only
- Limited performance documentation
- No formal standards for repaired products
- Minimal data collection and analysis
- Limited performance tracking across lifecycles

NEXT STEPS FOR LEVEL 1

Begin by establishing basic performance metrics for repaired products. Focus on documenting current repair procedures and their outcomes. Create a pilot program to track performance over time.

Consider these targeted actions:

- Develop basic repair quality metrics
- Document current testing procedures
- Create performance tracking system
- Establish baseline measurements
- Begin collecting repair outcome data

Level 2 (Developing)

Organizations have begun establishing standardized repair procedures, similar to the early days in the fictional example in Hackney Wick. They're starting to collect repair data and track outcomes, though not yet systematically. They have basic protocols for testing and documentation, but struggle to scale these consistently. They recognize the importance of performance standards but haven't fully developed systems to maintain them across multiple product lifecycles.

Key characteristics:

- Established repair quality standards
- Basic performance tracking in place
- Some documentation of procedures
- Limited data analysis capabilities
- Growing focus on lifecycle performance

NEXT STEPS FOR LEVEL 2

Focus on developing comprehensive standards that account for multiple lifecycles. Implement systematic data collection and analysis. Create formal validation procedures.

Consider these targeted actions:

- Expand performance metrics beyond basic functionality
- Implement formal testing protocols
- Develop data analysis capabilities
- Create systematic documentation procedures
- Establish performance baselines across lifecycles

Level 3 (Advanced)

Organizations at this level reflect the mature hub operations in the fictional example, with testing protocols and performance tracking across multiple repairs. They collect and analyze repair data to improve procedures, similar to how the network in the fictional example began informing manufacturer design improvements. Their standards ensure consistent quality across multiple facilities while enabling continuous improvement through shared learning. Digital documentation and validation procedures are well established.

Key characteristics:

- Comprehensive lifecycle standards
- Advanced testing capabilities
- Strong data analysis program
- Clear documentation requirements
- Active performance optimization

NEXT STEPS FOR LEVEL 3
Work on expanding standards influence across the network. Create formal programs for continuous improvement. Develop industry-leading practices.
Consider these targeted actions:

- Establish advanced testing capabilities
- Create predictive performance models
- Develop network-wide standards
- Implement continuous improvement program
- Build industry partnerships

Level 4 (Leading)

Organizations show capabilities like those that the network in the fictional example achieved with the major appliance manufacturer partnership. They've developed industry-leading standards that influence product design and repair practices across their sector. Their repair data actively drives innovation in both repair techniques and original product design. They've created systems for validating performance across multiple lifecycles while continuously evolving standards based on network-wide insights.
Key characteristics:

- Industry-leading standards
- Innovative testing approaches
- Predictive performance modeling
- Network-wide implementation
- Continuous standards evolution

NEXT STEPS FOR LEVEL 4
Focus on driving industry transformation through open standards development, share knowledge to build wider capabilities and lead industry working groups.
Consider these targeted actions:

- Lead industry standards development
- Create open testing protocols
- Establish certification programs
- Drive network-wide adoption
- Develop predictive capabilities

Digital Interoperability to Repair at Scale

Creating common data standards that enable seamless sharing of product information across the circular network.

In Chapter 4, we explored how traditional documentation approaches needed to evolve to support complex networks of recovery and reuse. Systems should now capture, share, and apply repair knowledge across multiple locations.

The fictional example shows this change through their AR-guided repair procedures, where every successful repair contributes to a growing knowledge base. Their approaches show how effective documentation enables knowledge transfer, allowing apprentices to tackle complex repairs with expert guidance. This systematic approach to capturing and sharing knowledge became crucial as the network expanded from Hackney Wick to multiple specialized hubs across London.

Leading organizations today demonstrate similar transformations. Patagonia's repair documentation system provides detailed guides for both professionals and customers, enabling repairs at multiple levels. Similarly, iFixit has created an open documentation platform that supports repair communities worldwide, proving how standardized documentation can scale repair capabilities.

Finding Your Level

To assess your organization, you'll need input from multiple perspectives across your value chain. Schedule focused conversations with key stakeholders with the goal of understanding both the current state of repair in your organization and the barriers to advancing this capability.

Plan to speak with representatives from five key stakeholder groups. For each group, you'll see specific questions designed to uncover how this capability is valued and implemented across your organization. Take notes during these conversations—the patterns that emerge will help you identify your organization's current level and next steps.

After gathering responses to these questions, look for patterns:

- If most answers focus on basic data collection with manual sharing, you're likely at Level 1
- If you see digital tools in use but limited standardization across systems, you're probably at Level 2

- If data sharing consistently enables collaboration but isn't yet driving innovation, you're at Level 3
- If interoperable systems actively drive network-wide optimization, you've reached Level 4

FOR DOCUMENTATION TEAMS

1 How do we capture repair procedures?

2 What formats do we use for documentation?

3 How do we maintain documentation accuracy?

4 What tools support documentation creation?

5 How do we handle documentation versions?

FOR REPAIR TECHNICIANS

1 How accessible is repair documentation?

2 What documentation formats are most useful?

3 How do you contribute to documentation?

4 What gaps exist in current documentation?

5 How do you share repair insights?

FOR TRAINING TEAMS

1 How do you use documentation in training?

2 What documentation standards exist?

3 How do you measure documentation effectiveness?

4 What feedback systems exist?

5 How do you update training materials?

FOR KNOWLEDGE MANAGEMENT

1 How do we organize repair knowledge?

2 What systems manage documentation?

3 How do we ensure documentation quality?

4 What analytics track documentation use?

5 How do we handle knowledge transfer?

FOR NETWORK PARTNERS

1 How do you access shared documentation?

2 What standards guide documentation creation?

3 How do you contribute to documentation?

4 What barriers exist to documentation sharing?

5 How do you maintain documentation consistency?

Level 1 (Beginning)

Organizations maintain bare-bones repair documentation, often relying on individual technicians' personal notes or basic manuals. Like a traditional repair shop, knowledge exists primarily in technicians' heads instead of in shareable formats. Documentation is typically scattered across paper files, emails, and individual computers, making it difficult to access or update systematically. The focus is mainly on documenting mandatory procedures like warranty repairs.

Key characteristics:

- Basic written procedures exist
- Limited documentation accessibility
- Minimal standardization
- Static document formats
- Limited version control

NEXT STEPS FOR LEVEL 1

Start by establishing basic documentation standards. Focus on converting existing knowledge into accessible formats. Create a central repository for repair information.

Consider these targeted actions:

- Create a documentation template
- Establish central document repository
- Begin standardizing procedures
- Implement version control
- Start collecting repair insights

Level 2 (Developing)

Organizations operate with basic digital documentation systems in place but are still working out consistency issues. They've started creating standardized repair procedures and using digital platforms to share knowledge, but information often remains siloed within departments or locations. Like the initial repair stations in the fictional example, they're beginning to capture repair insights but haven't yet created systematic ways to share and apply this knowledge across multiple sites.

Key characteristics:

- Digital documentation system in place
- Basic standardization implemented
- Growing accessibility
- Some multimedia content
- Limited knowledge sharing

NEXT STEPS FOR LEVEL 2

Focus on developing comprehensive documentation standards, implementing systematic knowledge capture, and creating accessible digital platforms.

Consider these targeted actions:

- Expand digital documentation platform
- Create multimedia content standards
- Implement feedback systems
- Develop knowledge-sharing processes
- Establish documentation metrics

Level 3 (Advanced)

Organizations mirror the mature repair hub operations in the fictional example, maintaining digital documentation that supports multiple locations. Their systems effectively capture repair procedures through multiple formats, including AR guidance and video documentation. Like the network in the fictional example as it expanded across London, they've developed strong processes for turning individual repair successes into standardized procedures that can be shared and replicated across their network.

Key characteristics:

- Comprehensive digital platform
- Strong standardization
- High accessibility
- Rich multimedia content
- Active knowledge sharing

NEXT STEPS FOR LEVEL 3

Work on expanding documentation influence across networks. Create systems for continuous improvement and develop innovative documentation approaches.

Consider these targeted actions:

- Implement AR documentation tools
- Create collaborative authoring systems
- Develop predictive content suggestions
- Build cross-network documentation standards
- Establish innovation programs

Level 4 (Leading)

Organizations demonstrate capabilities like the network achieved in the fictional example through their manufacturer partnership. They've created industry-leading documentation systems that seamlessly integrate AR guidance, predictive maintenance data, and crowd-sourced repair insights. Their documentation actively improves based on repair outcomes and user feedback, while supporting knowledge sharing across their entire ecosystem. Like the expanding network in the fictional example, they're innovating in how repair knowledge is captured, shared, and applied.

Key characteristics:

- Industry-leading documentation systems
- Innovative formats and tools
- Predictive content delivery
- Network-wide implementation
- Continuous evolution

NEXT STEPS FOR LEVEL 4:
Focus on driving industry transformation through open documentation standards. Share knowledge to build wider capabilities and lead industry working groups.

Consider these targeted actions:

- Lead documentation standards development
- Create open documentation platforms
- Establish certification programs
- Drive network-wide adoption
- Develop AI-assisted documentation tools

Ecosystem Collaboration Protocols to Repair at Scale

Developing standard approaches for knowledge sharing and joint improvement across network partners.

In Chapter 4, we explored how traditional supplier relationships needed to expand to accelerate collaboration across circular networks. Moving forward, organizations that adopt knowledge sharing and continuous improvement across a network of partners will demonstrate this capability.

The fictional example shows this change through the partnerships with major manufacturers, where standardized approaches to sharing repair data led to improvements in both repair approaches and product design. Structured collaboration among education partners, community members, and repair professionals can unlock new value for all stakeholders. This approach became crucial as the network expanded from a single location to an integrated ecosystem spanning London.

Leading organizations today show similar capabilities. Toyota's collaboration with suppliers includes sharing best practices and improvement methodologies. For example, extending the Toyota Production System to Tier 1 and Tier 2 suppliers benefitted their entire network. Similarly, Interface's Net-Works program has developed structured protocols for collaborating with fishing communities to source recycled materials, establishing local community banks and a sustainable business model. Both examples show how standardized approaches can enable effective partnerships across different organizational contexts.

Finding Your Level

To assess your organization, you'll need input from multiple perspectives across your value chain. Schedule focused conversations with key stakeholders with the goal of understanding both the current state of repair in your organization and the barriers to advancing this capability.

Plan to speak with representatives from five key stakeholder groups. For each group, you'll see specific questions designed to uncover how this capability is valued and implemented across your organization. Take notes during these conversations—the patterns that emerge will help you identify your organization's current level and next steps.

After gathering responses to these questions, look for patterns:

- If most answers focus on individual partner management with minimal coordination, you're likely at Level 1

- If you see some structured partnerships but limited network integration, you're probably at Level 2

- If collaboration protocols enable consistent production but aren't yet driving innovation, you're at Level 3

- If ecosystem collaboration actively drives network-wide value creation, you've reached Level 4

FOR NETWORK PARTNERS

1 How clear are collaboration protocols?

2 What support do you receive?

3 How do you contribute improvements?

4 What challenges affect collaboration?

5 How do you measure partnership value?

FOR PARTNERSHIP TEAMS

1 How do we structure collaboration with partners?

2 What frameworks guide joint improvement efforts?

3 How do we measure collaboration effectiveness?

4 What systems support partner communication?

5 How do we align partner objectives?

FOR NETWORK COORDINATORS

1   How do you manage partner interactions?

2   What protocols guide knowledge sharing?

3   How do you track partner engagement?

4   What barriers exist to collaboration?

5   How do you measure network performance?

FOR OPERATIONS TEAMS

1   How do you work with external partners?

2   What standards guide joint operations?

3   How do you share operational insights?

4   What collaboration tools do you use?

5   How do you manage partner variations?

FOR INNOVATION TEAMS

1   How do you collaborate on improvements?

2   What frameworks support joint innovation?

3   How do you share development insights?

4   What barriers exist to joint innovation?

5   How do you scale successful innovations?

Level 1 (Beginning)

Organizations rely on informal, ad hoc collaboration approaches, similar to traditional supplier relationships. Like early repair shops before the innovation in the fictional example, they lack structured protocols for partner engagement or knowledge sharing. Collaboration depends heavily on individual relationships rather than systematic approaches. Partners operate largely independently, with limited coordination or joint improvement efforts.

Key characteristics:

• Informal collaboration approaches

• Limited partner engagement protocols

- Ad hoc knowledge sharing
- Minimal joint improvement efforts
- Individual relationship-based coordination

NEXT STEPS FOR LEVEL 1

Start by establishing basic collaboration frameworks. Focus on creating structured approaches to partner engagement. Develop initial protocols for knowledge sharing.

Consider these targeted actions:

- Create basic partnership guidelines
- Establish regular partner meetings
- Develop communication protocols
- Start tracking collaboration outcomes
- Identify key sharing opportunities

Level 2 (Developing)

Organizations have basic collaboration frameworks in place but are still working out consistency issues. They've started creating standardized approaches to partner engagement and knowledge sharing, but coordination remains challenging across multiple partners. Like the initial repair stations in the fictional example, they're beginning to see the value of systematic collaboration but haven't yet developed comprehensive protocols.

Key characteristics:

- Basic collaboration frameworks exist
- Growing partner engagement
- Some standardized protocols
- Limited network coordination
- Emerging joint improvement efforts

NEXT STEPS FOR LEVEL 2

Focus on developing comprehensive collaboration protocols. Implement systematic approaches to partner engagement. Create structured improvement frameworks.

Consider these targeted actions:

- Expand collaboration frameworks
- Create partner engagement standards
- Implement feedback systems
- Develop coordination processes
- Establish collaboration metrics

Level 3 (Advanced)

Organizations maintain collaboration protocols that enable effective part-ner engagement across their network. Their systems effectively coordinate multiple partners while supporting continuous improvement through struc-tured knowledge sharing. Like the network in the fictional example as it expanded across London, they've developed strong processes for scaling successful practices across diverse partners.

Key characteristics:

- Comprehensive collaboration protocols
- Strong partner engagement
- Effective network coordination
- Active knowledge sharing
- Systematic improvement processes

NEXT STEPS FOR LEVEL 3

Work on expanding collaboration influence across networks. Create systems for continuous improvement and develop innovative engagement approaches.

Consider these targeted actions:

- Implement advanced coordination tools
- Create collaborative innovation systems
- Develop network-wide standards
- Build cross-partner improvement programs
- Establish innovation frameworks

Level 4 (Leading)

Organizations create industry-leading collaboration protocols that enable effective coordination across diverse partners while driving continuous improvement. Their systems actively grow based on network learning, supporting innovation, and value creation across their ecosystem. Like the expanding network in the fictional example, they're continuously developing new approaches to partner engagement and joint improvement.

Key characteristics:

- Industry-leading collaboration protocols
- Innovative engagement approaches
- Network-wide implementation
- Continuous evolution
- Active partner innovation

NEXT STEPS FOR LEVEL 4

Focus on driving industry transformation through open collaboration standards. Share approaches to build wider capabilities and lead industry working groups.

Consider these targeted actions:

- Lead collaboration standards development
- Create open engagement frameworks
- Establish partner certification programs
- Drive network-wide adoption
- Develop predictive collaboration tools

Note

1   Hancock, M. (2024) SKF bearing remanufacturing revolution, ecogeneration, www.ecogeneration.com.au/skf-bearing-remanufacturing-revolution/ (archived at https://perma.cc/67D6-JKSH)

09

Governance Capabilities

Ensuring Circular Success to Repair at Scale

Governance forms the structure that enables circular ecosystems to operate and scale for the long term. Successful circular operations require frameworks for measuring value creation, ensuring consistent quality, and driving continuous improvement across diverse networks of partners. These governance systems expand isolated repair initiatives into engrained business models that can serve both community needs and industrial demands.

This section explores three interconnected governance capabilities that organizations need to develop: Value-Sharing Mechanisms, Quality Assurance Through Multiple Lives, and Continuous Evolution. As we examine each capability, we'll see how the network in the fictional example uses these governance capabilities to ensure fair value distribution, maintain consistent quality, and enable systematic improvement across their expanding ecosystem of partners. These capabilities work together to create the foundation for sustainable circular operations—where every participant benefits from extending product life, quality standards ensure reliable performance across multiple lifecycles, and systematic learning drives ongoing innovation.

Through the story explored in the fictional example, we see how effective governance allows the network to grow from a single community repair hub to an interconnected system that influences manufacturing practices and industry standards. The experience shows that while technical capabilities make circular operations possible, it's governance frameworks that make them sustainable and scalable. These frameworks create the trust, consistency, and continuous improvement that circular ecosystems need to thrive.

Value-Sharing Mechanisms to Repair at Scale

Creating frameworks that fairly distribute benefits among ecosystem partners who contribute to extending product life.

In Chapter 4, we explored how traditional value calculations expanded to support circular operations. Organizations discovered that circular operations required new frameworks for recognizing and rewarding multiple forms of value creation across partner networks. These frameworks need to balance immediate operational efficiency with long-term capability building.

When the team in the fictional example first launched the repair hub in Hackney Wick, they encountered a challenge that went beyond technical expertise. The success of the network depended on multiple contributors. These include local technicians sharing repair knowledge, community colleges providing apprentices, manufacturers supplying documentation, and small businesses trusting their equipment to a new model of maintenance. Traditional business contracts usually don't capture how value is created and shared across a network of partners.

This capability recognizes and fairly distributes value across networks of partners. In the fictional example case, the coffee shop owner benefited from faster, cheaper repairs while the repair hub gained expertise that could help other businesses. The apprenticeship program created value through workforce development, while manufacturers gained insights into product performance in real-world conditions. Creating capabilities to measure and share these diverse forms of value became essential to scaling the network from a single location to multiple specialized hubs across London.

Leading organizations today show these capabilities. For example, Michelin's fleet management program creates value-sharing frameworks across their tire-as-a-service network, where partners earn rewards based on their contributions to extending tire life and improving fleet efficiency.

Finding Your Level

To assess your organization, you'll need input from multiple perspectives across your value chain. Schedule focused conversations with key stakeholders with the goal of understanding both the current state of repair in your organization and the barriers to advancing this capability.

Plan to speak with representatives from five key stakeholder groups. For each group, you'll see specific questions designed to uncover how this capability is valued and implemented across your organization. Take notes during these conversations—the patterns that emerge will help you identify your organization's current level and next steps.

After gathering responses to these questions, look for patterns:

- If most answers focus on traditional transactional relationships, you're likely at Level 1
- If you see basic value-sharing initiatives but limited partner integration, you're probably at Level 2
- If value sharing consistently influences decisions but isn't yet driving innovation, you're at Level 3
- If collaborative value creation actively drives network strategy, you've reached Level 4

FOR PARTNER ORGANIZATIONS

1 How clearly do you understand the value-sharing framework?
2 What incentives exist for improving circular performance?
3 How are your contributions to innovation recognized?
4 What barriers exist to increasing circular value creation?
5 How effectively are benefits distributed across the network?

FOR OPERATIONS TEAMS

1 How do we track value added through repair and recovery?
2 What metrics exist for measuring circular performance?
3 How do we share efficiency gains with network partners?
4 What systems exist for rewarding innovation in circular processes?
5 How do we balance standardization with partner flexibility?

FOR FINANCE TEAMS

1 How do we value circular assets through multiple lifecycles?
2 What models exist for sharing circular revenue streams?
3 How do we account for long-term value creation?
4 What financial incentives support circular innovation?
5 How do we measure return on circular investments?

FOR SUSTAINABILITY TEAMS

1 How do we measure environmental and economic value?

2 What frameworks exist for measuring total impact?

3 How do we incentivize sustainable practices?

4 What metrics capture long-term value creation?

5 How do we share sustainability benefits across the network?

FOR EXECUTIVE LEADERSHIP

1 How do we measure value creation across our circular network?

2 What frameworks exist for sharing benefits with circular partners?

3 How do we balance short-term costs against long-term value creation?

4 What incentives exist to encourage circular innovation?

5 How do we evaluate partner contributions to circular success?

Level 1 (Beginning)

Organizations at this level view repair as a cost center and miss opportunities for shared value creation. These organizations maintain traditional transactional relationships that don't recognize the potential value of collaboration. Partners are managed through conventional supplier contracts that focus on unit costs rather than value creation opportunities.

Key characteristics:

- Traditional supplier contracts based on unit pricing
- Limited recognition of circular value creation
- No formal frameworks for sharing circular benefits
- Focus on immediate cost rather than long-term value
- Transactional relationship with partners

NEXT STEPS FOR LEVEL 1

Start by mapping current value flows and contributions across your partner network. Focus on identifying and documenting how different partners create and capture value. Create pilot programs to test new value-sharing mechanisms with key partners.

Consider these targeted actions:

- Map all forms of value creation in your circular network
- Identify key partners' contributions to circular success
- Develop basic metrics for measuring circular performance
- Create a pilot program for sharing circular benefits
- Begin tracking long-term value creation

Level 2 (Developing)

Organizations at this level look like the early days of establishing the first repair hub in the fictional example. Like the initial partnership with local technical colleges for apprenticeships, they've begun experimenting with new forms of value sharing but haven't yet developed comprehensive frameworks. They recognize the potential benefits of collaboration but struggle to consistently measure and distribute value across their network.

Key characteristics:

- Modified contracts including some circular metrics
- Basic benefit-sharing mechanisms established
- Limited recognition of indirect value creation
- Emerging focus on partner development
- Simple performance incentives in place

NEXT STEPS FOR LEVEL 2

Begin implementing structured frameworks for measuring partner contributions to circular success. Focus on developing clear metrics that capture both immediate and long-term value creation. Create formal systems for tracking and distributing benefits across the network.

Consider these targeted actions:

- Develop comprehensive circular value metrics
- Create structured innovation reward systems
- Establish partner development programs
- Implement long-term value-sharing frameworks
- Build network-wide performance tracking

Level 3 (Advanced)

Organizations at this level operate like the mature network of specialized repair hubs in the fictional example. Just as they created systems for sharing knowledge between locations and coordinating with manufacturers, these organizations have established clear frameworks for measuring and distributing value across their partner ecosystem. Their governance structures recognize multiple forms of value creation – from technical innovation to knowledge sharing to community development – and ensure fair distribution of benefits.

Key characteristics:

- Comprehensive circular value metrics established
- Clear frameworks for sharing benefits
- Active partner development programs
- Innovation incentives in place
- Long-term value creation tracked and rewarded

NEXT STEPS FOR LEVEL 3

Launch comprehensive value-sharing programs that recognize multiple forms of contribution. Focus on implementing automated systems for tracking and distributing benefits. Create innovation incentive programs that reward long-term value creation.

Consider these targeted actions:

- Implement predictive value creation models
- Create network-wide innovation programs
- Develop automated benefit distribution systems
- Establish circular investment frameworks
- Build partner capability development programs

Level 4 (Leading)

Organizations at this level have achieved what the network in the fictional example demonstrated through its manufacturer partnerships—creating new forms of value that benefit the entire ecosystem. Like how the repair data helped manufacturers improve product designs while their technical documentation enhanced repair capabilities, these organizations have developed frameworks that align incentives and share benefits across their network. They actively seek new ways to create and distribute value, seeing their partner ecosystem as a source of continuous innovation and improvement.

Key characteristics:

- Value creation measurement systems
- Automated benefit-sharing mechanisms
- Network-wide innovation programs
- Integrated partner development systems
- Predictive value creation modeling

NEXT STEPS FOR LEVEL 4

Start developing industry-leading frameworks for measuring and sharing circular value. Focus on creating open platforms that enable network-wide innovation and collaboration. Create certification programs that recognize partner excellence in circular value creation.

Consider these targeted actions:

- Pioneer new circular value metrics
- Develop industry-leading sharing frameworks
- Create open innovation platforms
- Establish circular investment funds
- Lead development of industry standards

Quality Assurance Through Multiple Lives to Repair at Scale

Implementing governance structures that maintain consistent quality standards across multiple product lifecycles.

In Chapter 4, we explored how traditional quality systems, which are designed for new production, struggled to address circular operations. Organizations found that ensuring consistent quality across multiple product lifecycles required new approaches to verification and compliance. Success meant developing frameworks that could maintain standards while adapting to the unique challenges of recovered products.

When the repair hub in the fictional example began refurbishing industrial equipment, they encountered a fundamental challenge in quality management. Traditional quality systems, designed to verify products against manufacturing specifications, didn't account for the complexities of restored equipment. When the team successfully repaired the coffee grinder for James's café, they needed to prove not just that it worked, but that it would perform reliably through another complete lifecycle. The situation became even more complex as they expanded to critical manufacturing equipment, where reliability directly impacted their customers' production lines.

Leading organizations today show these capabilities. For example, Abbott Laboratories' cardiac device remanufacturing program maintains rigorous quality standards across multiple device lifecycles, with digital tracking and validation systems to make sure each restored device meets or exceeds original specifications.

Finding Your Level

To assess your organization, you'll need input from multiple perspectives across your value chain. Schedule focused conversations with key stakeholders with the goal of understanding both the current state of repair in your organization and the barriers to advancing this capability.

Plan to speak with representatives from five key stakeholder groups. For each group, you'll see specific questions designed to uncover how this capability is valued and implemented across your organization. Take notes during these conversations—the patterns that emerge will help you identify your organization's current level and next steps.

After gathering responses to these questions, look for patterns:

- If most answers focus on basic quality checks without lifecycle tracking, you're likely at Level 1
- If you see quality systems for recovered materials but limited integration, you're probably at Level 2
- If quality assurance spans multiple lifecycles but isn't yet driving innovation, you're at Level 3
- If quality systems actively enable new business models, you've reached Level 4

FOR QUALITY TEAMS

1 How do we define quality standards for restored products?

2 What testing protocols exist for refurbished items?

3 How do we validate repairs across different facilities?

4 What systems track quality through multiple lifecycles?

5 How do we compare restored versus new product performance?

FOR OPERATIONS TEAMS

1 How are repair quality standards documented and shared?

2 What processes ensure consistent repair quality?

3 How do we validate new repair procedures?

4 What metrics track repair success rates?

5 How do we manage quality variation between facilities?

FOR TECHNICAL TEAMS

1 How do we verify component performance after repair?

2 What testing equipment supports quality verification?

3 How do we validate innovative repair methods?

4 What standards exist for component reuse?

5 How do we document quality requirements?

FOR CUSTOMERS

1 How do you measure repaired product performance?

2 What quality assurance do you expect for repairs?

3 How do you compare refurbished versus new quality?

4 What documentation supports your quality requirements?

5 How do you verify repair reliability?

FOR NETWORK PARTNERS

1 How are quality standards shared across facilities?

2 What support exists for meeting quality requirements?

3 How do you validate your repair processes?

4 What systems track quality performance?

5 How do you ensure consistent quality across locations?

Level 1 (Beginning)

Organizations at this level may show initial skepticism, unsure about the quality of repaired versus new equipment. These organizations lack systematic approaches to validating repair quality. They rely primarily on basic functional testing and struggle to provide confidence in long-term performance.

Key characteristics:

- Basic functional testing only
- Limited quality documentation for repairs
- No standardized repair validation process
- Quality tracking focused on immediate function
- Minimal performance history tracking

NEXT STEPS FOR LEVEL 1

Start by establishing basic testing protocols and quality standards for repairs. Focus on documenting successful repair procedures and outcomes systematically. Create simple but reliable validation processes that build confidence in repair quality.

Consider these targeted actions:

- Develop basic repair quality standards
- Create a repair validation checklist
- Start tracking repair success rates
- Implement basic performance testing
- Document repair procedures

Level 2 (Developing)

Organizations at this level reflect the early success with the community repair café in the fictional example, where they began developing systematic approaches to quality assurance. The team has started creating standardized testing procedures and documenting successful repairs but haven't yet scaled these practices across their full operation.

Key characteristics:

- Standard testing procedures established
- Basic repair quality documentation

- Initial performance tracking systems
- Some validation processes defined
- Limited quality data collection

NEXT STEPS FOR LEVEL 2

Begin implementing comprehensive quality tracking systems across repair operations. Focus on developing standardized testing procedures for different types of repairs. Create formal validation processes that ensure consistent quality outcomes.

Consider these targeted actions:

- Expand testing protocols
- Implement quality tracking system
- Develop comprehensive documentation standards
- Create repair validation processes
- Build performance history database

Level 3 (Advanced)

Organizations at this level operate like the mature repair hub network in the fictional example, with quality assurance systems across multiple locations. Similar to how the team handled critical industrial equipment repairs, they maintain comprehensive testing protocols and validation processes that ensure consistent quality across all repairs. Their systems track performance through multiple lifecycles, building confidence in repaired equipment reliability.

Key characteristics:

- Comprehensive testing protocols
- Detailed quality documentation
- Advanced performance tracking
- Validated repair procedures
- Multi-lifecycle quality monitoring

NEXT STEPS FOR LEVEL 3

Launch advanced quality monitoring systems that track performance across multiple lifecycles. Focus on implementing automated testing and validation procedures. Create network-wide quality databases that enable continuous improvement.

Consider these targeted actions:

- Implement predictive quality monitoring
- Develop cross-facility quality standards
- Create automated testing systems
- Establish quality improvement programs
- Build network-wide quality database

Level 4 (Leading)

Organizations at this level have achieved what the network in the fictional example demonstrated through their manufacturer partnerships—quality assurance systems that often exceed original manufacturing standards. Like how the repair hub's data helped improve product designs, these organizations use quality monitoring to drive continuous improvement across their network, influencing both repair procedures and original product specifications.

Key characteristics:

- Industry-leading quality standards
- Predictive performance monitoring
- Automated testing and validation
- Network-wide quality systems
- Continuous improvement integration

NEXT STEPS FOR LEVEL 4

Start developing industry-leading quality standards for circular operations. Focus on creating open frameworks that enable quality validation across networks. Create certification programs that establish repair quality benchmarks for your industry.

Consider these targeted actions:

- Pioneer new quality standards
- Develop industry testing protocols
- Create open quality frameworks
- Lead industry standardization efforts
- Establish certification programs

Continuous Evolution to Repair at Scale

Establishing processes for ongoing improvement and adaptation of circular practices based on network learning.

In Chapter 4, we explored how traditional governance structures, built for linear supply chains, couldn't support continuous improvement in circular networks. Organizations learned that success required frameworks for capturing and scaling innovations across partner ecosystems. These structures need to coordinate complex networks while encouraging ongoing development of circular capabilities.

When the repair hub network in the fictional example began collaborating with manufacturers, they encountered a challenge that went beyond daily operations. Each successful repair generated insights that could improve future products, while every new product design affected repair procedures. Meetings with manufacturers that started as simple information exchanges evolved into dynamic sessions where repair technicians and design engineers collaborated on innovations. The team in the fictional example realized that success in circular operations required more than just maintaining current capabilities—it needed systematic approaches to continuous learning and evolution.

Leading organizations today show these capabilities. For example, Samsung's circular operations program creates governance structures that systematically capture innovations from their repair and recovery network, using these insights to improve both product design and maintenance procedures.

Finding Your Level

To assess your organization, you'll need input from multiple perspectives across your value chain. Schedule focused conversations with key stakeholders with the goal of understanding both the current state of repair in your organization and the barriers to advancing this capability.

Plan to speak with representatives from five key stakeholder groups. For each group, you'll see specific questions designed to uncover how this capability is valued and implemented across your organization. Take notes during these conversations—the patterns that emerge will help you identify your organization's current level and next steps.

After gathering responses to these questions, look for patterns:

- If most answers focus on reactive improvements without systematic capture, you're likely at Level 1

- If you see improvement systems but limited network learning, you're probably at Level 2
- If continuous evolution influences operations but isn't yet transformative, you're at Level 3
- If systematic innovation actively drives network growth, you've reached Level 4

FOR NETWORK PARTNERS

1 How are improvement ideas shared across the network?
2 What support exists for implementing innovations?
3 How do you contribute to network learning?
4 What barriers exist to continuous improvement?
5 How are successful innovations scaled?

FOR TECHNICAL TEAMS

1 How do we capture technical learning?
2 What processes exist for validating improvements?
3 How do we share technical innovations?
4 What systems support knowledge transfer?
5 How do we measure technical progress?

FOR LEARNING AND DEVELOPMENT

1 How do we develop new capabilities?
2 What frameworks support continuous learning?
3 How do we measure capability growth?

FOR LEADERSHIP TEAMS

1 How do we systematically capture and implement improvements?
2 What frameworks exist for scaling successful innovations?
3 How do we measure the impact of improvement initiatives?
4 What resources support continuous learning?
5 How do we balance stability with innovation?

FOR INNOVATION TEAMS

1 How do we identify opportunities for improvement?

2 What processes support testing new approaches?

3 How do we validate and scale successful innovations?

4 What systems capture and share learning?

5 How do we measure innovation success?

6 How do we scale successful training?

Level 1 (Beginning)

Organizations at this level focus on maintaining current operations without systematic approaches to improvement, and view innovation as occasional projects rather than continuous processes. Learning happens informally and improvements often stay isolated within individual teams.

Key characteristics:

- Ad hoc approach to improvements
- Limited knowledge-sharing systems
- Informal learning processes
- Isolated pockets of innovation
- Minimal network collaboration

NEXT STEPS FOR LEVEL 1:

Start by establishing basic systems for capturing improvement ideas and learning. Focus on creating simple processes that enable knowledge sharing between teams. Create regular forums for discussing and implementing improvements.

Consider these targeted actions:

- Begin documenting improvement opportunities
- Set up basic knowledge-sharing platforms
- Create improvement review meetings
- Start tracking innovation impact
- Establish learning networks

Level 2 (Developing)

Organizations at this level reflect the early days of establishing repair procedures and training programs in the fictional example. Like the initial
partnerships with technical colleges, they've begun creating structured
approaches to learning and improvement but haven't yet developed comprehensive systems for scaling innovations across their network.

Key characteristics:

- Basic improvement processes established
- Initial knowledge-sharing systems
- Structured learning programs
- Some innovation tracking
- Limited network collaboration

NEXT STEPS FOR LEVEL 2

Begin implementing formal systems for capturing and sharing improvements. Focus on developing metrics that track the impact of innovations.
Create structured processes for scaling successful improvements across the
network.

Consider these targeted actions:

- Develop innovation-tracking systems
- Launch formal improvement programs
- Create knowledge management platforms
- Establish innovation metrics
- Build partner collaboration forums

Level 3 (Advanced)

Organizations at this level operate like the mature repair hub network in the
fictional example, with systems for driving continuous improvement. Similar
to how the team integrated apprentice training with experienced technician
knowledge, they maintain comprehensive frameworks for capturing, validating, and scaling innovations across their network.

Key characteristics:

- Comprehensive improvement systems
- Advanced knowledge-sharing platforms

- Integrated learning programs
- Systematic innovation tracking
- Active network collaboration

NEXT STEPS FOR LEVEL 3

Launch advanced systems for predicting and driving improvements. Focus on creating platforms that enable network-wide innovation. Create frameworks that accelerate the scaling of successful improvements.

Consider these targeted actions:

- Implement predictive improvement systems
- Develop network innovation platforms
- Create rapid scaling processes
- Establish innovation centers
- Build advanced learning networks

Level 4 (Leading)

Organizations at this level have achieved what the network in the fictional example demonstrated through their influence on manufacturing practices—creating ecosystems that drive continuous improvement across entire industries. Like how the repair data led to improved product designs, these organizations have developed systems that transform individual insights into industry-wide advances.

Key characteristics:

- Industry-leading improvement systems
- Open innovation platforms
- Network-wide learning programs
- Predictive improvement tracking
- Ecosystem-wide collaboration

NEXT STEPS FOR LEVEL 4

Start developing industry-leading frameworks for driving continuous improvement. Focus on creating open platforms that enable ecosystem-wide innovation. Create systems that accelerate the adoption of improvements across industries.

Consider these targeted actions:

- Pioneer improvement methodologies
- Launch open innovation platforms
- Create industry learning networks
- Establish innovation standards
- Build ecosystem improvement programs

PART THREE

The Capability to Manufacture In-Market

FICTIONAL EXAMPLE
Global to Local

Maya stood at her familiar spot on the mezzanine of the Hackney Wick facility, but her attention wasn't on the busy repair floor below. Instead, she studied a holographic display showing a web of lines connecting cities across Britain. Each line represented component shipments to their repair network.

"Have you noticed?" Tom asked, joining her at the railing. "80 percent of our repair parts are traveling an average of 4,000 miles before they reach us. We've solved one problem only to uncover a bigger one."

Maya nodded. Their repair network had grown impressively—seven facilities across London, partnerships with major manufacturers, and a growing army of skilled technicians. But this morning's sustainability report highlighted an uncomfortable reality: While they were extending product life, they were still deeply dependent on global supply chains for replacement parts.

"Look at this," she said, pointing to a cluster of data points. "Last week alone, we had 300 orders for the same power controller. We're trucking them in from Southampton after they've crossed half the world. The specs are standardized, the testing protocols are clear..."

"You think we could make them here?"

"Not just here," Maya replied, expanding the holographic display to show their network. "What if each repair hub could also be a manufacturing node? We already have the digital infrastructure tracking component specifications. Our technicians understand the quality requirements. The AR systems we use for repairs could guide local production."

Two months later, Maya walked through their transformed component storage area. Where shelves of spare parts once stood, a compact manufacturing cell hummed quietly. A hybrid manufacturing system—part 3D printer, part precision CNC machine—worked on their hundredth locally produced power controller.

Through AR glasses, every dimension, tolerance, and material property was visible in perfect detail. The system matched these against original manufacturer specifications, highlighting areas for inspection in real-time.

"Ninety-seven percent first-pass yield across the last 100 units," Rachel reported. "Even better—we're using 40 percent reclaimed materials from our own recovery operations."

Their success attracted attention. Six months in, they received an unexpected proposal from a consortium of medical device manufacturers. They wanted the network to produce sterile components for medical devices.

"Actually," explained Dr. Obi, their quality expert, "it's not as different as you might think. Look at the core attributes." She isolated several key specifications. "The tolerances are tighter, yes, and the cleaning protocols more stringent. But the fundamental manufacturing principles are the same."

Their standardization system proved remarkably adaptable. What started as a way to maintain consistent quality across their network evolved into a sophisticated framework that could translate specifications across industries. The key was focusing on fundamental, measurable attributes rather than industry-specific terminology.

In their new network control center, Maya watched as production orders flowed across their manufacturing system. "Incoming urgent order," the AI system announced. "Medical component required at St. Thomas's Hospital within three hours. Evaluating optimal production routing."

The system analyzed multiple factors simultaneously: Which facilities had necessary certifications for medical production, current capacity at each location, material availability, and transport time. Within seconds, the order was routed to their Croydon facility.

"Three factors," the AI explained. "They just completed a medical production run, so the clean room is already prepared. They have a full stock of required materials. And the new routing would disrupt a critical aerospace component sequence."

Their network had become more than a collection of manufacturing cells. It was a living system, constantly learning and adapting—all while keeping production as local as possible. Each facility maintained core capabilities while sharing capacity across industries.

Through her AR display, Maya watched the finished component being prepared for delivery. From digital file to physical product in under an hour, produced within miles of where it was needed. Around them, a micro-ecosystem had developed—material recovery operations, quality testing labs, training spaces, and even a small material science research center partnering with local universities.

"This is manufacturing reimagined," Maya explained to visiting manufacturers. "Not just making products locally, but creating sustainable loops of material, knowledge, and value within our communities."

The revolution that had started with a broken coffee grinder had come full circle, breathing new life into local manufacturing while proving that production could be both distributed and precise, local and world-class.

10

People and Culture Capabilities
Manufacturing In-Market

The transition to local manufacturing begins with people. As seen in the fictional example, success comes from developing leaders who understand distributed production, creating new technical roles that blend digital and physical skills, and fostering continuous learning across facilities. While technology enables local production at scale, it's the human capabilities— from AR-guided specialists to cross-trained technicians—that bring these systems to life. Leading organizations recognize that investing in these three core human capabilities creates the foundation for lasting transformation: Circular leadership, evolved technical roles, and continuous learning culture.

Circular Leadership to Manufacture In-Market

Developing leaders who understand value exists beyond single-use lifecycles. This encompasses training supply chain professionals to identify opportunities for material reuse, repair, and reintegration.

In Chapter 4, we explored how traditional manufacturing mindsets treat products as having a single, linear lifecycle—raw materials in, finished goods out, and eventual disposal. Now, it's possible to imagine an operation where manufacturing becomes distributed, local, and responsive to community needs.

The fictional example shows this capability through the journey from repair hubs to local manufacturing. Their success with power controllers led to manufacturing medical components, showing how distributed production could maintain rigorous quality standards while dramatically shortening supply chains.

Leading organizations today show similar capabilities. Local Motors operates micro-factories that produce vehicles using a combination of 3D printing and traditional techniques, proving that complex products can be made locally at scales as low as 200 units per year. Their process results in vehicles with about 90 percent fewer parts and shorter production times than traditional methods.[1] Similarly, Arrival's micro-factories for electric vehicles showcase how digital manufacturing technologies enable local production of sophisticated products.

Finding Your Level

To assess your organization, you'll need input from multiple perspectives across your value chain. Schedule focused conversations with key stakeholders with the goal of understanding both the current state of repair in your organization and the barriers to advancing this capability.

Plan to speak with representatives from five key stakeholder groups. For each group, you'll see specific questions designed to uncover how this capability is valued and implemented across your organization. Take notes during these conversations—the patterns that emerge will help you identify your organization's current level and next steps.

After gathering responses to these questions, look for patterns:

- If most answers focus on traditional centralized manufacturing and global sourcing, you're likely at Level 1
- If you see pilot programs for local production but limited integration, you're probably at Level 2
- If local manufacturing consistently influences decisions but isn't yet driving strategy, you're at Level 3
- If distributed local manufacturing is actively driving innovation and business models, you've reached Level 4

FOR MANUFACTURING TEAMS

1 How do we evaluate opportunities for local production?
2 What systems support distributed manufacturing?
3 How do we maintain quality across multiple locations?
4 What prevents greater localization of production?
5 How do we incorporate local capabilities into manufacturing planning?

FOR SUPPLY CHAIN PARTNERS

1 How do local manufacturing capabilities influence partner selection?
2 What local production networks exist in our supply chain?
3 How do we collaborate on local manufacturing initiatives?
4 What prevents greater manufacturing localization?
5 How do we share manufacturing knowledge across the network?

FOR QUALITY TEAMS

1 What percentage of our production is local?
2 How do we manage quality across distributed sites?
3 What capabilities exist for local quality assurance?
4 How do we track quality metrics across locations?
5 What barriers prevent increased local production?

FOR INNOVATION TEAMS

1 How do we measure the impact of local manufacturing?
2 What targets exist for local production?
3 How do we verify manufacturing capabilities?
4 What role does local production play in our innovation strategy?
5 How do we develop new local manufacturing capabilities?

FOR EXECUTIVE LEADERSHIP

1 How does manufacturing location factor into our business strategy?
2 What investments are we making in local production capabilities?
3 How do we measure the value of local manufacturing?
4 What role does local production play in our risk management?
5 How do we balance economies of scale with local responsiveness?

Level 1 (Beginning)

Organizations at this level view manufacturing primarily through a centralized, global lens—similar to how traditional manufacturers operated before the distributed production network in the fictional example emerged. Like the early skeptics of local manufacturing, these organizations see economies of scale as the primary driver of production decisions. Manufacturing strategy prioritizes centralization over local responsiveness, and production capabilities aren't systematically developed at local levels.

Key characteristics:

- Manufacturing viewed primarily through centralized lens
- No formal evaluation of local production opportunities
- Limited local manufacturing capabilities
- Production data focused on central facilities

NEXT STEPS FOR LEVEL 1

Review your assessment results with your leadership team. The goal is to create a shared understanding of your current state and align local manufacturing opportunities.

Consider these targeted actions:

- Start collecting data on local market demands and response times
- Identify the top three products suitable for local production
- Create a pilot program for one local manufacturing cell
- Engage with the operations team to understand localization challenges

Level 2 (Developing)

Organizations at this level look like the earliest days of the fictional example of local manufacturing, when they were just beginning to demonstrate the value of distributed production. Like the first manufacturing cell experiments, they've started basic local production but haven't fully integrated distributed thinking into their manufacturing strategy. Similar to the initial challenges with quality assurance, these organizations struggle with maintaining consistency across locations but recognize the potential benefits.

Key characteristics:

- Basic local manufacturing programs established
- Some distributed production exists but may be limited
- Limited integration with central manufacturing strategy
- Basic quality systems for local production started

Focus on integrating local manufacturing thinking into your operations. Build connections between distributed sites and central planning. Create formal processes for maintaining quality across locations.

Consider these targeted actions:

- Develop distributed manufacturing metrics dashboard
- Include local production in strategic planning
- Create and implement distributed quality standards
- Launch local manufacturing specialist training program
- Establish process for evaluating local production opportunities

Level 3 (Advanced)

Organizations at this level operate like the maturing manufacturing network in the fictional example, with local production fully integrated as a strategic priority. Just as the network expanded to specialized facilities across London, these organizations maintain comprehensive quality systems and actively seek local manufacturing opportunities. Like the system of AR-guided production and real-time quality verification, they actively use production data to influence manufacturing decisions and see local production as a value creator.

Key characteristics:

- Local manufacturing integrated into corporate strategy
- Comprehensive quality systems across locations
- Active development of local production capabilities
- Production data influences manufacturing decisions

NEXT STEPS FOR LEVEL 3
Work on expanding local manufacturing influence across your organization. Create formal programs for capturing production innovations. Develop networks to scale local capabilities. Begin sharing knowledge beyond your organization.

Consider these targeted actions:

- Establish manufacturing innovation program with dedicated resources
- Create automated quality monitoring systems

- Develop strategy for scaling local production networks
- Implement comprehensive design-for-distributed-manufacturing guidelines
- Set organization-wide local production performance metrics

Level 4 (Leading)

Organizations at this level have achieved what the network accomplished in the fictional example through their manufacturer partnerships—developing local manufacturing to become a key capability. Like the expanding network of specialized production facilities, they've developed sophisticated systems for maintaining quality across distributed operations. Similar to how the success in the fictional example led manufacturers to design for local production, these organizations influence their entire industry's approach to manufacturing strategy.

Key characteristics:

- Local manufacturing drives innovation and strategy
- Advanced quality monitoring and prediction systems
- Active development of distributed production capabilities
- Industry leadership in local manufacturing

NEXT STEPS FOR LEVEL 4

Focus on leading industry transformation toward distributed manufacturing models. Share knowledge openly to build local production ecosystems. Develop new business models based on distributed manufacturing capabilities.

Consider these targeted actions:

- Create an open platform for sharing manufacturing knowledge
- Develop industry-standard quality protocols for distributed production
- Launch local manufacturing-based business models
- Establish distributed production innovation centers
- Lead development of industry standards for local manufacturing
- Create local manufacturing capability development programs

New Circular Supply Chain Roles to Manufacture In-Market

Building teams that excel at coordinating across traditionally separate domains. This involves bringing together specialists from across supply chain functions to collaborate on circular solutions.

In Chapter 4, we explored how traditional supply chain roles need to expand for circular operations, with professionals developing expertise across multiple product lifecycles. Production specialists should combine traditional manufacturing skills with digital design capabilities and materials science expertise.

The fictional example shows this capability through the manufacturing specialists who evolved from basic parts production to become digital manufacturing experts. These professionals learned to work with AR-guided production systems, material composition analysis, and quality verification protocols. The apprenticeship program further shows this capability, training a new generation of technicians who understand both traditional manufacturing techniques and advanced digital production tools.

Leading organizations today show similar capabilities. Protolabs' digital manufacturing specialists combine traditional machining knowledge with advanced CAD/CAM expertise to enable rapid local production across multiple technologies including CNC machining, 3D printing, and injection molding. Similarly, Fast Radius's manufacturing engineers work across various processes—from additive manufacturing to CNC machining—while leveraging a Cloud Manufacturing Platform that integrates design, production, and fulfillment. This platform uses data analytics and a learning engine to continuously improve manufacturing processes, ensuring efficient production across their network of micro-factories.

Finding Your Level

To assess your organization, you'll need input from multiple perspectives across your value chain. Schedule focused conversations with key stakeholders with the goal of understanding both the current state of repair in your organization and the barriers to advancing this capability.

Plan to speak with representatives from five key stakeholder groups. For each group, you'll see specific questions designed to uncover how this capability is valued and implemented across your organization. Take notes during these conversations—the patterns that emerge will help you identify your organization's current level and next steps.

After gathering responses to these questions, look for patterns:

- If most answers focus on traditional manufacturing roles and skills, you're likely at Level 1
- If you see emerging hybrid roles but limited systematic development, you're probably at Level 2
- If new manufacturing roles consistently influence operations but aren't yet driving innovation, you're at Level 3
- If specialized local manufacturing roles are actively driving transformation, you've reached Level 4

FOR MANUFACTURING TEAMS

1 How do we identify needs for new manufacturing roles?
2 What systems support skills development?
3 How do we maintain expertise across locations?
4 What prevents development of new capabilities?
5 How do we incorporate new technologies into training?

FOR HR/TRAINING TEAMS

1 What percentage of roles involve advanced manufacturing skills?
2 How do we develop new manufacturing competencies?
3 What career paths exist for manufacturing specialists?
4 How do we track skills development?
5 What barriers prevent new role creation?

FOR TECHNOLOGY TEAMS

1 How do we integrate new technologies into roles?
2 What targets exist for digital manufacturing skills?
3 How do we verify technical competencies?
4 What role does automation play in workforce planning?
5 How do we develop digital manufacturing capabilities?

FOR QUALITY TEAMS

1 How do manufacturing roles support quality objectives?

2 What advanced skills exist in our quality systems?

3 How do we collaborate on skills development?

4 What prevents greater technical specialization?

5 How do we share expertise across locations?

FOR EXECUTIVE LEADERSHIP

1 How do we develop new manufacturing capabilities in our workforce?

2 What investments are we making in skills development?

3 How do we measure the effectiveness of new roles?

4 What role do specialized skills play in our manufacturing strategy?

5 How do we balance traditional and new manufacturing competencies?

Level 1 (Beginning)

Organizations at this level maintain traditional manufacturing roles similar to how factories operated before the distributed production network emerged, and see workforce development primarily through the lens of conventional production skills.

Key characteristics:

- Manufacturing roles focused on traditional production tasks
- Limited integration of digital manufacturing skills
- Training focused on standard operating procedures
- Minimal cross-functional skill development
- Roles designed around centralized production models
- Quality assurance separate from production roles

NEXT STEPS FOR LEVEL 1

Review your assessment results with your leadership team. The goal is to create a shared understanding of your current workforce capabilities and opportunities for new manufacturing roles.

Consider these targeted actions:

- Identify key skills needed for local manufacturing
- Create a pilot program for digital manufacturing training
- Engage with technology teams to understand future skill requirements

Level 2 (Developing)

Organizations at this level look like the earliest days of the fictional example of local manufacturing, when they began transforming repair technicians into production specialists. Like the first manufacturing cell operators, they've started developing hybrid roles but haven't fully integrated new capabilities into their workforce strategy.

Key characteristics:

- Basic digital manufacturing skills emerging
- Some cross-functional roles established
- Limited integration with advanced technologies
- Traditional career paths still dominant
- Growing emphasis on technical problem-solving
- Initial development of quality-focused production roles

NEXT STEPS FOR LEVEL 2

Focus on systematically developing new manufacturing capabilities across your workforce. Build connections between traditional and emerging roles.

Consider these targeted actions:

- Develop digital manufacturing training program
- Create hybrid role definitions combining production and technical skills
- Establish a mentoring program for advanced manufacturing skills

Level 3 (Advanced)

Organizations at this level operate like the maturing manufacturing network in the fictional example, with specialized roles fully integrated into operations. Just as the network developed AR-guided production specialists, these organizations actively cultivate advanced manufacturing capabilities across their workforce.

Key characteristics:

- Advanced manufacturing roles standardized
- Comprehensive digital skill development
- Active cultivation of specialized expertise
- Data-driven decision-making embedded in roles
- Strong integration of quality and production capabilities
- Career paths support technical specialization

NEXT STEPS FOR LEVEL 3

Work on expanding manufacturing capabilities across your organization. Create formal programs for developing specialized expertise.

Consider these targeted actions:

- Establish advanced manufacturing certification program
- Create knowledge-sharing networks across locations
- Develop strategy for scaling technical capabilities

Level 4 (Leading)

Organizations at this level have achieved what the network accomplished in the fictional example through their apprenticeship development programs— transforming manufacturing roles into a core competitive advantage. Like the expanding network of technical experts, they've developed sophisticated systems for building and maintaining advanced manufacturing capabilities.

Key characteristics:

- Manufacturing roles drive innovation and strategy
- Advanced technical capabilities widespread
- Active development of future manufacturing skills
- Industry leadership in workforce development
- Seamless integration of digital and physical expertise
- Roles designed for continuous learning and adaptation

NEXT STEPS FOR LEVEL 4

Focus on leading industry transformation in manufacturing capabilities. Share expertise to build workforce development ecosystems.

Consider these targeted actions:

- Create an open platform for manufacturing skills development
- Launch advanced manufacturing apprenticeship programs
- Lead development of industry skill standards

Continuous Learning Culture to Manufacture In-Market

Creating an environment where teams actively share knowledge about repair techniques, material innovations, and process improvements across the circular network.

In Chapter 4, we explored how traditional organizational approaches often become barriers to circular success. Breaking down these silos can enable local production, showing how diverse teams—from materials scientists to production specialists to quality engineers—can work together effectively to manufacture complex components locally.

The fictional example shows this capability through their cross-functional approach to developing new manufacturing capabilities. When they began producing medical components, their teams combined insights from repair technicians, materials recovery specialists, and manufacturing engineers. Interaction between different facilities enables knowledge sharing between sites that accelerates innovation, with improvements in production techniques spreading rapidly across the network.

Leading organizations today show similar capabilities. Jabil's Blue Sky Innovation Centers create collaborative spaces where manufacturing engineers work directly with designers and materials scientists to develop new production techniques using advanced technologies. Similarly, DMG Mori's open innovation centers unite production specialists, software developers, and process engineers to enhance distributed manufacturing capabilities, proving that breaking down traditional roles accelerates technical innovation.

Finding Your Level

To assess your organization, you'll need input from multiple perspectives across your value chain. Schedule focused conversations with key stakeholders with the goal of understanding both the current state of repair in your organization and the barriers to advancing this capability.

Plan to speak with representatives from five key stakeholder groups. For each group, you'll see specific questions designed to uncover how this capability is valued and implemented across your organization. Take notes during these conversations – the patterns that emerge will help you identify your organization's current level and next steps.

After gathering responses to these questions, look for patterns:

- If most answers focus on traditional training and limited knowledge sharing, you're likely at Level 1
- If you see emerging collaboration but limited systematic learning, you're probably at Level 2
- If continuous learning influences operations but isn't yet driving innovation, you're at Level 3
- If learning culture actively drives manufacturing transformation, you've reached Level 4

FOR MANUFACTURING TEAMS

1 How do we capture and share production insights?
2 What systems support continuous learning?
3 How do we spread best practices across locations?
4 What prevents better knowledge sharing?
5 How do we incorporate learnings into procedures?

FOR TRAINING TEAMS

1 How do we facilitate cross-functional learning?
2 What collaborative learning programs exist?
3 How do we track knowledge transfer?
4 What barriers prevent effective learning?
5 How do we develop learning capabilities?

FOR INNOVATION TEAMS

1 How does learning culture support innovation?
2 What mechanisms exist for sharing discoveries?
3 How do we scale successful innovations?

4 What role does collaboration play in development?

5 How do we capture and spread new insights?

FOR QUALITY TEAMS

1 How do we learn from quality issues?

2 What knowledge-sharing networks exist?

3 How do we collaborate on improvements?

4 What prevents faster learning cycles?

5 How do we spread quality insights?

FOR EXECUTIVE LEADERSHIP

1 How does knowledge sharing influence our manufacturing strategy?

2 What investments are we making in learning infrastructure?

3 How do we measure the impact of continuous learning?

4 What role does collaboration play in our innovation process?

5 How do we balance standardization with local innovation?

Level 1 (Beginning)

Organizations at this level maintain traditional approaches to learning similar to how factories operated before the distributed production network emerged. Like early manufacturing operations, these organizations see knowledge as centrally controlled and distributed through formal channels only.

Key characteristics:

- Learning primarily through formal training
- Limited cross-facility knowledge sharing
- Improvements driven by central authority
- Minimal collaborative innovation
- Standard procedures rarely updated
- Knowledge silos between departments

NEXT STEPS FOR LEVEL 1

Review your assessment results with your leadership team. The goal is to create a shared understanding of your current learning culture and opportunities for improvement.

Consider these targeted actions:

- Create a basic knowledge-sharing platform
- Establish regular cross-functional meetings
- Implement simple improvement suggestion system
- Start documenting local manufacturing insights

Level 2 (Developing)

Organizations at this level look like the earliest days of the fictional example of local manufacturing, when facilities began sharing production insights. Like the first manufacturing cells, they've started basic knowledge sharing but haven't developed systematic learning processes.

Key characteristics:

- Basic collaboration between facilities
- Some cross-functional learning exists
- Limited systems for sharing insights
- Traditional barriers still prominent
- Growing emphasis on local improvements
- Initial development of learning networks

NEXT STEPS FOR LEVEL 2

Focus on systematically developing learning capabilities across your organization. Build connections between facilities and functions.

Consider these targeted actions:

- Develop a collaborative learning platform
- Create cross-facility improvement teams
- Launch a peer learning program
- Establish a process for sharing best practices

Level 3 (Advanced)

Organizations at this level operate like the maturing manufacturing network in the fictional example, with learning fully integrated into operations. Just as the network shared innovations between facilities, these organizations actively cultivate knowledge exchange and continuous improvement.

Key characteristics:

- Active knowledge sharing across network
- Systematic approach to learning
- Regular cross-facility collaboration
- Innovation driven by local insights
- Strong feedback loops established
- Learning integrated into daily operations

NEXT STEPS FOR LEVEL 3

Work on expanding learning influence across your organization. Create formal programs for scaling innovations.

Consider these targeted actions:

- Establish an innovation-sharing network
- Create a systematic improvement process
- Develop knowledge management strategy
- Launch a cross-facility innovation program

Level 4 (Leading)

Organizations at this level have achieved what the network accomplished in the fictional example through their learning culture—transforming knowledge sharing into a core capability. Like the expanding network of innovative facilities, they've developed sophisticated systems for capturing and scaling improvements.

Key characteristics:

- Learning drives manufacturing strategy
- Advanced collaboration capabilities
- Active development of new knowledge
- Industry leadership in innovation
- Seamless knowledge transfer
- Culture of continuous improvement

NEXT STEPS FOR LEVEL 4

Focus on leading industry transformation through collaborative learning. Share knowledge to build learning ecosystems.

Consider these targeted actions:

- Create an open innovation platform
- Launch industry learning network
- Develop a collaborative improvement system
- Lead development of learning standards

Note

1   IACMI (2021) 3D-Printed, Self-Driving Vehicles Built in a Micro Factory, Manufacturing USA, www.manufacturingusa.com/studies/3d-printed-self-driving-vehicles (archived at https://perma.cc/CEK3-RT7Z)

11

Process Capabilities

Orchestrating Circular Flows to Manufacture In-Market

Local manufacturing requires reimagining how production flows. The network in the fictional example demonstrates how organizations can transform traditional processes into dynamic systems that support distributed production. Success comes from developing three core capabilities: Circular value streams that connect local material flows with global knowledge sharing, smart recovery protocols that maintain quality across locations, and resource optimization systems that maximize network efficiency. Leading organizations recognize that these process capabilities enable them to manufacture locally while also maintaining the global quality standards and efficiency they require for customers.

The Circular Value Stream to Manufacture In-Market

Expanding traditional value stream mapping to capture circular opportunities, including repair loops, material recovery, and reintegration points.

In Chapter 4, we explored how circular value streams function more like water cycles than traditional linear flows. Materials and digital specifications can flow among operations, production cells, and end users, creating value at each transformation.

The fictional example shows this capability through the power controller production, where recovered materials from Croydon feed manufacturing cells in Park Royal and Hackney Wick. Their digital value stream enables production specifications to flow instantly between facilities, while physical materials move efficiently within local loops. When one facility discovers a production improvement, the value ripples across the entire network.

Leading organizations today show similar capabilities in creating circular value stream processes to support local manufacturing. Additive Industries' MetalFAB system gives an example of distributed manufacturing value streams where digital designs flow globally while production takes place locally, optimizing local capabilities. Similarly, EOS's End-to-End Production Network supports the exchange of manufacturing specifications between certified partners, making sure that production can happen within regional boundaries while promoting collaboration across facilities.

Finding Your Level

To assess your organization's circular value stream capabilities for local manufacturing, gather input from key stakeholders across your operations. Schedule focused conversations with representatives from each group, aiming to understand both current approaches to production flows and opportunities for localizing manufacturing.

After gathering responses to these questions, look for patterns:

- If most answers focus on traditional linear production with centralized manufacturing, you're likely at Level 1
- If you see some local production initiatives but limited integration, you're probably at Level 2
- If local manufacturing consistently informs decisions but isn't yet driving strategy, you're at Level 3
- If distributed production is actively driving innovation and operations, you've reached Level 4

FOR MANUFACTURING TEAMS

1 How do we manage production across different locations?
2 What systems support local manufacturing capabilities?
3 How do we maintain quality across production sites?
4 What prevents greater localization of production?
5 How do we share manufacturing knowledge between sites?

FOR SUPPLY CHAIN TEAMS

1 How do we optimize production network design?
2 What data drives facility location decisions?

3   How do we measure network performance?

4   What barriers exist to local production?

5   How do we coordinate material flows for distributed manufacturing?

FOR ENGINEERING TEAMS

1   How do product designs consider manufacturing location?

2   What prevents products from being made locally?

3   How do we validate production at new locations?

4   What design changes would enable local manufacturing?

5   How do we maintain consistency across production sites?

FOR QUALITY TEAMS

1   How do we ensure consistency across manufacturing locations?

2   What systems verify production quality at different sites?

3   How do we validate new production locations?

4   What prevents quality consistency across sites?

5   How do we share quality knowledge across locations?

FOR OPERATIONS LEADERSHIP

1   How do we currently decide where to manufacture products?

2   What percentage of our production could be localized?

3   How do we measure the impact of production location decisions?

4   What prevents us from manufacturing closer to demand?

5   How do we balance centralized and local production?

Level 1 (Beginning)

Organizations at this level operate traditional centralized manufacturing models, similar to the pre-distributed manufacturing era in the fictional example, and see manufacturing as requiring large, centralized facilities. Production location decisions prioritize scale economies over proximity to demand, and manufacturing knowledge isn't systematically shared between facilities.

Key characteristics:

- Centralized production model
- Limited local manufacturing capabilities
- Production knowledge siloed within facilities
- Minimal sharing of manufacturing expertise

NEXT STEPS FOR LEVEL 1

Review your assessment results with your leadership team. The goal is to create a shared understanding of your current state and align opportunities for local manufacturing.

Consider these targeted actions:

- Map current production locations against demand
- Identify products suitable for local manufacturing pilots
- Analyze transportation costs and lead times
- Create initial digital manufacturing documentation
- Start collecting production knowledge systematically

I'll continue with the remaining maturity levels for the circular value stream capability, maintaining the practical, action-oriented approach.

Level 2 (Developing)

Organizations at this level look like the earliest days of the fictional example of local manufacturing, when they were just beginning to produce power controllers locally. Like the initial manufacturing cells, they've started small-scale local production but haven't fully integrated it into their manufacturing strategy. These organizations struggle with maintaining consistency across sites but recognize the potential value of distributed production.

Key characteristics:

- Pilot local manufacturing initiatives started
- Basic digital production documentation exists
- Limited coordination between production sites
- Some sharing of manufacturing knowledge
- Initial quality validation processes for local production

Focus on systematically developing local manufacturing capabilities. Build connections between production sites. Create formal processes for sharing manufacturing knowledge and validating quality.

Consider these targeted actions:

- Develop standardized production documentation
- Create a manufacturing knowledge-sharing platform
- Implement cross-site quality verification systems
- Launch a local manufacturing training program
- Establish metrics for measuring local production performance

Level 3 (Advanced)

Organizations at this level operate like the maturing manufacturing network in the fictional example, with local production fully integrated as a strategic priority. Just as the network expanded to specialized facilities across London, these organizations maintain production documentation and actively seek opportunities for local manufacturing. Like the system of AR-guided production and quality verification, they actively use digital tools to ensure consistent quality across sites.

Key characteristics:

- Local manufacturing integrated into production strategy
- Comprehensive digital production documentation
- Active knowledge sharing between facilities
- Standardized quality verification across sites
- Clear metrics for distributed manufacturing performance

Work on expanding local manufacturing influence across your organization. Create formal programs for capturing production innovations. Develop networks to scale manufacturing capabilities. Begin sharing knowledge beyond your organization.

Consider these targeted actions:

- Establish manufacturing innovation program with dedicated resources
- Create automated production knowledge-sharing systems

- Develop strategy for scaling local production network
- Implement comprehensive design-for-distributed-manufacturing guidelines
- Set organization-wide local manufacturing performance metrics

Level 4 (Leading)

Organizations at this level have achieved what the network accomplished in the fictional example through their medical device manufacturing—developing local production into a core capability. Like the network of specialized manufacturing cells, they've created systems for maintaining quality across distributed facilities. Similar to how the success in the fictional example led manufacturers to redesign products for local production, these organizations influence their entire industry's approach to manufacturing.

Key characteristics:

- Distributed manufacturing drives production strategy
- Advanced digital production systems
- Active development of local manufacturing capabilities
- Industry leadership in distributed production
- Continuous innovation in manufacturing methods

NEXT STEPS FOR LEVEL 4

Focus on creating industry capabilities toward distributed manufacturing models. Share knowledge openly to build manufacturing ecosystems. Develop new business models based on local production capabilities.

Consider these targeted actions:

- Create an open platform for sharing manufacturing knowledge
- Develop industry-standard production protocols
- Launch distributed manufacturing-based business models
- Establish local manufacturing innovation centers
- Lead development of industry standards for distributed production
- Create manufacturing capability development programs for suppliers

Smart Recovery Protocols to Manufacture In-Market

Standardizing how teams assess, repair, and reintegrate materials and products, ensuring consistent quality across multiple lifecycles.

In Chapter 4, we explored how traditional manufacturing processes struggled with incorporating recovered materials. Protocols that enable local production using reclaimed resources show how smart manufacturing systems can adapt processes to material variations.

The fictional example shows this transformation through their ability to manufacture medical components using recovered titanium. Their systems continuously adjust production parameters based on material properties, using AI and real-time monitoring to ensure consistent quality. When manufacturing cells in different locations work with varying material batches, their protocols automatically optimize processing parameters.

Leading organizations today show similar capabilities.

Carpenter Technology's PowderLife system enables distributed manufacturing with recycled metal powders through effective material monitoring and process adaptation, supporting sustainable practices. Similarly, Markforged's adaptive manufacturing systems automatically adjust production parameters based on material variations, ensuring consistent quality when utilizing recovered resources.

Finding Your Level

To assess your organization's smart recovery protocol capabilities for local manufacturing, gather input from key stakeholders across your operations. Schedule focused conversations with representatives from each group, aiming to understand both current approaches to manufacturing processes and opportunities for intelligent adaptation to material and condition variations.

After gathering responses to these questions, look for patterns:

- If most answers focus on fixed manufacturing processes with limited adaptation, you're likely at Level 1

- If you see some intelligent process control but limited integration, you're probably at Level 2

- If adaptive manufacturing consistently informs operations but isn't yet driving innovation, you're at Level 3
- If smart recovery protocols are actively driving process improvement and quality, you've reached Level 4

FOR PROCESS ENGINEERS

1 How do our manufacturing processes adapt to material variations?
2 What systems monitor and adjust production parameters?
3 How do we optimize processes for different conditions?
4 What prevents greater process adaptation?
5 How do we capture and share process improvements?

FOR QUALITY TEAMS

1 How do we verify quality with varying input materials?
2 What systems ensure consistent output across conditions?
3 How do we validate process adaptations?
4 What prevents better quality consistency?
5 How do we measure process capability?

FOR MATERIALS TEAMS

1 How do we characterize input material variations?
2 What data drives process parameter adjustments?
3 How do we verify material-process compatibility?
4 What prevents better material utilization?
5 How do we optimize material recovery processes?

FOR MANUFACTURING TEAMS

1 How do production systems handle material variability?
2 What automation supports process adaptation?
3 How do we maintain consistency across batches?
4 What barriers exist to process flexibility?
5 How do we share process knowledge?

FOR TECHNOLOGY TEAMS

1   What systems support adaptive manufacturing?

2   How do we integrate process monitoring and control?

3   What analytics guide parameter adjustments?

4   What prevents better process automation?

5   How do we manage process data?

Level 1 (Beginning)

Organizations at this level operate with fixed manufacturing processes, similar to the traditional approach before the adaptive manufacturing systems. Like early manufacturing cells, these organizations struggle to handle material variations and maintain consistency across conditions. Manufacturing parameters remain static, with limited ability to adjust for changing inputs or conditions.

Key characteristics:

- Fixed manufacturing processes
- Limited process monitoring
- Manual parameter adjustments
- Minimal data collection
- Basic quality control

NEXT STEPS FOR LEVEL 1

Review your assessment results with your engineering team. The goal is to create a shared understanding of current process capabilities and identify opportunities for smart adaptation.

Consider these targeted actions:

- Implement basic process monitoring
- Start collecting parameter adjustment data
- Identify key process variables
- Map material variation impacts
- Begin standardizing quality measurements

Level 2 (Developing)

Organizations at this level look like the early manufacturing cells, when they first began implementing adaptive controls. Like the initial systems, they've started basic process monitoring and adjustment but haven't fully integrated intelligent control. Similar to the early challenges with medical components, these organizations struggle with maintaining consistency but recognize the value of adaptive manufacturing.

Key characteristics:

- Basic process monitoring implemented
- Some automated parameter control
- Initial data collection systems
- Growing understanding of material impacts
- Developing quality verification methods

NEXT STEPS FOR LEVEL 2

Focus on developing adaptive manufacturing capabilities. Build connections between process monitoring and control. Create formal systems for optimizing parameters based on conditions.

Consider these targeted actions:

- Implement real-time process monitoring
- Develop automated parameter adjustment systems
- Create material characterization protocols
- Launch process optimization program
- Establish adaptive control metrics

Level 3 (Advanced)

Organizations at this level operate like the maturing manufacturing network in the fictional example, with smart recovery protocols fully integrated into operations. Just as the network handled medical device production, these organizations maintain process control and actively optimize manufacturing parameters. Like the AI-driven systems, they actively use data to ensure consistent quality across varying conditions.

Key characteristics:

- Comprehensive process monitoring
- Automated parameter optimization
- Advanced material characterization

- Consistent quality across conditions
- Clear performance metrics

Next Steps for Level 3

Work on expanding smart recovery protocols across your operations. Create formal programs for capturing process innovations. Develop systems to scale adaptive capabilities. Begin sharing knowledge beyond your organization.
Consider these targeted actions:

- Establish a process innovation program
- Create automated optimization systems
- Develop strategy for scaling adaptive manufacturing
- Implement comprehensive process control guidelines
- Set organization-wide adaptation metrics

Level 4 (Leading)

Organizations at this level have achieved what the network accomplished in the fictional example with medical device manufacturing—turning adaptive, local manufacturing into a capability. Like the production cells, they've developed intelligent systems that maintain perfect quality across varying conditions. Similar to how the success in the fictional example led to new manufacturing possibilities, these organizations influence their industry's approach to process control.
Key characteristics:

- Intelligent process adaptation drives operations
- Advanced monitoring and control systems
- Active development of adaptive capabilities
- Industry leadership in process innovation
- Continuous optimization of manufacturing methods

NEXT STEPS FOR LEVEL 4
Focus on creating industry capabilities toward intelligent manufacturing. Share knowledge openly to build adaptive manufacturing ecosystems. Develop new capabilities based on smart recovery protocols.

Consider these targeted actions:

- Create an open platform for sharing process knowledge
- Develop industry-standard adaptation protocols
- Launch new manufacturing capabilities
- Establish process innovation centers
- Lead development of industry standards
- Create development programs for suppliers

Resource Optimization to Manufacture In-Market

Developing processes that maximize the use of existing materials through sharing, repair, and alternative sourcing.

In Chapter 4, we explored how circular operations require coordination of resources across networks. Intelligent orchestration of production capacity, materials, and expertise across multiple facilities can optimize local manufacturing resources to meet diverse needs.

The fictional example illustrates this through their dynamic production routing. When urgent medical device components were needed, their system orchestrated production across facilities based on capacity, capability, and material availability. Their network continuously optimizes resource utilization, balancing workloads between facilities while minimizing transportation distances.

Leading organizations today demonstrate similar capabilities. Xometry's distributed manufacturing platform optimizes production routing across thousands of local manufacturers based on capability, capacity, and location. Similarly, 3D Hubs' manufacturing network uses AI to orchestrate production across local facilities, optimizing resource utilization while reducing transportation needs.

Finding Your Level

To assess your organization's resource optimization capabilities for local manufacturing, gather input from key stakeholders across your operations. Schedule focused conversations with representatives from each group, aiming to understand both current approaches to resource allocation and opportunities for network-wide optimization.

After gathering responses to these questions, look for patterns:

- If most answers focus on individual facility optimization with limited coordination, you're likely at Level 1
- If you see some network coordination but limited system-wide optimization, you're probably at Level 2
- If network optimization consistently informs decisions but isn't yet driving strategy, you're at Level 3
- If dynamic resource optimization is actively driving network performance, you've reached Level 4

FOR OPERATIONS LEADERSHIP

1 How do we balance resources across our network?
2 What systems guide capacity allocation decisions?
3 How do we measure network-wide efficiency?
4 What prevents better resource utilization?
5 How do we coordinate between facilities?

FOR PRODUCTION PLANNING TEAMS

1 How do we optimize production loading?
2 What data drives resource allocation?
3 How do we balance network capacity?
4 What barriers exist to better coordination?
5 How do we handle demand fluctuations?

FOR LOGISTICS TEAMS

1 How do we optimize material flows between sites?
2 What systems support network coordination?
3 How do we minimize transportation needs?
4 What prevents better network efficiency?
5 How do we manage inventory across locations?

FOR FACILITY MANAGERS

1 How do we share resources with other sites?
2 What guides local capacity decisions?

3 How do we coordinate with other facilities?

4 What prevents better resource sharing?

5 How do we optimize local operations?

FOR TECHNOLOGY TEAMS

1 What systems support network optimization?

2 How do we track resource utilization?

3 What analytics guide allocation decisions?

4 What prevents better coordination?

5 How do we manage network data?

Level 1 (Beginning)

Organizations at this level optimize resources primarily within individual facilities, similar to traditional manufacturing before the networked approach. Like early manufacturing operations, these organizations struggle to coordinate across locations and balance resources effectively. Each facility operates largely independently, with limited visibility into network-wide opportunities.

Key characteristics:

- Facility-level optimization only
- Limited network coordination
- Manual resource allocation
- Minimal cross-facility sharing
- Basic efficiency metrics

NEXT STEPS FOR LEVEL 1

Review your assessment results with your operations team. The goal is to create a shared understanding of current resource utilization and identify opportunities for network optimization.

Consider these targeted actions:

- Map current resource utilization
- Start tracking cross-facility metrics
- Identify sharing opportunities

- Begin standardizing capacity measurements
- Create basic network visibility

Level 2 (Developing)

Organizations at this level look like the early manufacturing network, when they first began coordinating between facilities. Like the initial system, they've started basic network coordination but haven't fully integrated dynamic optimization. Similar to the early challenges with medical device production, these organizations struggle with balancing resources but recognize the value of network-wide optimization.

Key characteristics:

- Basic network coordination established
- Some resource sharing between sites
- Initial network metrics tracking
- Growing cross-facility communication
- Developing optimization methods

NEXT STEPS FOR LEVEL 2

Focus on systematically developing network optimization capabilities. Build connections between facilities. Create formal systems for coordinating resources across the network.

Consider these targeted actions:

- Implement network monitoring systems
- Develop resource-sharing protocols
- Create capacity planning tools
- Launch network efficiency program
- Establish coordination metrics

Level 3 (Advanced)

Organizations at this level operate like the maturing manufacturing network in the fictional example, with resource optimization fully integrated into operations. These organizations maintain coordination and actively optimize network-wide resources. Like the AI-driven systems, they use data to ensure efficient resource utilization across all locations.

Key characteristics:

- Comprehensive network optimization
- Automated resource balancing
- Advanced capacity planning
- Consistent efficiency across sites
- Clear network performance metrics

NEXT STEPS FOR LEVEL 3
Work on expanding optimization capabilities across your network. Create formal programs for capturing efficiency improvements. Develop systems to scale coordination capabilities. Begin sharing knowledge beyond your organization.

Consider these targeted actions:

- Establish a network innovation program
- Create automated optimization systems
- Develop strategy for scaling coordination
- Implement comprehensive planning guidelines
- Set network-wide performance metrics

Level 4 (Leading)

Organizations at this level have achieved what the network accomplished in the fictional example with synchronized production—developing resource optimization into a core comparative advantage. Like the network, they've developed intelligent systems that maintain perfect coordination across multiple facilities. Similar to how the success in the fictional example led to new manufacturing possibilities, these organizations influence their industry's approach to network optimization.

Key characteristics:

- Dynamic optimization drives network performance
- Advanced coordination systems
- Active development of optimization capabilities
- Industry leadership in network efficiency
- Continuous improvement of resource utilization

NEXT STEPS FOR LEVEL 4

Focus on creating industry capabilities toward intelligent network optimization. Share knowledge openly to build efficient manufacturing ecosystems. Develop new capabilities based on dynamic resource allocation.

Consider these targeted actions:

- Create an open platform for sharing optimization knowledge
- Develop industry-standard coordination protocols
- Launch new network capabilities
- Establish optimization innovation centers
- Lead development of industry standards
- Create development programs for partners

12

Technology Capabilities

Digital Enablement to Manufacture In-Market

Digital systems form the backbone of local manufacturing networks. The fictional example shows how technology enables consistent production across distributed facilities through three core capabilities: Digital product memory that captures and shares manufacturing knowledge, predictive recovery intelligence that maintains quality through AI-driven optimization, and network orchestration platforms that coordinate production across locations. Leading organizations recognize that these technology capabilities transform traditional manufacturing constraints, enabling local production with global quality standards.

Digital Product Memory to Manufacture In-Market

Creating comprehensive digital records that track a product's complete history through multiple lifecycles, repairs, and material changes.

In Chapter 4, we explored how traditional manufacturing systems needed to change in order to manage production across distributed networks. Digital systems can create a "product memory" that gives a consistent approach and information across multiple facilities.

The fictional example shows this capability through the manufacturing cells' ability to capture and share detailed production knowledge. Every component manufactured carries a complete digital record—from material composition to processing parameters to quality verification results. When the Park Royal facility perfected new production parameters, this knowledge was instantly available to other facilities, ensuring consistent approaches across the network.

Leading organizations today demonstrate similar capabilities in creating digital product memories to support local manufacturing. Authentise's Manufacturing Execution System generates detailed digital records of every production run, enhancing traceability and supporting consistent quality and approaches across distributed facilities. Similarly, AMFG's production management platform maintains comprehensive digital records that support workflow automation and make sure that manufacturing knowledge can be accurately replicated across locations.

Finding Your Level

To assess your organization, you'll need input from multiple perspectives across your value chain. Schedule focused conversations with key stakeholders with the goal of understanding both the current state of repair in your organization and the barriers to advancing this capability.

Plan to speak with representatives from five key stakeholder groups. For each group, you'll see specific questions designed to uncover how this capability is valued and implemented across your organization. Take notes during these conversations – the patterns that emerge will help you identify your organization's current level and next steps.

After gathering responses to these questions, look for patterns:

- If most answers focus on basic production records with minimal digital tracking, you're likely at Level 1
- If you see digital tools in use but limited integration across facilities, you're probably at Level 2
- If digital tracking consistently informs production but isn't yet driving innovation, you're at Level 3
- If digital product memory actively drives manufacturing strategy and improvement, you've reached Level 4

FOR PRODUCTION TEAMS

1 How do we capture and store manufacturing process data?
2 What digital tools track production parameters?
3 How do we share production knowledge between facilities?
4 What prevents better use of production data?
5 How do we validate and maintain data consistency?

FOR QUALITY TEAMS

1   How do we use digital records for quality assurance?

2   What metrics track production consistency?

3   How do we verify manufacturing data accuracy?

4   What role does data play in process improvement?

5   How do we maintain quality standards across facilities?

FOR ENGINEERING TEAMS

1   How do we document manufacturing specifications?

2   What systems manage production parameters?

3   How do we capture process improvements?

4   What barriers exist to knowledge sharing?

5   How do we validate new production processes?

FOR TECHNOLOGY TEAMS

1   What platforms manage our production data?

2   How do we ensure data security and accessibility?

3   What analytics capabilities support manufacturing?

4   How do we integrate data across facilities?

5   What prevents better digital integration?

FOR SUPPLY CHAIN PARTNERS

1   How do we share production specifications?

2   What digital systems connect our facilities?

3   How do we verify manufacturing consistency?

4   What prevents better data sharing?

5   How do we collaborate on process improvements?

Level 1 (Beginning)

Organizations at this level maintain basic digital records of production parameters, similar to traditional manufacturing documentation. Like the facilities the team in the fictional example first encountered, these organizations track essential specifications but lack comprehensive digital memory systems. Production knowledge often resides in individual facilities or with specific operators rather than in shared digital systems.

Key characteristics:

- Basic digital production records
- Limited sharing of manufacturing data
- Minimal integration between facilities
- Production knowledge primarily in human memory

NEXT STEPS FOR LEVEL 1

Review your assessment results with your production and technology teams. Focus on establishing basic digital tracking systems and identifying opportunities for better knowledge sharing.

Consider these targeted actions:

- Implement basic digital production logging
- Start documenting key process parameters
- Create central repository for manufacturing data
- Engage operators to capture tribal knowledge

Level 2 (Developing)

Organizations at this level look like the early manufacturing cells, with digital tools tracking production but limited integration across facilities. Like the initial challenges with sharing manufacturing knowledge, these organizations have started building digital memory systems but struggle with consistency and accessibility.

Key characteristics:

- Digital tracking of key parameters
- Some sharing of production data
- Basic integration between systems
- Growing digital knowledge base

NEXT STEPS FOR LEVEL 2

Focus on expanding digital tracking capabilities and improving integration between facilities. Build systems for sharing production knowledge effectively.

Consider these targeted actions:

- Implement real-time parameter monitoring
- Develop standardized data collection
- Create knowledge-sharing protocols
- Establish cross-facility data standards
- Launch digital training program

Level 3 (Advanced)

Organizations at this level operate like the maturing network, with comprehensive digital memory systems informing production decisions. Similar to the synchronized manufacturing cells, these organizations maintain detailed digital records that enable consistent production across facilities.

Key characteristics:

- Comprehensive digital tracking
- Integrated production systems
- Active knowledge sharing
- Data-driven decision-making

NEXT STEPS FOR LEVEL 3

Work on leveraging digital memory for innovation and improvement. Create systems for capturing and scaling process improvements across facilities.

Consider these targeted actions:

- Implement predictive analytics
- Develop AI-assisted process control
- Create a digital innovation platform
- Establish automated knowledge sharing
- Launch cross-facility improvement program

Level 4 (Leading)

Organizations at this level have achieved what the network accomplished in the fictional example through their medical device production—using digital memory to drive manufacturing innovation and consistency. Like the network's ability to instantly share and verify production knowledge, these organizations maintain digital systems that enable continuous improvement while ensuring consistent quality.

Key characteristics:

- Advanced digital memory systems
- AI-driven process optimization
- Automated knowledge sharing
- Industry-leading digital capabilities

NEXT STEPS FOR LEVEL 4

Focus on pushing the boundaries of digital manufacturing memory. Lead industry transformation toward connected, intelligent production systems.

Consider these targeted actions:

- Create open digital memory platforms
- Develop industry-standard protocols
- Launch digital innovation centers
- Establish cross-industry collaborations
- Lead development of digital standards

Predictive Recovery Intelligence to Manufacture In-Market

Using AI and analytics to determine optimal repair strategies and material reuse opportunities based on product condition and market needs.

In Chapter 4, we explored how traditional manufacturing approaches needed to grow beyond centralized control. Intelligent systems that combine AI-powered process control, real-time quality monitoring, and analytics can maintain consistent production across distributed facilities.

The fictional example shows this capability through the synchronized production runs across facilities.

Leading organizations today show similar capabilities. Oqton's autonomous manufacturing platform uses AI to optimize production parameters and predict quality issues across distributed facilities. Similarly, Inkbit's manufacturing systems use machine learning and real-time monitoring to maintain consistent quality across multiple production locations.

Finding Your Level

To assess your organization, you'll need input from multiple perspectives across your value chain. Schedule focused conversations with key stakeholders with the goal of understanding both the current state of repair in your organization and the barriers to advancing this capability.

Plan to speak with representatives from five key stakeholder groups. For each group, you'll see specific questions designed to uncover how this capability is valued and implemented across your organization. Take notes during these conversations—the patterns that emerge will help you identify your organization's current level and next steps.

After gathering responses to these questions, look for patterns:

- If most responses indicate reactive process control with minimal prediction, you're likely at Level 1
- If you see basic analytics in use but limited prediction capability, you're probably at Level 2
- If predictive systems inform production but aren't yet driving automation, you're at Level 3
- If AI-driven prediction actively optimizes manufacturing, you've reached Level 4

FOR PROCESS ENGINEERS

1 How do we predict potential production issues?
2 What analytics tools support process control?
3 How do we optimize manufacturing parameters?
4 What prevents better process prediction?
5 How do we validate predictive models?

FOR QUALITY TEAMS

1 How do we anticipate quality issues?
2 What predictive metrics track production?
3 How do we prevent manufacturing defects?
4 What role does AI play in quality control?
5 How do we maintain consistent prediction accuracy?

FOR OPERATIONS TEAMS

1 How do we optimize production parameters?

2 What systems predict maintenance needs?

3 How do we prevent production disruptions?

4 What barriers exist to predictive control?

5 How do we validate system recommendations?

FOR DATA SCIENCE TEAMS

1 What predictive models support manufacturing?

2 How do we ensure model accuracy?

3 What machine learning capabilities exist?

4 How do we integrate AI into production?

5 What prevents better predictive systems?

FOR MANUFACTURING PARTNERS

1 How do we share predictive insights?

2 What systems coordinate process optimization?

3 How do we validate predictive improvements?

4 What prevents better prediction sharing?

5 How do we collaborate on system development?

Level 1 (Beginning)

Organizations at this level operate primarily through reactive process control, similar to traditional manufacturing approaches. Like the facilities the team in the fictional example first encountered, these organizations respond to issues after they occur rather than predicting and preventing them. Manufacturing optimization relies heavily on human expertise rather than intelligent systems.

Key characteristics:

- Reactive process control
- Limited use of analytics
- Minimal predictive capability
- Manual parameter optimization

NEXT STEPS FOR LEVEL 1

Review your assessment results with your process and data teams. Focus on establishing basic analytics capabilities and identifying opportunities for prediction.

Consider these targeted actions:

- Implement basic process monitoring
- Start collecting parameter data
- Create simple analytical models
- Identify key prediction opportunities

Level 2 (Developing)

Organizations at this level look like the early manufacturing cells, with basic analytics informing production but limited predictive capability. They have started building predictive systems but struggle with accuracy and integration.

Key characteristics:

- Basic analytics in place
- Some predictive monitoring
- Growing use of data science
- Early AI implementation

NEXT STEPS FOR LEVEL 2

Focus on expanding predictive capabilities and improving model accuracy. Build systems for sharing and validating predictions effectively.

Consider these targeted actions:

- Implement real-time analytics
- Develop initial predictive models
- Create validation protocols
- Establish prediction standards
- Launch AI pilot program

Level 3 (Advanced)

Organizations at this level operate with comprehensive predictive systems informing production decisions. Similar to the synchronized manufacturing cells, these organizations maintain models that enable consistent optimization across facilities.

Key characteristics:

- Advanced predictive analytics
- Integrated AI systems
- Active parameter optimization
- Data-driven process control

NEXT STEPS FOR LEVEL 3

Work on leveraging predictive intelligence for automation and innovation. Create systems for scaling AI capabilities across facilities.

Consider these targeted actions:

- Implement AI-driven control
- Develop automated optimization
- Create predictive platforms
- Establish cross-facility learning
- Launch intelligent automation program

Level 4 (Leading)

Organizations at this level have achieved what the network accomplished in the fictional example through their medical device production—using AI to maintain perfect consistency across distributed facilities. Like the network's ability to automatically optimize processes, these organizations maintain predictive systems that enable continuous improvement while supporting reliable production.

Key characteristics:

- Advanced AI systems
- Automated optimization
- Predictive maintenance
- Industry-leading capabilities

NEXT STEPS FOR LEVEL 4

Focus on pushing the boundaries of intelligent manufacturing. Lead industry capabilities toward AI-driven production systems.

Consider these targeted actions:

- Create open AI platforms
- Develop prediction standards
- Launch innovation centers
- Establish industry collaborations
- Lead development of AI protocols

Network Orchestration Platform to Manufacture In-Market

Building integrated systems that coordinate material flows, repairs, and reintegration across the circular ecosystem.

In Chapter 4, we explored how traditional systems optimized individual facilities rather than entire networks. Intelligent orchestration can be very powerful, with platforms coordinating production across multiple locations while optimizing for resource utilization and knowledge sharing.

The fictional example shows this capability through the ability to balance production loads dynamically across facilities. Their platform automatically routes orders based on capacity, capability, and location, while ensuring consistent quality across all production nodes. When one facility discovers a process improvement, the platform immediately propagates this knowledge across the network.

Leading organizations today demonstrate similar capabilities. Hubs provides a robust platform that connects users with a vast network of local workshops, allowing them to upload 3D models for on-demand manufacturing. Similarly, Fictiv operates as a comprehensive manufacturing solution that orchestrates production across a global network of vetted partners. With capabilities spanning CNC machining, 3D printing, and injection molding, for example, Fictiv simplifies the sourcing process for mechanical parts.

Finding Your Level

To assess your organization, you'll need input from multiple perspectives across your value chain. Schedule focused conversations with key stakeholders with the goal of understanding both the current state of repair in your organization and the barriers to advancing this capability.

Plan to speak with representatives from five key stakeholder groups. For each group, you'll see specific questions designed to uncover how this capability is valued and implemented across your organization. Take notes during these conversations—the patterns that emerge will help you identify your organization's current level and next steps.

After gathering responses to these questions, look for patterns:

- If most responses indicate isolated facility management with minimal coordination, you're likely at Level 1
- If you see basic network coordination but limited optimization, you're probably at Level 2
- If network orchestration guides operations but isn't yet fully automated, you're at Level 3
- If AI-driven orchestration actively optimizes the entire network, you've reached Level 4

FOR NETWORK OPERATIONS TEAMS

1 How do we coordinate production across facilities?
2 What systems manage network capacity?
3 How do we optimize resource allocation?
4 What prevents better network coordination?
5 How do we balance workloads across sites?

FOR PRODUCTION PLANNERS

1 How do we manage multi-facility scheduling?
2 What tools support capacity planning?
3 How do we handle urgent production needs?
4 What barriers exist to network optimization?
5 How do we coordinate material flows?

FOR LOGISTICS TEAMS

1 How do we optimize network transportation?
2 What systems track material movement?
3 How do we coordinate deliveries?

4 What prevents better flow optimization?

5 How do we manage network inventory?

1 What platforms manage network operations?

2 How do we ensure system integration?

3 What orchestration capabilities exist?

4 How do we coordinate across platforms?

5 What prevents better automation?

1 How do we share capacity information?

2 What systems coordinate production?

3 How do we optimize joint operations?

4 What prevents better collaboration?

5 How do we manage shared resources?

Level 1 (Beginning)

Organizations at this level manage facilities independently, similar to traditional manufacturing approaches. Like the disconnected operations the team in the fictional example first encountered, these organizations coordinate production manually with minimal network-level optimization. Resource allocation relies heavily on individual facility decisions rather than network orchestration.

Key characteristics:

- Independent facility management
- Manual coordination
- Limited network visibility
- Basic resource allocation

NEXT STEPS FOR LEVEL 1

Review your assessment results with your operations and technology teams. Focus on establishing basic network coordination and identifying opportunities for optimization.

Consider these targeted actions:

- Implement basic network monitoring
- Start tracking capacity across sites
- Create shared production calendar
- Identify key coordination points

Level 2 (Developing)

Organizations at this level look like the early manufacturing network, with basic coordination between facilities but limited optimization. Like the initial challenges with balancing production loads, these organizations have started building network orchestration but struggle with real-time coordination.

Key characteristics:

- Basic network coordination
- Some resource optimization
- Growing cross-facility visibility
- Early automated scheduling

NEXT STEPS FOR LEVEL 2

Focus on expanding network visibility and improving coordination capabilities. Build systems for optimizing resource allocation effectively.

Consider these targeted actions:

- Implement real-time capacity tracking
- Develop network planning tools
- Create coordination protocols
- Establish optimization standards
- Launch an automation program

Level 3 (Advanced)

Organizations at this level operate like the maturing network, with comprehensive orchestration systems guiding production decisions. Similar to the ability to balance urgent medical device production across facilities, these organizations maintain coordination that enables efficient network operation.

Key characteristics:

- Advanced network orchestration
- Integrated capacity planning
- Active resource optimization
- Data-driven coordination

NEXT STEPS FOR LEVEL 3
Work on leveraging network orchestration for automation and innovation. Create systems for optimizing entire network operations.
Consider these targeted actions:

- Implement AI-driven coordination
- Develop automated load balancing
- Create a network optimization platform
- Establish predictive planning
- Launch cross-facility optimization

Level 4 (Leading)

Organizations at this level have achieved what the network accomplished in the fictional example through their medical device production—using intelligent orchestration to optimize operations across all facilities. Like the network's ability to automatically route and balance production, these organizations maintain systems that enable continuous optimization while ensuring efficient resource use.
Key characteristics:

- Advanced orchestration systems
- Automated optimization
- Network-wide coordination
- Industry-leading capabilities

NEXT STEPS FOR LEVEL 4
Focus on pushing the boundaries of network orchestration. Lead industry transformation toward intelligent manufacturing networks.

Consider these targeted actions:

- Create open orchestration platforms
- Develop network standards
- Launch coordination centers
- Establish industry collaborations
- Lead development of orchestration protocols

13

Standards Capabilities

*Common Language for Circularity
to Manufacture In-Market*

Common standards enable trust in local manufacturing. The network in the fictional example demonstrates how shared protocols and metrics allow distributed production to scale while maintaining consistency. Success comes from three core capabilities: Multi-life performance metrics that verify quality across locations, digital interoperability frameworks that enable seamless information sharing, and ecosystem collaboration protocols that coordinate diverse partners. Leading organizations recognize that these standards capabilities create the shared language needed for local manufacturing to thrive.

Multi-Life Performance Metrics to Manufacture In-Market

Establishing clear standards for measuring product and material performance across multiple use cycles.

In Chapter 4, we explored how traditional manufacturing standards focused on new production and needed to evolve. This evolution can be supported through performance metrics that evaluate not just production quality, but the complete lifecycle impact of locally manufactured components.

The fictional example shows this transformation through their production of medical components. Their standards evaluate immediate manufacturing quality while tracking how components perform through multiple use cycles. When they began manufacturing power controllers, their metrics encompassed both production consistency and long-term performance data from repair operations, creating a feedback loop that improved both manufacturing and product design.

Leading organizations today demonstrate similar transformations. Desktop Metal's manufacturing certification program includes metrics for both initial production quality and long-term component performance. Similarly, Materialise's manufacturing standards integrate production specifications with lifecycle performance data, ensuring components meet both immediate and long-term requirements.

Finding Your Level

To assess your organization, you'll need input from multiple perspectives across your value chain. Schedule focused conversations with key stakeholders with the goal of understanding both the current state of repair in your organization and the barriers to advancing this capability.

Plan to speak with representatives from five key stakeholder groups. For each group, you'll see specific questions designed to uncover how this capability is valued and implemented across your organization. Take notes during these conversations—the patterns that emerge will help you identify your organization's current level and next steps.

After gathering responses to these questions, look for patterns:

- If most answers focus on traditional single-life quality metrics, you're likely at Level 1
- If you see some lifecycle considerations but limited integration with manufacturing standards, you're probably at Level 2
- If performance metrics consistently consider multiple lifecycles but aren't yet driving manufacturing strategy, you're at Level 3
- If multi-life metrics actively guide manufacturing decisions and innovation, you've reached Level 4

FOR QUALITY TEAMS

1 How do we measure product performance across multiple lifecycles?

2 What standards exist for evaluating locally manufactured components?

3 How do we validate long-term performance of manufactured items?

4 What prevents better integration of lifecycle data into standards?

5 How do we incorporate repair data into manufacturing metrics?

FOR MANUFACTURING TEAMS

1 How do our quality standards account for local production?

2 What metrics track manufacturing consistency across facilities?

3 How do we verify long-term component performance?

4 What prevents better use of lifecycle performance data?

5 How do we standardize quality across distributed manufacturing?

FOR ENGINEERING TEAMS

1 How do design standards consider multiple lifecycles?

2 What performance data influences manufacturing specifications?

3 How do we validate designs for local production?

4 What barriers exist to lifecycle-based standards?

5 How do we incorporate field performance into specifications?

FOR SUPPLY CHAIN TEAMS

1 How do we measure supplier performance across lifecycles?

2 What standards govern local manufacturing partners?

3 How do we verify consistent quality across locations?

4 What prevents better integration of supplier performance data?

5 How do we standardize requirements across our network?

FOR SUSTAINABILITY TEAMS

1 How do we measure lifecycle environmental impact?

2 What standards exist for circular manufacturing?

3 How do we verify sustainability claims?

4 What role do lifecycle metrics play in decision-making?

5 How do we standardize impact measurement?

Level 1 (Beginning)

Organizations at this level apply traditional single-life performance metrics, similar to how manufacturing facilities initially approached quality before the local production network. These organizations focus primarily on initial production quality rather than long-term performance. Standards emphasize conformance to original specifications without considering multiple lifecycles or local manufacturing variations.

Key characteristics:

- Performance metrics focused on initial production
- Limited consideration of lifecycle performance
- Quality standards designed for centralized manufacturing
- No formal tracking of long-term component performance

NEXT STEPS FOR LEVEL 1

Review your assessment results with your quality and engineering teams. Focus on developing basic frameworks for evaluating recovered materials on their own terms rather than just comparing to virgin material standards.

Consider these targeted actions:

- Document current material testing procedures
- Identify key performance attributes for recovered materials
- Start tracking basic material transformation data
- Create a pilot testing protocol for one recovered material
- Begin collecting performance history for recovered materials

Level 2 (Developing)

Organizations at this level mirror the earliest days of the fictional example of local manufacturing, when they were just beginning to validate quality across distributed facilities. Like the first power controller production, they've started considering lifecycle performance but haven't fully integrated these insights into manufacturing standards. Similar to the initial challenges with medical device manufacturers, these organizations struggle with maintaining consistent quality across locations while recognizing the potential of local production.

Key characteristics:

- Basic lifecycle performance tracking established
- Some consideration of local manufacturing requirements
- Limited integration of repair data into standards
- Initial development of distributed quality protocols

NEXT STEPS FOR LEVEL 2

Focus on systematically integrating predictive analytics across operations. Build connections between different systems and create formal processes for validating predictions.

Consider these targeted actions:

- Implement real-time parameter monitoring
- Develop standardized data collection
- Create knowledge-sharing protocols
- Establish cross-facility data standards
- Launch a digital training program

Level 3 (Advanced)

Organizations at this level operate like the maturing manufacturing network in the fictional example, with multi-life performance metrics fully integrated into their production standards. Just as the network expanded to manufacture medical components across multiple facilities, these organizations maintain comprehensive lifecycle tracking and actively use performance data to improve manufacturing standards. Like the system of synchronized production cells, they actively verify quality across distributed locations while optimizing for long-term performance.

Key characteristics:

- Lifecycle performance integrated into manufacturing standards
- Comprehensive quality verification across facilities
- Active use of repair data to improve production
- Performance metrics influence manufacturing decisions

NEXT STEPS FOR LEVEL 3

Work on expanding predictive influence across your network. Create formal programs for advancing analytical capabilities. Develop more sophisticated models. Begin sharing insights across partners.

Consider these targeted actions:

- Establish a predictive analytics program
- Create cross-industry performance standards
- Develop automated performance-tracking systems

- Implement comprehensive lifecycle testing protocols
- Set performance-based circular economy targets

Level 4 (Leading)

Organizations at this level have achieved what the network accomplished in the fictional example through their medical device manufacturing—transforming multi-life performance metrics into a competitive advantage. Like the expanding network of specialized production cells, they've developed sophisticated systems for measuring and ensuring quality across multiple lifecycles and locations. Similar to how the success in the fictional example led to cross-industry adoption, these organizations influence their entire industry's approach to manufacturing standards.

Key characteristics:

- Performance metrics drive manufacturing innovation
- Advanced prediction of lifecycle performance
- Industry-leading quality standards for distributed production
- Active development of new manufacturing verification methods

NEXT STEPS FOR LEVEL 4

Focus on leading industry transformation toward circular quality models. Share frameworks openly to build verification ecosystems. Develop new approaches to lifecycle quality assurance.

Consider these targeted actions:

- Lead development of industry performance standards
- Create open platforms for sharing performance data
- Develop new circular metrics for industry adoption
- Establish innovation centers for measurement methods
- Launch performance-based circular business models

Digital Interoperability to Manufacture In-Market

Creating common data standards that enable seamless sharing of product information across the circular network.

In Chapter 4, we explored how traditional documentation approaches needed to evolve to support distributed manufacturing. Standardized digital protocols enable consistent production across multiple facilities while protecting intellectual property.

The fictional example illustrates this through their ability to share production specifications securely across facilities. Their digital standards ensure that manufacturing parameters, quality requirements, and verification protocols are consistently interpreted and applied at every production node. When they began manufacturing medical components, these standards enabled multiple facilities to maintain identical quality levels.

Leading organizations today show similar capabilities. The ISO 23247 series for digital twin manufacturing creates comprehensive protocols that standardize information sharing across facilities, defining clear frameworks for exchanging data about personnel, equipment, materials, and processes. Similarly, the OPC UA Companion Specifications, particularly when integrated with MTConnect standards, provide a universal communication language that allows diverse manufacturing systems and devices to exchange information efficiently. These standards ensure that different technological platforms can interact transparently, maintaining high levels of data integrity and enabling more sophisticated, interconnected production ecosystems.

Finding Your Level

To assess your organization, you'll need input from multiple perspectives across your value chain. Schedule focused conversations with key stakeholders with the goal of understanding both the current state of repair in your organization and the barriers to advancing this capability.

Plan to speak with representatives from five key stakeholder groups. For each group, you'll see specific questions designed to uncover how this capability is valued and implemented across your organization. Take notes during these conversations—the patterns that emerge will help you identify your organization's current level and next steps.

After gathering responses to these questions, look for patterns:

- If most digital information exists in isolated systems, you're likely at Level 1
- If you see some data standardization but limited integration across facilities, you're probably at Level 2

- If digital standards enable consistent production but aren't yet driving innovation, you're at Level 3
- If interoperable systems actively advance manufacturing capabilities, you've reached Level 4

FOR TECHNOLOGY TEAMS

1 How do manufacturing systems share data across facilities?
2 What standards govern digital information exchange?
3 How do we maintain data consistency across platforms?
4 What prevents better system integration?
5 How do we protect intellectual property while sharing data?

FOR MANUFACTURING TEAMS

1 How do production systems communicate across locations?
2 What digital standards support local manufacturing?
3 How do we share production specifications securely?
4 What barriers exist to digital collaboration?
5 How do we standardize process parameters?

FOR QUALITY TEAMS

1 How do we share quality data between facilities?
2 What standards verify production consistency?
3 How do we validate digital manufacturing data?
4 What prevents better-quality information sharing?
5 How do we standardize quality verification?

FOR ENGINEERING TEAMS

1 How do design systems integrate with production?
2 What standards govern manufacturing specifications?
3 How do we share product data across facilities?
4 What technical barriers limit interoperability?
5 How do we standardize design parameters?

FOR IT SECURITY TEAMS

1 How do we secure shared manufacturing data?

2 What standards protect intellectual property?

3 How do we validate data access and use?

4 What security concerns limit sharing?

5 How do we standardize data protection?

Level 1 (Beginning)

Organizations at this level maintain isolated digital systems, similar to how facilities operated before the networked production cells. Like early attempts at distributed manufacturing, these organizations struggle with sharing production data across locations. Digital information remains siloed, making consistent local manufacturing difficult.

Key characteristics:

- Isolated manufacturing systems
- Limited digital data sharing
- No standardized production formats
- Manual transfer of manufacturing information

NEXT STEPS FOR LEVEL 1

Review your assessment results with your technology and operations teams. Focus on establishing basic visibility into network-wide data flows and identifying opportunities for greater integration.

Consider these targeted actions:

- Map current data flows and systems
- Identify key data-sharing needs
- Create a pilot for standardized data exchange
- Begin documenting data standards
- Evaluate secure sharing platforms

Level 2 (Developing)

Organizations at this level look like the earliest days of the fictional example of networked manufacturing, when they began connecting production cells across facilities. Like the first power controller production network, they've started standardizing digital information but haven't achieved seamless integration. Similar to the initial challenges with medical device production, these organizations recognize the need for better digital integration while working to establish consistent standards.

Key characteristics:

- Basic data sharing established
- Some standardized digital formats
- Limited system integration
- Initial security protocols

NEXT STEPS FOR LEVEL 2

Focus on expanding data-sharing capabilities and improving integration between systems. Build frameworks for validating and sharing data effectively across the network.

Consider these targeted actions:

- Develop standardized data protocols
- Create a data quality verification system
- Establish a baseline for partner data exchange
- Launch a pilot for automated sharing
- Begin implementing common data standards

Level 3 (Advanced)

Organizations at this level operate like the mature manufacturing network, with standardized digital systems enabling consistent production across locations. Just as the network expanded to produce medical components, these organizations maintain sophisticated data-sharing protocols while ensuring security and quality. Like the synchronized production cells, they enable seamless information flow while protecting intellectual property.

Key characteristics:

- Standardized digital infrastructure
- Comprehensive data-sharing protocols
- Active system integration
- Secure information exchange

NEXT STEPS FOR LEVEL 3

Work on expanding data influence across your network. Create formal programs for capturing and sharing insights. Build systems to scale data capabilities.

Consider these targeted actions:

- Establish predictive data analytics
- Create cross-industry sharing standards
- Develop automated validation systems
- Implement comprehensive data governance
- Set interoperability performance targets

Level 4 (Leading)

Organizations at this level have achieved what the network accomplished in the fictional example through their medical device manufacturing—developing digital interoperability into a key capability. Like the expanding network of production cells, they've developed sophisticated systems for sharing and standardizing manufacturing data. Similar to how success in the fictional example led to cross-industry adoption, these organizations influence their industry's approach to digital manufacturing standards.

Key characteristics:

- Digital systems drive innovation
- Advanced interoperability standards
- Industry-leading data sharing
- Active development of new protocols

NEXT STEPS FOR LEVEL 4

Focus on leading industry transformation toward standardized data sharing. Share knowledge openly to build data-sharing ecosystems. Develop new approaches based on network-wide integration.

Consider these targeted actions:

- Lead development of industry data standards
- Create open platforms for secure sharing
- Develop new interoperability frameworks

- Establish innovation centers for data exchange
- Launch data-driven circular business models

Ecosystem Collaboration Protocols to Manufacture In-Market

Developing standard approaches for knowledge sharing and joint improvement across network partners.

In Chapter 4, we explored how traditional supplier relationships needed to evolve to enable effective collaboration across manufacturing networks. Structured protocols enable diverse partners to work together effectively in distributed production.

The fictional example shows this capability through the partnerships with medical device manufacturers. Their collaboration protocols enable secure sharing of production specifications, quality requirements, and performance data across organizational boundaries. When they expanded into new component types, these protocols helped quickly establish trust with new manufacturing partners.

Leading organizations today show similar capabilities. The COMPOSITION Collaborative Ecosystem is one example. It implements a Marketplace Management System that provides secure, transparent data exchange between manufacturing stakeholders. Similarly, the Biden administration's Universal Data Exchange initiative creates a standardized language for supply chain interactions. By encouraging manufacturers to develop universal data translation mechanisms and leveraging Industrial Internet of Things (IIoT) technologies, this initiative enables granular, contextualized data collection that supports adaptive and interconnected production environments.

Finding Your Level

To assess your organization, you'll need input from multiple perspectives across your value chain. Schedule focused conversations with key stakeholders with the goal of understanding both the current state of repair in your organization and the barriers to advancing this capability.

Plan to speak with representatives from five key stakeholder groups. For each group, you'll see specific questions designed to uncover how this capability is valued and implemented across your organization. Take notes during these conversations—the patterns that emerge will help you identify your organization's current level and next steps.

After gathering responses to these questions, look for patterns:

- If most collaboration happens through informal channels, you're likely at Level 1
- If you see some structured partnerships but limited network integration, you're probably at Level 2
- If collaboration protocols enable consistent production but aren't yet driving innovation, you're at Level 3
- If ecosystem partnerships actively advance manufacturing capabilities, you've reached Level 4

FOR PARTNERSHIP TEAMS

1 How do we structure manufacturing collaborations?
2 What protocols govern partner interactions?
3 How do we measure partnership effectiveness?
4 What prevents better network integration?
5 How do we standardize collaboration approaches?

FOR MANUFACTURING TEAMS

1 How do we work with external production partners?
2 What standards guide partner manufacturing?
3 How do we share production knowledge?
4 What barriers exist to partner collaboration?
5 How do we maintain consistency across partners?

FOR INNOVATION TEAMS

1 How do partnerships drive manufacturing innovation?
2 What protocols support collaborative development?
3 How do we share improvements across networks?
4 What prevents better innovation sharing?
5 How do we standardize improvement processes?

FOR QUALITY TEAMS

1 How do we ensure partner quality standards?

2 What protocols verify partner capabilities?

3 How do we validate collaborative production?

4 What quality concerns limit partnerships?

5 How do we standardize partner requirements?

FOR LEGAL TEAMS

1 How do we structure partnership agreements?

2 What protocols protect intellectual property?

3 How do we manage collaborative rights?

4 What legal barriers limit collaboration?

5 How do we standardize partner contracts?

Level 1 (Beginning)

Organizations at this level maintain informal partnerships, similar to traditional supplier relationships before the networked production model. Like early attempts at distributed manufacturing, these organizations lack structured protocols for collaboration, making consistent local production difficult across partners.

Key characteristics:

- Informal collaboration approaches
- Limited partnership structures
- No standardized protocols
- Basic contractual relationships

NEXT STEPS FOR LEVEL 1

Review your assessment results with your partnership teams. The goal is to create a shared understanding of current collaboration patterns and align standardization opportunities.

Consider these targeted actions:

- Map current partner relationships
- Identify collaboration opportunities

- Create a pilot ecosystem initiative
- Begin documenting shared practices
- Evaluate collaboration platforms

Level 2 (Developing)

Organizations at this level look like the earliest days of the fictional example of partner integration, when they began coordinating production across facilities. Like the first power controller partnerships, they've started establishing protocols but haven't achieved seamless collaboration. Similar to the initial challenges with medical device manufacturing, these organizations recognize the need for better partnership structures while working to establish consistent standards.

Key characteristics:

- Basic collaboration protocols established
- Some standardized partnership approaches
- Limited network integration
- Initial quality verification systems

NEXT STEPS FOR LEVEL 2

Focus on systematically developing collaboration capabilities across your network. Build frameworks for coordinating and optimizing partner interactions effectively.

Consider these targeted actions:

- Develop collaboration frameworks
- Create shared metrics system
- Establish baseline for ecosystem initiatives
- Launch a pilot for structured engagement
- Begin implementing common standards

Level 3 (Advanced)

Organizations at this level operate like the mature manufacturing network, with standardized protocols enabling consistent collaboration across partners. Just as the network expanded to produce medical components, these organizations maintain sophisticated partnership structures while ensuring quality and innovation. Like the synchronized production cells, they enable seamless collaboration while protecting partner interests.

Key characteristics:

- Standardized collaboration frameworks
- Comprehensive partnership protocols
- Active network integration
- Structured innovation sharing

NEXT STEPS FOR LEVEL 3

Work on expanding collaboration influence across your ecosystem. Create formal programs for capturing and scaling partnership innovations. Develop frameworks to accelerate network optimization.

Consider these targeted actions:

- Establish ecosystem innovation programs
- Create cross-industry collaboration standards
- Develop automated coordination systems
- Implement comprehensive governance
- Set ecosystem performance targets

Level 4 (Leading)

Organizations at this level have achieved what the network accomplished in the fictional example through their medical device manufacturing—developing ecosystem collaboration into a key capability. Like the expanding network of production partners, they've developed sophisticated protocols for coordinating manufacturing across networks. Similar to how the success in the fictional example led to cross-industry adoption, these organizations influence their industry's approach to partnership standards.

Key characteristics:

- Partnerships drive innovation
- Advanced collaboration protocols
- Industry-leading network integration
- Active development of new standards

NEXT STEPS FOR LEVEL 4

Focus on leading industry transformation toward ecosystem collaboration. Share frameworks openly to build collaborative networks. Develop new approaches based on network-wide engagement.

Consider these targeted actions:

- Lead development of industry collaboration standards
- Create open platforms for ecosystem engagement
- Develop new partnership frameworks
- Establish innovation centers for collaboration
- Launch ecosystem-based business models

14

Governance Capabilities

Ensuring Circular Success to Manufacture In-Market

Effective governance frameworks ensure local manufacturing can scale successfully. The network in the fictional example shows how new approaches to oversight and coordination enable distributed production through three core capabilities: Value-sharing mechanisms that align incentives across partners, quality assurance systems that maintain standards through multiple lifecycles, and continuous evolution frameworks that drive ongoing improvement. Leading organizations recognize that these governance capabilities create the foundation for trusted local manufacturing networks.

Value-Sharing Mechanisms to Manufacture In-Market

Creating frameworks that fairly distribute benefits among ecosystem partners who contribute to extending product life.

In Chapter 4, we explored how traditional value calculations needed to expand for circular operations. Frameworks that recognize and reward value creation across distributed production networks, from material recovery to final manufacturing, should be implemented.

The fictional example shows this capability through the expansion into medical device manufacturing. Their value-sharing model recognizes multiple contributors—from material recovery teams providing certified titanium to production specialists developing new manufacturing techniques. When one facility develops process improvements, their framework ensures benefits are distributed across the network while incentivizing continued innovation.

Leading organizations today show similar capabilities. John Deere's Digital Ecosystem unites software companies, dealers, and service providers, fostering collaborative innovation in agricultural tools while ensuring equitable value distribution. Similarly, the P&G and EY alliance leverages P&G's manufacturing expertise to create software, with EY as the market channel, demonstrating how partnerships can fairly distribute benefits across the ecosystem while enhancing overall manufacturing efficiency.

Finding Your Level

To assess your organization, you'll need input from multiple perspectives across your value chain. Schedule focused conversations with key stakeholders with the goal of understanding both the current state of repair in your organization and the barriers to advancing this capability.

Plan to speak with representatives from five key stakeholder groups. For each group, you'll see specific questions designed to uncover how this capability is valued and implemented across your organization. Take notes during these conversations—the patterns that emerge will help you identify your organization's current level and next steps.

After gathering responses to these questions, look for patterns:

- If most answers focus on traditional supplier contracts and basic cost structures, you're likely at Level 1
- If you see some profit-sharing initiatives but limited network integration, you're probably at Level 2
- If value sharing consistently influences decisions but isn't yet driving strategy, you're at Level 3
- If distributed value creation is actively driving your manufacturing network, you've reached Level 4

FOR EXECUTIVE LEADERSHIP

1 How do we measure and distribute value across our manufacturing network?

2 What investments are we making in value-sharing mechanisms?

3 How do we incentivize innovation across manufacturing locations?

4 What role does value sharing play in partner selection?

5 How do we balance local value creation with network efficiency?

FOR MANUFACTURING TEAMS

1 How do we recognize value creation at different production sites?

2 What systems support tracking value contributions?

3 How do we share benefits from manufacturing innovations?

4 What prevents more equitable value distribution?

5 How do we measure site-specific value creation?

FOR FINANCE TEAMS

1 How do we calculate value distribution across locations?

2 What metrics track value creation in manufacturing?

3 How do we account for non-financial value contributions?

4 How do we evaluate network-wide benefits?

5 What barriers exist to implementing value sharing?

FOR PARTNER ORGANIZATIONS

1 How is value shared when innovations improve network performance?

2 What mechanisms exist for collaborative value creation?

3 How are benefits distributed from joint improvements?

4 What prevents deeper value-sharing collaboration?

5 How do we measure shared value creation?

FOR LOCAL COMMUNITIES

1 How do manufacturing operations create local value?

2 What mechanisms share benefits with the community?

3 How do we measure local economic impact?

4 What prevents greater local value creation?

5 How do we balance local and network benefits?

Level 1 (Beginning)

Organizations at this level maintain traditional transactional relationships with manufacturing partners, similar to how facilities operated before the network demonstrated the power of shared value creation. These organizations focus on direct costs and immediate returns rather than network-wide value creation. Value sharing is limited to basic supplier contracts and standard pricing structures.

Key characteristics:

- Traditional supplier-customer relationships
- Value measured primarily through direct costs
- Limited recognition of network contributions
- Basic financial metrics only

NEXT STEPS FOR LEVEL 1

Review your assessment results with your leadership team. The goal is to create a shared understanding of your current state and align value-sharing opportunities.

Consider these targeted actions:

- Map value-creation points across your manufacturing network
- Identify the top three opportunities for shared value creation
- Create a pilot value-sharing program with one key partner
- Engage with manufacturing teams to understand value barriers

Level 2 (Developing)

Organizations at this level look like the earliest days of the fictional example of local manufacturing, when they were just beginning to demonstrate how shared value creation could drive network performance. They've started basic profit-sharing programs but haven't fully integrated value sharing into their network strategy. Similar to the initial challenges with manufacturers, these organizations recognize the potential of distributed value creation but struggle with implementation.

Key characteristics:

- Basic value-sharing programs established
- Some profit sharing with key partners
- Limited integration across network
- Traditional metrics with some value-sharing elements

NEXT STEPS FOR LEVEL 2

Focus on systematically integrating value sharing into your manufacturing strategy. Build connections between facilities and partners. Create formal processes for tracking and distributing value creation.

Consider these targeted actions:

- Develop a value-sharing metrics dashboard
- Include value-creation potential in partner selection
- Create and implement shared benefit calculations
- Launch a value-sharing pilot program
- Establish a process for measuring network contributions

Level 3 (Advanced)

Organizations at this level operate like the maturing manufacturing network in the fictional example, with value sharing fully integrated into their strategy. Just as the network expanded to specialized facilities across London, these organizations maintain comprehensive systems for tracking and sharing value creation. Like the approach to medical device manufacturing, they actively use value sharing to drive innovation and collaboration.

Key characteristics:

- Value sharing integrated into strategy
- Comprehensive tracking of value creation
- Active development of shared benefits
- Network value metrics influence decisions

NEXT STEPS FOR LEVEL 3

Work on expanding value-sharing influence across your network. Create formal programs for capturing and distributing innovation benefits. Develop frameworks to scale value-sharing capabilities.

Consider these targeted actions:

- Establish innovation-sharing program with dedicated resources
- Create automated value distribution systems
- Develop strategy for scaling value sharing
- Implement comprehensive benefit-sharing guidelines
- Set network-wide value-creation metrics

Level 4 (Leading)

Organizations at this level have achieved what the network accomplished in the fictional example through their manufacturer partnerships—developing value sharing into a key capability. Like the expanding network of specialized facilities, they've developed systems for identifying and distributing value creation. Similar to how the success in the fictional example led manufacturers to redesign their business models, these organizations influence their entire industry's approach to value sharing.

Key characteristics:

- Value sharing drives network strategy
- Advanced value-creation tracking systems
- Active development of new sharing models
- Industry leadership in distributed benefits

NEXT STEPS FOR LEVEL 4

Focus on leading industry transformation toward shared value models. Share knowledge openly to build value-sharing ecosystems. Develop new business models based on distributed value creation.

Consider these targeted actions:

- Create an open platform for sharing value-creation models
- Develop industry-standard benefit-sharing protocols
- Launch value-sharing-based business models
- Establish innovation-sharing centers
- Lead development of industry value-sharing standards
- Create value-focused partner development programs

Quality Assurance Through Multiple
Lives to Manufacture In-Market

Implementing governance structures that maintain consistent quality standards across multiple product lifecycles.

In Chapter 4, we explored how traditional quality systems struggled with circular operations. Governance frameworks maintain consistent quality across distributed manufacturing locations while enabling continuous improvement.

The fictional example shows this capability through medical component production. Their quality governance ensures consistent standards across facilities while adapting to local conditions and capabilities. Their frameworks maintain identical quality levels while allowing each facility to optimize their specific processes.

Leading organizations today show similar capabilities. For example, Formlabs use their global quality system, which leverages a cloud-based data management capability to oversee production across diverse locations, ensuring uniform standards and traceability. Similarly, Carbon's framework combines centralized control with local optimization, allowing partners to adapt their processes while also adhering to strict quality guidelines. This governance model enables Carbon to maintain regulatory compliance and product consistency across its distributed network, which shows how companies can balance global standards with local manufacturing flexibility.

Finding Your Level

To assess your organization, you'll need input from multiple perspectives across your value chain. Schedule focused conversations with key stakeholders with the goal of understanding both the current state of repair in your organization and the barriers to advancing this capability.

Plan to speak with representatives from five key stakeholder groups. For each group, you'll see specific questions designed to uncover how this capability is valued and implemented across your organization. Take notes during these conversations—the patterns that emerge will help you identify your organization's current level and next steps.

After gathering responses to these questions, look for patterns:

- If most answers focus on basic quality control and end-of-line testing, you're likely at Level 1
- If you see some distributed quality initiatives but limited network integration, you're probably at Level 2
- If quality systems consistently operate across locations but aren't yet driving innovation, you're at Level 3
- If distributed quality management is actively driving your manufacturing strategy, you've reached Level 4

FOR QUALITY TEAMS

1 How do we maintain consistent quality across manufacturing locations?

2 What systems verify production standards across sites?

3 How do we share quality insights between facilities?

4 What prevents standardized quality management?

5 How do we measure quality consistency across the network?

FOR MANUFACTURING TEAMS

1 How do we implement quality standards at different sites?

2 What tools support quality verification during production?

3 How do we adapt quality processes for local conditions?

4 What barriers exist to consistent quality?

5 How do we track quality metrics across facilities?

FOR ENGINEERING TEAMS

1 How do quality requirements influence process design?

2 What systems ensure consistent specifications across sites?

3 How do we validate quality improvements network-wide?

4 What prevents better quality integration?

5 How do we standardize quality requirements?

FOR PARTNER ORGANIZATIONS

1 How do we align quality standards across organizations?

2 What mechanisms verify partner quality performance?

3 How are quality improvements shared across networks?

4 What prevents deeper quality collaboration?

5 How do we measure shared quality achievements?

FOR CERTIFICATION BODIES

1 How do we validate quality across distributed operations?

2 What systems verify compliance at multiple sites?

3 How do we maintain certification consistency?

4 What prevents standardized certification?

5 How do we evaluate network-wide quality?

Level 1 (Beginning)

Organizations at this level maintain traditional quality control approaches, similar to how facilities operated before the network demonstrated the power of distributed quality management. These organizations focus on end-of-line inspection rather than integrated quality systems. Quality management is limited to basic checks and standardized tests.

Key characteristics:

- Traditional quality control methods
- Quality measured at end of production
- Limited integration between sites
- Basic quality metrics only

NEXT STEPS FOR LEVEL 1

Review your assessment results with your quality team. The goal is to create a shared understanding of your current state and align quality management opportunities.

Consider these targeted actions:

- Map quality control points across your manufacturing network
- Identify the top three quality standardization opportunities
- Create a pilot quality-sharing program with one facility
- Engage with manufacturing teams to understand quality barriers

Level 2 (Developing)

Organizations at this level look like the earliest days of the fictional example of local manufacturing, when they were just beginning to demonstrate how distributed quality management could ensure consistent production. Like the first manufacturing cells, they've started basic quality-sharing programs but haven't fully integrated quality systems across their network. Similar to the initial challenges with medical device manufacturing, these organizations recognize the potential of networked quality management but struggle with implementation.

Key characteristics:

- Basic quality-sharing programs established
- Some standardization between sites
- Limited integration across network
- Traditional metrics with some shared elements

NEXT STEPS FOR LEVEL 2

Focus on systematically integrating quality management across your manufacturing network. Build connections between facilities and quality teams. Create formal processes for sharing and implementing quality improvements.

Consider these targeted actions:

- Develop a network quality metrics dashboard
- Include quality capability in site selection
- Create and implement shared quality standards
- Launch quality improvement-sharing program
- Establish process for measuring network quality

Level 3 (Advanced)

Organizations at this level operate like the maturing manufacturing network in the fictional example, with quality management fully integrated across facilities. Just as the network expanded to specialized production across London, these organizations maintain comprehensive systems for ensuring consistent quality. Like the approach to medical component manufacturing, they actively use quality systems to drive innovation and improvement.

Key characteristics:

- Quality management integrated across network
- Comprehensive quality-tracking systems
- Active development of shared standards
- Network quality metrics drive decisions

NEXT STEPS FOR LEVEL 3

Work on expanding quality influence across your network. Create formal programs for capturing and sharing quality improvements. Develop frameworks to scale quality capabilities.

Consider these targeted actions:

- Establish quality innovation program with dedicated resources
- Create automated quality verification systems
- Develop strategy for scaling quality management
- Implement comprehensive quality-sharing guidelines
- Set network-wide quality performance metrics

Level 4 (Leading)

Organizations at this level have achieved what the network accomplished in the fictional example through their medical device manufacturing—and quality management becomes a comparative advantage. Like the expanding network of specialized facilities, they've developed systems for ensuring consistent quality across all operations. Similar to how the success in the fictional example led manufacturers to trust local production, these organizations influence their entire industry's approach to quality management.

Key characteristics:

- Quality management drives network strategy
- Advanced quality verification systems
- Active development of new standards
- Industry leadership in distributed quality

NEXT STEPS FOR LEVEL 4

Focus on leading industry transformation toward distributed quality models. Share knowledge openly to build quality management ecosystems. Develop new approaches based on networked quality systems.

Consider these targeted actions:

- Create an open platform for sharing quality knowledge
- Develop industry-standard quality protocols
- Launch quality-driven business models
- Establish quality innovation centers
- Lead development of industry quality standards
- Create quality-focused partner development programs

Continuous Evolution to Manufacture In-Market

Establishing processes for ongoing improvement and adaptation of circular practices based on network learning.

In Chapter 4, we explored how traditional governance structures couldn't support continuous improvement in circular networks. Frameworks should capture and scale innovations across their distributed production system while maintaining consistent quality.

The fictional example shows this capability through the expanding component portfolio. Their governance structure enables rapid scaling of new manufacturing capabilities while ensuring quality standards are maintained. When one facility develops an improved production technique, their framework ensures this innovation is effectively validated and implemented across the network.

Leading organizations today show similar capabilities. For example, Velo3D shows this with its end-to-end solution, including the Assure quality assurance software, which enables real-time monitoring and optimization of production processes across its network. This system allows for quick identification and correction of issues, facilitating ongoing production improvements. Similarly, Stratasys uses a "Mindful Manufacturing™" approach that emphasizes data collection, analysis, and continuous improvement across its extensive 3D printing network.

Finding Your Level

To assess your organization, you'll need input from multiple perspectives across your value chain. Schedule focused conversations with key stakeholders with the goal of understanding both the current state of repair in your organization and the barriers to advancing this capability.

Plan to speak with representatives from five key stakeholder groups. For each group, you'll see specific questions designed to uncover how this capability is valued and implemented across your organization. Take notes during these conversations—the patterns that emerge will help you identify your organization's current level and next steps.

After gathering responses to these questions, look for patterns:

- If most answers focus on basic improvement processes and individual site innovations, you're likely at Level 1

- If you see some network learning but limited systematic evolution, you're probably at Level 2
- If continuous improvement consistently operates across locations but isn't yet transformative, you're at Level 3
- If network-wide evolution is actively driving your manufacturing strategy, you've reached Level 4

FOR INNOVATION TEAMS

1 How do we capture and scale manufacturing improvements?
2 What systems support innovation sharing across sites?
3 How do we validate and implement new approaches?
4 What prevents faster evolution of capabilities?
5 How do we measure innovation impact across networks?

FOR MANUFACTURING TEAMS

1 How do we share process improvements between facilities?
2 What mechanisms support continuous learning?
3 How do we implement innovations from other sites?
4 What barriers exist to rapid evolution?
5 How do we track improvement impacts?

FOR TECHNOLOGY TEAMS

1 How do we enable systematic innovation sharing?
2 What platforms support network-wide learning?
3 How do we scale technical improvements?
4 What prevents faster technology evolution?
5 How do we measure innovation adoption?

FOR PARTNER ORGANIZATIONS

1 How do we collaborate on continuous improvement?
2 What mechanisms share innovations across networks?
3 How are joint improvements implemented?

4 What prevents faster collaborative evolution?

5 How do we measure shared innovation impact?

FOR RESEARCH AND DEVELOPMENT

1 How do manufacturing insights influence R&D?

2 What systems connect shop floor learning to development?

3 How do we accelerate innovation cycles?

4 What prevents faster capability development?

5 How do we evaluate evolution effectiveness?

Level 1 (Beginning)

Organizations at this level maintain traditional improvement approaches, similar to how facilities operated before the network demonstrated the power of systematic evolution. Like early manufacturing cells, these organizations focus on individual site improvements rather than network-wide evolution. Innovation sharing is limited to basic documentation and occasional meetings.

Key characteristics:

- Traditional improvement processes
- Innovation primarily at individual sites
- Limited sharing between facilities
- Basic improvement metrics only

NEXT STEPS FOR LEVEL 1

Review your assessment results with your leadership team. The goal is to create a shared understanding of your current state and align evolution opportunities.

Consider these targeted actions:

- Map innovation flows across your manufacturing network
- Identify the top three improvement-sharing opportunities
- Create a pilot evolution program with one facility
- Engage with manufacturing teams to understand innovation barriers

Level 2 (Developing)

Organizations at this level look like the earliest days of the fictional example of local manufacturing, when they were just beginning to demonstrate how networked learning could accelerate evolution. Like the first manufacturing cells, they've started basic improvement sharing but haven't fully integrated evolution across their network. Similar to the initial challenges with medical device manufacturing, these organizations recognize the potential of systematic evolution but struggle with implementation.

Key characteristics:

- Basic improvement sharing established
- Some learning between sites
- Limited network-wide evolution
- Traditional metrics with some innovation tracking

NEXT STEPS FOR LEVEL 2

Focus on systematically integrating evolution across your manufacturing network. Build connections between facilities and innovation teams. Create formal processes for scaling improvements.

Consider these targeted actions:

- Develop network evolution metrics dashboard
- Include innovation sharing in site operations
- Create and implement learning systems
- Launch improvement scaling program
- Establish a process for measuring network evolution

Level 3 (Advanced)

Organizations at this level operate like the maturing manufacturing network in the fictional example, with evolution fully integrated across facilities. Just as the network expanded to specialized production across London, these organizations maintain comprehensive systems for sharing and scaling improvements. Like the approach to medical component manufacturing, they actively use network learning to drive innovation.

Key characteristics:

- Evolution integrated across network
- Comprehensive improvement tracking
- Active development of shared learning
- Network evolution metrics drive decisions

NEXT STEPS FOR LEVEL 3

Work on expanding evolution influence across your network. Create formal programs for capturing and scaling innovations. Develop frameworks to accelerate capability development.

Consider these targeted actions:

- Establish an innovation scaling program with dedicated resources
- Create automated improvement-sharing systems
- Develop strategy for accelerating evolution
- Implement comprehensive learning frameworks
- Set network-wide innovation metrics

Level 4 (Leading)

Organizations at this level have achieved what the network accomplished in the fictional example through their distributed manufacturing—creating a capability of continuous evolution. Like the expanding network of specialized facilities, they've developed systems for scaling improvements across all operations. Similar to how the success in the fictional example led manufacturers to trust local production, these organizations influence their entire industry's approach to evolution.

Key characteristics:

- Evolution drives network strategy
- Advanced improvement scaling systems
- Active development of new capabilities
- Industry leadership in systematic innovation

NEXT STEPS FOR LEVEL 4

Focus on leading industry transformation toward systematic evolution. Share knowledge openly to build learning ecosystems. Develop new approaches based on network-wide innovation.

Consider these targeted actions:

- Create an open platform for sharing evolution approaches
- Develop industry-standard learning protocols
- Launch evolution-driven business models
- Establish innovation scaling centers
- Lead development of industry evolution standards
- Create learning-focused partner development programs

PART FOUR

The Capability to Circulate Locally

FICTIONAL EXAMPLE·
The Urban Mining Revolution

Maya stood on the rooftop of the warehouse in Hackney Wick, watching the morning sun sparkle off the solar panels that now covered most of London's industrial buildings. A year after launching their repair network, her team had transformed this space into something even more ambitious: London's first integrated urban mining hub, taking products, components and materials from the city for reuse.

Below her, electric delivery pods moved silently between collection points, bringing in everything from old mobile phones to construction debris. Each item contained valuable materials that, until recently, would have been lost to landfills or shipped overseas for processing. Now they were becoming the lifeblood of a new kind of supply chain—one that kept materials circulating within the city itself.

Fresh from the success of their repair network, she'd noticed something interesting in their data: Even with excellent repair capabilities, they were still dependent on global supply chains for raw materials. When the latest semiconductor shortage hit, it had sparked an idea. "We've got more gold sitting in London's abandoned phones than in most mining operations," she had told the skeptical executives. "And that's just the beginning. The steel in our buildings, the rare earth elements in our electronics, the glass in our windows—our cities are becoming our new mines."

The board had been intrigued but cautious. "Urban mining sounds fascinating," one director had said, "but how do you make it commercially viable?"

Through the AR overlay in her glasses, Maya could see the optimized paths of their electric pods as they moved through the city. Each one would visit multiple collection points—electronics retailers, office buildings, construction sites—gathering materials that would have once been considered waste. Through the skylights, she could see their advanced optical sorting systems beginning their daily calibration, identifying and separating materials with incredible precision. These machines, which could identify material compositions with advanced spectroscopy, were the key to making urban mining commercially viable. But the real innovation wasn't just technological— it was in creating a new kind of circular supply chain, one that operated entirely within the city's boundaries.

Three months later, their network had grown beyond expectations. Construction companies were using their platform to track and trade recovered materials between sites. Fashion brands had established collection points for used clothing. Their new material recovery line was processing titanium for medical applications while their AI systems maintained detailed records of every parameter. Each item in their system carried what they called a "digital twin plus"—not just tracking its physical properties and location, but also its complete history, verification records, and future potential. Their recovery network now included dozens of collection points across London—repair cafes, electronics retailers, community centers, and even dedicated "urban mining points" in high-traffic areas.

The real breakthrough came when their AI system discovered that recovered materials from one industry could meet specifications for another. Their success with recovering rare earth elements from electric vehicle motors had led manufacturers to redesign products specifically for eventual recovery. Each component was now tagged with its exact material composition, with critical materials concentrated in easily removable modules.

As the morning's first collection routes started, Maya checked the impact metrics on their wall display: "50 percent reduction in new material demand," "90 percent decrease in transportation emissions," "200+ new technical jobs created." The revolution in how we source materials was starting, one city block at a time.

15

People and Culture Capabilities

Circulating Locally

Developing the capability for local recovery begins with people. As seen in the fictional example's network, success comes from transforming mindsets from "take-make-waste" to seeing cities as material mines. While technology enables recovery, it's the human capabilities—from materials scientists using advanced spectroscopy to logistics specialists optimizing collection routes—that make these systems work. Leading organizations recognize that investing in three core capabilities creates the foundation for effective urban mining operations: Circular leadership, new supply chain roles, and continuous learning culture.

Circular Leadership to Circulate Locally

Developing leaders who understand value exists beyond single-use lifecycles. This encompasses training supply chain professionals to identify opportunities for material reuse, repair, and reintegration.

In Chapter 4, we explored how traditional supply chains treated materials as consumable inputs, shown by the decades of "take-make-waste" thinking that shaped industrial development. This mindset created supply chains optimized for material consumption rather than preservation. A change is possible—one where cities become sources of valuable materials rather than sites of waste accumulation.

The local recovery network in the fictional example shows how this change creates value across multiple stakeholders. This integrated model shows how local recovery capabilities can grow at scale, creating jobs while dramatically reducing the need for virgin resource extraction.

This change shows what leading organizations are already showcasing today. For example, Interface's ReEntry program recovers materials from used carpet tiles for remanufacturing, showing that urban mining approaches can work for industrial materials at scale. This program, which has diverted over 360 million pounds of carpet from landfills since 1994, uses sophisticated processes to separate and recycle different components.[1]

Finding Your Level

To assess your organization, you'll need input from multiple perspectives across your value chain. Schedule focused conversations with key stakeholders with the goal of understanding both the current state of repair in your organization and the barriers to advancing this capability.

Plan to speak with representatives from five key stakeholder groups. For each group, you'll see specific questions designed to uncover how this capability is valued and implemented across your organization. Take notes during these conversations—the patterns that emerge will help you identify your organization's current level and next steps.

After gathering responses to these questions, look for patterns:

- If most answers focus on basic recycling and waste disposal, you're likely at Level 1
- If you see material recovery initiatives but limited integration with core operations, you're probably at Level 2
- If material recovery consistently influences decisions but it isn't yet driving strategy, you're at Level 3
- If urban mining is actively driving innovation and business models, you've reached Level 4

FOR MATERIALS/ENGINEERING TEAMS

1 How do we identify opportunities for material recovery?
2 What systems support material identification and sorting?
3 How do we evaluate recovered material quality?
4 What prevents greater use of recovered materials?
5 How do we incorporate recovery potential into material selection?

FOR OPERATIONS TEAMS

1 What percentage of our materials comes from recovery operations?

2 How do we manage material recovery processes?

3 What capabilities exist for processing recovered materials?

4 How do we track material flows through our operations?

5 What barriers prevent increased material recovery?

FOR SUSTAINABILITY TEAMS

1 How do we measure the impact of material recovery?

2 What targets exist for recovered material use?

3 How do we verify recovery process effectiveness?

4 What role does recovery play in our environmental goals?

5 How do we communicate recovery benefits to stakeholders?

FOR SUPPLY CHAIN PARTNERS

1 How do recovery capabilities influence partner selection?

2 What material recovery networks exist in our supply chain?

3 How do we collaborate on recovery initiatives?

4 What prevents greater recovery collaboration?

5 How do we share recovery knowledge across the network?

FOR EXECUTIVE LEADERSHIP

1 How does material recovery factor into our business strategy?

2 What investments are we making in urban mining capabilities?

3 How do we measure the value of recovered materials?

4 What role does material recovery play in our risk management?

5 How do we balance short-term costs with long-term material security?

Level 1 (Beginning)

Organizations at this level view material recovery primarily as waste management, similar to how cities might initially approach discarded electronics before a more formalized recovery hub is put into place. These organizations see materials as consumable inputs rather than circular assets. Material selection prioritizes initial cost over recovery potential, and material flows aren't systematically tracked or analyzed.

Key characteristics:

- Materials viewed primarily as consumable inputs
- No formal material tracking beyond basic waste reporting
- Material recovery limited to basic recycling
- Material flow data not systematically collected

NEXT STEPS FOR LEVEL 1

Review your assessment results with your leadership team. The goal is to create a shared understanding of your current state and align material recovery opportunities.

Consider these targeted actions:

- Start collecting basic material flow data (types, volumes, disposal costs)
- Identify the top three most valuable materials in your waste stream
- Create a pilot recovery program for one material type
- Engage with the operations team to understand recovery challenges

Level 2 (Developing)

Organizations at this level look like the earliest days in the fictional example of local recovery, when they were just beginning to show the value of recovered materials. Like the first material recovery efforts, they've started basic collection and sorting operations but haven't fully integrated circular thinking into their material strategy. These organizations struggle with trusting recovered materials but recognize their potential value.

Key characteristics:

- Basic material recovery programs established
- Some material tracking exists but may be incomplete
- Limited integration of recovered materials into production
- Basic material flow data collection started but not fully utilized

NEXT STEPS FOR LEVEL 2

Focus on integrating circular material thinking into your operations. Build connections between recovery teams and procurement. Create formal processes for tracking material flows and quality verification.

Consider these targeted actions:

- Develop material recovery metrics dashboard
- Include recovery potential in material selection criteria
- Create and implement material testing standards
- Launch a recovery specialist training program
- Establish processes for evaluating recovered material quality

Level 3 (Advanced)

Organizations at this level operate with material recovery fully integrated as a strategic priority. Just as the network expanded to specialized facilities across London, these organizations maintain material tracking and actively seek recovery opportunities. They actively use material flow data to influence procurement decisions and see recovery as a value creator.

Key characteristics:

- Recovery integrated into material strategy
- Comprehensive material-tracking systems in place
- Active sourcing of recovered materials
- Material flow data influences procurement decisions

NEXT STEPS FOR LEVEL 3

Work on expanding recovery ideation across your organization. Create formal programs for capturing recovery innovations. Develop networks to scale recovery capabilities and begin sharing knowledge beyond your organization.

Consider these targeted actions:

- Establish material innovation program with dedicated resources
- Create automated material-tracking systems
- Develop strategy for scaling recovery networks
- Implement comprehensive design-for-recovery guidelines
- Set organization-wide recovery-based performance metrics

Level 4 (Leading)

Organizations at this level have achieved what the network in the fictional example accomplished through their manufacturer partnerships—transforming urban mining into a core competitive advantage. Like the expanding network of specialized recovery facilities, they've developed systems for identifying and capturing material value. Similar to how the success in the fictional example led manufacturers to design for recovery, these organizations influence their entire industry's approach to material use.

Key characteristics:

- Recovery drives material innovation and strategy
- Advanced material tracking and prediction systems
- Active development of urban mining capabilities
- Industry leadership in circular material flows

NEXT STEPS FOR LEVEL 4

Focus on leading industry change toward circular material models. Share knowledge openly to build recovery ecosystems. Develop new business models based on urban mining capabilities.

Consider these targeted actions:

- Create an open platform for sharing recovery knowledge
- Develop industry-standard material testing protocols
- Launch circular material-based business models
- Establish urban mining innovation centers
- Lead development of industry recovery standards
- Create recovery-focused supplier development programs

New Circular Supply Chain Roles to Circulate Locally

Building teams that excel at coordinating across traditionally separate domains. This involves bringing together specialists from across supply chain functions to collaborate on circular solutions.

In Chapter 4, we explored how traditional supply chain roles need to expand for circular operations, with professionals developing expertise across multiple product lifecycles. Materials scientists and logistics specialists can combine traditional skills with advanced analytics and digital tracking capabilities.

The fictional example shows the capability of new circular supply chain roles through the example organization's approach to material recovery. What started as basic sorting evolved into material science, with specialists using advanced spectroscopy and AI-powered systems to identify and grade recovered materials. These professionals don't just separate materials—they understand their molecular structure, predict their performance in different applications, and optimize their recovery processes.

Leading organizations today show similar capabilities. BASF's ChemCycling program employs advanced chemical recycling processes to transform plastic waste into pyrolysis oil, which is then used to create virgin-quality materials for various products. Similarly, Umicore's precious metals recovery operations require sophisticated metallurgical expertise to process complex waste streams, recovering up to 17 different metals from a wide range of industrial by-products and consumer recyclables.[2]

Finding Your Level

To assess your organization, you'll need input from multiple perspectives across your value chain. Schedule focused conversations with key stakeholders with the goal of understanding both the current state of repair in your organization and the barriers to advancing this capability.

Plan to speak with representatives from five key stakeholder groups. For each group, you'll see specific questions designed to uncover how this capability is valued and implemented across your organization. Take notes during these conversations—the patterns that emerge will help you identify your organization's current level and next steps.

After gathering responses to these questions, look for patterns:

- If most answers focus on traditional linear supply chain roles, you're likely at Level 1
- If you see some specialized circular roles but limited integration, you're probably at Level 2
- If circular roles consistently influence operations but aren't yet driving innovation, you're at Level 3
- If circular roles are actively driving business change, you've reached Level 4

FOR HR/TRAINING TEAMS

1 What circular economy skills are we developing internally?
2 How do we identify needs for new circular roles?
3 What training programs support circular capabilities?

4 How do we assess circular economy competencies?

5 What barriers exist to developing circular roles?

FOR OPERATIONS TEAMS

1 What specialized circular roles exist in our operations?

2 How do we integrate circular expertise into existing teams?

3 What skills gaps exist for circular operations?

4 How do we capture and share circular knowledge?

5 What prevents broader adoption of circular roles?

FOR TECHNICAL TEAMS

1 What circular technical capabilities are we developing?

2 How do we combine traditional and circular expertise?

3 What tools support our circular specialists?

4 How do we validate circular technical skills?

5 What technical barriers limit circular roles?

FOR SUPPLY CHAIN PARTNERS

1 What circular roles exist across our partner network?

2 How do we collaborate on circular capability development?

3 What skills do we share across the network?

4 How do we coordinate circular training?

5 What prevents greater development of circular roles?

FOR EXECUTIVE LEADERSHIP

1 How do we develop circular economy capabilities in our workforce?

2 What investments are we making in training for circular roles?

3 How do we measure the impact of new circular positions?

4 What role do circular skills play in our talent strategy?

5 How do we balance traditional and circular economy expertise?

Level 1 (Beginning)

Organizations at this level maintain traditional linear supply chain roles, similar to how businesses operated before the expansion in the fictional example began. Like the initial skepticism toward local recovery specialists, these organizations rely on conventional job descriptions and skill sets. Training focuses on traditional supply chain efficiency rather than circular capabilities.

Key characteristics:

- Traditional linear supply chain roles dominate
- No formal circular economy training exists
- Limited recognition of circular skill requirements
- Circular knowledge not systematically developed

NEXT STEPS FOR LEVEL 1

Review your assessment results with your HR and operations teams. The goal is to create a shared understanding of needed circular capabilities and align development priorities.

Consider these targeted actions:

- Identify key circular economy skill gaps
- Create a pilot training program for circular principles
- Define one new circular role for pilot implementation
- Engage with operations to understand circular skill needs

Level 2 (Developing)

Organizations at this level have started creating dedicated circular positions but haven't fully integrated these roles across operations. Similar to the early challenges, these organizations struggle with balancing traditional and circular capabilities.

Key characteristics:

- Some specialized circular roles established
- Basic circular training programs exist
- Limited integration of circular specialists
- Initial circular knowledge capture started

NEXT STEPS FOR LEVEL 2

Focus on systematically integrating circular roles into your operations. Build connections between traditional and circular teams. Create formal processes for developing and sharing circular expertise.

Consider these targeted actions:

- Develop circular competency framework
- Create cross-training programs between traditional and circular roles
- Establish formal circular career paths
- Launch a circular knowledge-sharing platform
- Implement circular skills assessment tools

Level 3 (Advanced)

Organizations at this level operate with circular roles fully integrated as core positions. Just as the network developed material scientists and recovery specialists, these organizations maintain comprehensive circular training programs and actively develop new circular capabilities. Like the system of integrated expertise in the fictional example, they actively combine traditional and circular knowledge.

Key characteristics:

- Circular roles integrated across operations
- Comprehensive circular training programs
- Active development of new circular capabilities
- Circular expertise influences strategic decisions

NEXT STEPS FOR LEVEL 3

Work on expanding circular influence across your organization. Create formal programs for developing circular innovations. Build networks to scale circular capabilities. Begin sharing expertise beyond your organization.

Consider these targeted actions:

- Establish circular innovation teams
- Create advanced circular certification programs
- Develop strategy for scaling circular capabilities
- Implement comprehensive circular skill requirements
- Set organization-wide circular performance metrics

Level 4 (Leading)

Organizations at this level have achieved what the network in the fictional example accomplished—transforming circular roles into a core competitive advantage. Like the expanding network of specialists, they've developed systems for building and sharing circular expertise. Similar to how the success in the fictional example influenced entire industries, these organizations lead in developing new circular capabilities.

Key characteristics:

- Circular roles drive organizational strategy
- Advanced circular capability development systems
- Active creation of new circular positions
- Industry leadership in circular workforce development

NEXT STEPS FOR LEVEL 4

Focus on leading industry change toward circular capabilities. Share knowledge openly to build circular expertise. Develop new organizational models based on circular roles.

Consider these targeted actions:

- Create an open platform for circular knowledge sharing
- Develop industry-standard circular certifications
- Launch circular economy centers of excellence
- Establish circular innovation hubs
- Lead development of industry skill standards
- Create circular capability development networks

Continuous Learning Culture to Circulate Locally

Creating an environment where teams actively share knowledge about repair techniques, material innovations, and process improvements across the circular network.

In Chapter 4, we explored how traditional organizational reporting structures can hinder circular success. Challenging these structures with diverse teams working together, from material scientists to logistics specialists to AI systems engineers, can maximize resource recovery and value creation.

Leading organizations today show similar capabilities. Veolia's resource recovery operations create learning environments where waste management expertise meets advanced technologies across various industries. Their teams work with diverse clients to improve recovery rates and find new applications for recovered materials. Similarly, Sims Metal Management has developed training programs that combine traditional recycling knowledge with digital systems, creating professionals who understand both material processing and environmental best practices.

Finding Your Level

To assess your organization, you'll need input from multiple perspectives across your value chain. Schedule focused conversations with key stakeholders with the goal of understanding both the current state of repair in your organization and the barriers to advancing this capability.

Plan to speak with representatives from five key stakeholder groups. For each group, you'll see specific questions designed to uncover how this capability is valued and implemented across your organization. Take notes during these conversations—the patterns that emerge will help you identify your organization's current level and next steps.

After gathering responses to these questions, look for patterns:

- If most answers focus on individual knowledge retention, you're likely at Level 1
- If you see some knowledge sharing but limited systematic learning, you're probably at Level 2
- If learning consistently influences operations but isn't yet driving innovation, you're at Level 3
- If continuous learning is actively driving organizational evolution, you've reached Level 4

FOR LEARNING/DEVELOPMENT TEAMS

1 What systems support knowledge capture and sharing?

2 How do we identify critical knowledge areas?

3 What barriers prevent effective knowledge transfer?

4 How do we validate learning effectiveness?

5 What prevents broader adoption of learning practices?

FOR OPERATIONS TEAMS

1 How do teams share operational insights?

2 What processes support cross-functional learning?

3 How do we capture process improvements?

4 What prevents knowledge flow between teams?

5 How do we implement learned improvements?

FOR TECHNICAL TEAMS

1 How do we document technical innovations?

2 What tools support knowledge sharing?

3 How do we validate shared technical knowledge?

4 What prevents technical knowledge transfer?

5 How do we maintain knowledge accuracy?

FOR NETWORK PARTNERS

1 How do we share knowledge across organizations?

2 What platforms enable collaborative learning?

3 How do we protect IP while sharing insights?

4 What prevents network-wide learning?

5 How do we validate shared knowledge?

FOR EXECUTIVE LEADERSHIP

1 How do we foster knowledge sharing across our organization?

2 What investments support continuous learning?

3 How do we measure the impact of shared knowledge?

4 What role does learning play in our innovation strategy?

5 How do we balance expertise protection with knowledge sharing?

Level 1 (Beginning)

Organizations at this level maintain isolated pockets of knowledge, similar to how separate facilities operated before the network in the fictional example emerged. Like the initial resistance to sharing recovery techniques, these organizations rely on individual expertise and experience. Knowledge sharing happens informally and inconsistently.

Key characteristics:

- Knowledge remains largely individual
- No formal knowledge-sharing systems
- Limited documentation of insights
- Learning happens primarily through experience

NEXT STEPS FOR LEVEL 1

Review your assessment results with your leadership team. The goal is to create a shared understanding of knowledge-sharing opportunities and align learning priorities.

Consider these targeted actions:

- Start documenting key processes and insights
- Create a pilot knowledge-sharing platform
- Identify critical knowledge areas
- Engage teams to understand learning barriers

Level 2 (Developing)

Organizations at this level mirror the early days in the fictional example. Like the initial efforts to document successful repairs, they've started creating knowledge-sharing systems but haven't fully integrated learning across operations. These organizations struggle with balancing knowledge protection and sharing.

Key characteristics:

- Basic knowledge-sharing systems established
- Some documentation processes exist
- Limited cross-functional learning
- Initial knowledge capture started but inconsistent

NEXT STEPS FOR LEVEL 2

Focus on systematically integrating learning across your operations. Build connections between different knowledge areas. Create formal processes for capturing and sharing insights.

Consider these targeted actions:

- Develop a knowledge management framework
- Create cross-functional learning programs
- Establish formal documentation standards
- Launch a knowledge-sharing platform
- Implement learning validation processes

Level 3 (Advanced)

Organizations at this level operate like the mature network in the fictional example, with learning fully integrated across operations. These organizations maintain comprehensive knowledge-sharing systems and actively seek learning opportunities. Like the AI-enabled knowledge sharing in the fictional example, they systematically capture and distribute insights.

Key characteristics:

- Learning integrated across operations
- Comprehensive knowledge-sharing systems
- Active cross-functional collaboration
- Learning consistently drives improvement

NEXT STEPS FOR LEVEL 3

Work on expanding learning influence across your organization. Create formal programs for capturing innovations, build networks to scale knowledge sharing and begin sharing insights beyond your organization.

Consider these targeted actions:

- Establish innovation capture programs
- Create advanced learning platforms
- Develop strategy for scaling knowledge sharing
- Implement comprehensive documentation standards
- Set organization-wide learning metrics

Level 4 (Leading)

Organizations at this level have achieved what the network in the fictional example accomplished—transforming learning into a core competitive advantage. Like the expanding network of expertise, they've developed systems for capturing and sharing knowledge. Similar to how the success in the fictional example influenced entire industries, these organizations lead the development of new learning capabilities.

Key characteristics:

- Learning drives organizational strategy
- Advanced knowledge-sharing systems
- Active development of learning networks
- Industry leadership in continuous improvement

NEXT STEPS FOR LEVEL 4

Focus on leading industry change through learning. Share knowledge openly to build learning ecosystems. Develop new organizational models based on continuous learning.

Consider these targeted actions:

- Create open platforms for knowledge sharing
- Develop industry-standard learning protocols
- Launch learning innovation centers
- Establish cross-industry knowledge networks
- Lead development of sharing standards
- Create learning-focused partner programs

Note

1 Herlihy, J. (2018) Interface supports California AB 1158, Floor Covering Weekly, www.floorcoveringweekly.com/main/features/interface-supports-california-ab-1158-22833 (archived at https://perma.cc/9JUJ-LR3G)
2 Umicore (n.d.) How We Work, https://pmr.umicore.com/en/how-we-work/ (archived at https://perma.cc/E3CY-BCS7)

16

Process Capabilities

Orchestrating Circular Flows to Circulate Locally

Urban mining requires reimagining how materials flow through cities. Traditional linear processes must evolve into dynamic, multi-directional flows that maximize resource value. While technology provides tools, it is process capabilities—from AI-optimized sorting to cross-industry material matching—that enable effective recovery at scale. Leading organizations recognize that three core process capabilities—circular value streams, smart recovery protocols, and resource optimization—form the backbone of successful urban mining operations.

The Circular Value Stream to Circulate Locally

Expanding traditional value stream mapping to capture circular opportunities, including repair loops, material recovery, and reintegration points.

In Chapter 4, we explored how circular value streams function more like water cycles than traditional linear flows. Materials can flow through multiple states of transformation—from collection through processing to reintegration into new products.

Examples of this capability are seen in the market in several ways: Recovered gold moving from electronic waste into new circuit boards, construction materials being redirected between building sites, and rare earth elements being extracted and refined for multiple applications.

Leading organizations today show similar capabilities. Aurubis's multi-metal recycling operations manage complex material flows across their network, processing diverse inputs into high-purity metals for multiple industries. Similarly, Redwood Materials has created value streams for battery materials, recovering and refining critical materials for reuse in new electric vehicle batteries.

Finding Your Level

To assess your organization, you'll need input from multiple perspectives across your value chain. Schedule focused conversations with key stakeholders with the goal of understanding both the current state of repair in your organization and the barriers to advancing this capability.

Plan to speak with representatives from five key stakeholder groups. For each group, you'll see specific questions designed to uncover how this capability is valued and implemented across your organization. Take notes during these conversations—the patterns that emerge will help you identify your organization's current level and next steps.

After gathering responses to these questions, look for patterns:

- If most answers focus on linear material flows, you're likely at Level 1
- If you see some material recovery but limited integration, you're at Level 2
- If circular flows consistently influence operations but aren't optimized, you're at Level 3
- If circular value streams actively drive operations, you've reached Level 4

FOR OPERATIONS TEAMS

1 How do we track materials through multiple cycles?
2 What systems manage circular material flows?
3 How do we optimize recovery pathways?
4 What prevents greater material circulation?
5 How do we measure circular efficiency?

FOR TECHNICAL TEAMS

1 What tools support circular material tracking?
2 How do we analyze material transformation options?
3 What data guides circular routing decisions?
4 How do we validate material quality through cycles?
5 What technical barriers limit circulation?

FOR QUALITY TEAMS

1 How do we verify recovered material quality?

2 What standards govern material reuse?

3 How do we track material degradation?

4 What prevents quality assurance in circular flows?

5 How do we maintain consistency across cycles?

FOR SUPPLY CHAIN PARTNERS

1 How do we coordinate circular material flows?

2 What information do we share about materials?

3 How do we optimize network-wide circulation?

4 What prevents greater material sharing?

5 How do we align circular objectives?

FOR EXECUTIVE LEADERSHIP

1 How do we map and measure circular material flows?

2 What value do we capture from recovered materials?

3 How do we identify circular opportunities?

4 What metrics track circular value creation?

5 How do we balance linear and circular flows?

Level 1 (Beginning)

Organizations at this level operate primarily linear material flows—similar to how businesses worked before the urban mining hub network in the fictional example. Like early manufacturers in the fictional example who saw materials as one-way inputs, these organizations track materials only until point of sale or disposal. They have limited visibility into what happens to materials after first use, and recovery opportunities are largely missed.

Key characteristics:

- Linear material flows dominate operations
- No formal tracking of material cycles or transformations
- Limited visibility of recovery opportunities

- Material value measured only in first use cycle
- Basic waste tracking without recovery focus

NEXT STEPS FOR LEVEL 1

Review your assessment results with leadership. Focus on building awareness of circular value opportunities and start mapping basic material flows beyond first use.

Consider these targeted actions:

- Map current material flows through operations
- Identify the top three materials with recovery potential
- Create a pilot program for tracking one material type
- Begin measuring basic recovery metrics
- Engage the operations team to identify circular opportunities

Level 2 (Developing)

Organizations at this level mirror the early days in the fictional example in Hackney Wick, when they first began tracking materials through their facility. Like the initial efforts with recovered electronics, they've started monitoring some materials through multiple uses but haven't yet optimized these circular flows. These organizations see the potential of circular value but struggle to fully capture it.

Key characteristics:

- Basic material recovery flows tracked
- Some circular pathways documented
- Limited integration of recovery data
- Initial value capture from recovered materials
- Beginning to connect multiple material cycles

NEXT STEPS FOR LEVEL 2

Focus on systematically mapping circular value streams, build connections between different material pathways, and create formal processes for tracking material transformations.

Consider these targeted actions:

- Develop comprehensive circular flow metrics
- Create integrated material tracking system

- Establish standard recovery documentation
- Launch detailed value stream mapping
- Implement continuous flow monitoring
- Build cross-functional material teams

Level 3 (Advanced)

Organizations at this level operate like the maturing network in the fictional example, when they began connecting multiple facilities across London. Just as the system tracked materials flowing between recovery operations, these organizations actively monitor and optimize materials through multiple cycles. Like the digital tracking system in the fictional example, they can identify and capture value across various material transformations.

Key characteristics:

- Circular flows fully integrated across operations
- Comprehensive material tracking systems
- Active optimization of recovery pathways
- Value captured across multiple cycles
- Predictive analysis of material flows

NEXT STEPS FOR LEVEL 3

Work on expanding circular value influence across your network. Create formal programs for identifying new value opportunities. Build systems to scale circular flows.

Consider these targeted actions:

- Establish advanced tracking technologies
- Create predictive analytics platforms
- Develop network optimization tools
- Implement cross-cycle performance metrics
- Set network-wide material standards
- Launch value innovation programs

Level 4 (Leading)

Organizations at this level have achieved what the network in the fictional example accomplished in its full maturity—developing circular value streams into a comparative advantage. Like the fully integrated urban mining system in the fictional example, they've developed capabilities for maximizing value across multiple material cycles. Similar to how success in the fictional example influenced manufacturer behavior, these organizations lead their industries in circular value creation.

Key characteristics:

- Circular flows drive organizational strategy
- Advanced material intelligence systems
- Network-wide value optimization
- Industry leadership in circular innovation
- Predictive value capture capabilities

NEXT STEPS FOR LEVEL 4

Focus on leading industry transformation toward circular value models, share insights openly to build circular ecosystems, and develop new business models based on circular value streams.

Consider these targeted actions:

- Create open platforms for sharing flow data
- Develop industry-standard tracking protocols
- Launch circular value innovation centers
- Establish cross-industry learning networks
- Lead development of value stream standards
- Create circular value-focused partner programs

Smart Recovery Protocols to Circulate Locally

Standardizing how teams assess, repair, and reintegrate materials and products, ensuring consistent quality across multiple lifecycles.

In Chapter 4, we explored how traditional recovery approaches often fall short when scaling to handle diverse materials and complex sorting requirements. Smart recovery operations combine advanced analytics with processing technologies to maximize material recovery and value.

Supply chain innovators show this capability: AI-powered optical sorting systems identifying material compositions, advanced spectroscopy analyzing material properties, and machine learning optimizing recovery processes.

Leading organizations show similar capabilities today. Tomra's sensor-based sorting systems use advanced technologies to identify and separate materials with high precision in mining operations. Their solutions rely on color cameras, X-ray transmission sensors, and multi-channel scanning lasers to sort ore prior to downstream wet processing. Similarly, Boliden's electronic recycling operations use protocols to recover multiple metals from complex waste streams while maintaining high purity levels. At their Rönnskär smelter, for example, they process electronic material, including circuit boards from computers and mobile phones. Their specially designed process allows them to extract copper and precious metals.

Find Your Level

To assess your organization, you'll need input from multiple perspectives across your value chain. Schedule focused conversations with key stakeholders with the goal of understanding both the current state of repair in your organization and the barriers to advancing this capability.

Plan to speak with representatives from five key stakeholder groups. For each group, you'll see specific questions designed to uncover how this capability is valued and implemented across your organization. Take notes during these conversations—the patterns that emerge will help you identify your organization's current level and next steps.

After gathering responses to these questions, look for patterns:

- If most answers focus on basic material sorting with limited verification methods, you're likely at Level 1
- If you see some intelligent recovery systems but limited ability to handle diverse material streams, you're probably at Level 2
- If sophisticated material recovery consistently enables reliable urban mining but isn't yet creating cross-industry opportunities, you're at Level 3
- If advanced recovery intelligence actively discovers and enables new value streams across local material networks, you've reached Level 4

FOR RECOVERY TEAMS

1 How do automated systems assist recovery?
2 What protocols guide recovery decisions?

3 How do we capture recovery insights?

4 What prevents more efficient recovery?

5 How do we improve recovery rates?

FOR OPERATIONS TEAMS

1 What automated systems support recovery?

2 How do we optimize recovery processes?

3 What data guides recovery decisions?

4 How do we validate recovery success?

5 What prevents more intelligent recovery?

FOR TECHNICAL TEAMS

1 What tools enable smart recovery?

2 How do we analyze recovery options?

3 What AI/ML systems support recovery?

4 How do we maintain recovery systems?

5 What technical barriers limit intelligence?

FOR QUALITY TEAMS

1 How do we verify automated recovery?

2 What standards govern smart systems?

3 How do we validate AI decisions?

4 What prevents quality assurance?

5 How do we maintain consistency?

FOR EXECUTIVE LEADERSHIP

1 How do we evaluate recovery technologies?

2 What investments support smart recovery?

3 How do we measure recovery effectiveness?

4 What role does AI play in recovery?

5 How do we measure recovery costs and benefits?

Level 1 (Beginning)

Organizations at this level operate with basic manual recovery processes, similar to traditional recycling operations before the AI-enabled systems in the fictional example. Like the early days before smart sorting, these organizations rely on simple separation techniques and human inspection. Similar to facilities stuck in traditional recycling models, they miss significant value recovery opportunities due to limited processing capabilities.

Key characteristics:

- Manual recovery processes dominate
- No automated material identification
- Limited recovery process optimization
- Basic quality verification only
- Minimal data collection on recovery

NEXT STEPS FOR LEVEL 1

Review your assessment results with leadership and focus on identifying opportunities for process automation and building basic data collection systems.

Consider these targeted actions:

- Map current recovery processes
- Identify opportunities for automation
- Start collecting recovery performance data
- Begin standardizing quality checks
- Evaluate basic sorting technologies

Level 2 (Developing)

Organizations at this level mirror the early experimentation with automated systems in the fictional example. They've started implementing some smart technologies but haven't fully integrated them into operations and are learning to balance automation with verification needs.

Key characteristics:

- Some automated recovery systems
- Basic process data collection
- Limited AI/ML implementation

- Initial quality verification protocols
- Emerging predictive capabilities

NEXT STEPS FOR LEVEL 2

Focus on expanding automated recovery capabilities, build connections between different systems, and create formal processes for validating automated decisions.

Consider these targeted actions:

- Develop comprehensive recovery metrics
- Implement AI-powered sorting systems
- Establish automated quality controls
- Launch a recovery optimization program
- Create predictive maintenance systems
- Build cross-functional automation teams

Level 3 (Advanced)

Organizations at this level use technologies to maximize recovery value, and can maintain consistent quality while handling complex recovery challenges.

Key characteristics:

- Advanced AI/ML recovery systems deployed
- Comprehensive process optimization
- Real-time quality verification
- Predictive recovery planning
- Automated decision-making protocols

NEXT STEPS FOR LEVEL 3

Work on expanding smart recovery across your network, create formal programs for developing new recovery capabilities, and build systems to scale automation.

Consider these targeted actions:

- Establish advanced AI/ML platforms
- Create recovery innovation programs
- Develop cross-facility optimization

- Implement predictive analytics
- Set network-wide recovery standards
- Launch technology validation systems

Level 4 (Leading)

Organizations at this level have achieved what supply chain networks can accomplish at full maturity—developing smart recovery into a key capability They have developed capabilities for handling any recovery challenge. Similar to how success in the fictional example influenced manufacturer specifications, these organizations lead their industries in recovery innovation.

Key characteristics:

- AI-driven recovery strategy
- Advanced material intelligence
- Network-wide optimization
- Industry leadership in recovery innovation
- Cross-industry recovery capabilities

NEXT STEPS FOR LEVEL 4

Focus on developing industry-leading capabilities of intelligent recovery, share capabilities to build recovery ecosystems, and develop new business models based on smart recovery.

Consider these targeted actions:

- Create open AI/ML recovery platforms
- Develop industry-standard protocols
- Launch recovery innovation centers
- Establish cross-industry networks
- Lead development of recovery standards
- Create recovery technology programs

Resource Optimization to Circulate Locally

Developing processes that maximize the use of existing materials through sharing, repair, and alternative sourcing.

In Chapter 4, we explored how circular operations require coordination of resources across networks of partners and facilities. Effective resource orchestration enables product and material recovery at scale.

The fictional example shows how resource optimization through their network created new value streams that wouldn't be visible in traditional linear systems.

Leading organizations today demonstrate similar capabilities. Suez's resource management operations use AI-powered systems to optimize material flows across their network, improving efficiency and environmental performance. Their CoDAI (Collaborative Data & Artificial Intelligence) platform catalogs AI projects and algorithms, allowing users to find and test existing solutions for various applications, including industrial IoT and facility device management. Similarly, Remondis has developed advanced systems for coordinating material flows between collection, processing, and end-user facilities. This system considers factors such as disposal costs, material types and quantities, and seasonal variations in waste generation to determine the most efficient recycling plant for each waste type.

FIND YOUR LEVEL

To assess your organization, you'll need input from multiple perspectives across your value chain. Schedule focused conversations with key stakeholders with the goal of understanding both the current state of repair in your organization and the barriers to advancing this capability.

Plan to speak with representatives from five key stakeholder groups. For each group, you'll see specific questions designed to uncover how this capability is valued and implemented across your organization. Take notes during these conversations—the patterns that emerge will help you identify your organization's current level and next steps.

After gathering responses to these questions, look for patterns:

- If most answers focus on basic material collection with minimal coordination, you're likely at Level 1
- If you see some local material flows optimization but limited integration across recovery streams, you're probably at Level 2
- If material circulation consistently drives local operations but isn't yet enabling cross-industry flows, you're at Level 3
- If sophisticated resource optimization actively enables new value creation across local material networks, you've reached Level 4

FOR OPERATIONS TEAMS

1 What systems support resource optimization?

2 How do we balance multiple objectives?

3 What data guides allocation decisions?

4 How do we validate optimization results?

5 What prevents better optimization?

FOR TECHNICAL TEAMS

1 What tools enable network optimization?

2 How do we analyze resource flows?

3 What AI/ML systems support decisions?

4 How do we maintain optimization systems?

5 What technical barriers limit optimization?

FOR NETWORK TEAMS

1 How do we coordinate resource sharing?

2 What protocols guide allocation?

3 How do we capture network insights?

4 What prevents efficient sharing?

5 How do we improve network performance?

FOR QUALITY TEAMS

1 How do we verify optimization results?

2 What standards govern resource sharing?

3 How do we validate system decisions?

4 What prevents quality assurance?

5 How do we maintain consistency?

FOR EXECUTIVE LEADERSHIP

1 How do we optimize resource allocation?

2 What investments support optimization?

3 How do we measure network efficiency?

4 What role does AI play in optimization?

5 How do we balance local and network needs?

Level 1 (Beginning)

Organizations at this level operate with basic resource management—similar to traditional facilities before the network optimization in the fictional example. Like siloed operations, they optimize locally without considering network effects. Similar to early local recovery attempts, they miss opportunities for resource sharing and collaborative efficiency.

Key characteristics:

- Local optimization only
- No network resource sharing
- Limited coordination between sites
- Basic efficiency metrics
- Minimal cross-facility planning

NEXT STEPS FOR LEVEL 1

Review your assessment results with leadership and focus on identifying network opportunities and building basic coordination capabilities.

Consider these targeted actions:

- Map current resource flows
- Identify sharing opportunities
- Start collecting network data
- Begin standardizing metrics
- Evaluate coordination tools

Level 2 (Developing)

Organizations at this level mirror the early network coordination efforts in the fictional example. When supply chains first attempt to balance loads between facilities, they may run into issues where their network is optimized in pieces but they haven't yet achieved full integration. These organizations they are learning to balance local and network needs.

Key characteristics:

- Basic network coordination
- Some resource sharing

- Limited optimization tools
- Initial coordination protocols
- Emerging network metrics

NEXT STEPS FOR LEVEL 2

Focus on expanding network optimization capabilities, build connections between facilities and create formal processes for resource sharing.

Consider these targeted actions:

- Develop network performance metrics
- Implement coordination platforms
- Establish sharing protocols
- Launch optimization programs
- Create predictive planning tools
- Build cross-facility teams

Level 3 (Advanced)

Organizations at this level operate like the maturing network in the fictional example, when AI began optimizing resources across London. Like the integrated facility network, these organizations actively balance resources across multiple sites. Similar to the success with multi-industry optimization, they can effectively coordinate complex resource flows.

Key characteristics:

- Advanced network optimization
- Comprehensive resource sharing
- Real-time coordination
- Predictive resource planning
- Automated balancing protocols

NEXT STEPS FOR LEVEL 3

Work on expanding network optimization across your ecosystem, create formal programs for developing new coordination capabilities, and build systems to scale optimization.

Consider these targeted actions:

- Establish advanced optimization platforms
- Create network innovation programs

- Develop cross-network balancing
- Implement predictive analytics
- Set network-wide standards
- Launch coordination systems

Level 4 (Leading)

Organizations at this level have achieved what the network in the fictional example accomplished at full maturity—resource optimization as a key capability. Like the fully integrated network that could dynamically balance loads across industries, they've developed capabilities for maximizing resource use. Similar to how success in the fictional example influenced city-wide resource planning, these organizations lead their industries in network optimization.

Key characteristics:

- AI-driven network strategy
- Advanced resource intelligence
- Ecosystem-wide optimization
- Industry leadership in coordination
- Cross-industry balancing capabilities

NEXT STEPS FOR LEVEL 4

Focus on leading industry capabilities through network optimization. Share capabilities to build optimization ecosystems and develop new business models based on resource coordination.

Consider these targeted actions:

- Create open optimization platforms
- Develop industry-standard protocols
- Launch coordination innovation centers
- Establish cross-industry networks
- Lead development of sharing standards
- Create optimization technology programs

17

Technology Capabilities

Digital Enablement to Circulate Locally

Digital systems are essential for urban mining at scale. Technology must expand beyond basic tracking to create a product and material memory that supports advanced recovery and reuse. While people and processes drive operations, it's advanced technology capabilities that make complex material flows manageable. Leading organizations recognize that three core technology capabilities provide the infrastructure for effective urban mining: Digital product memory, predictive recovery intelligence, and network orchestration platforms.

Digital Product Memory to Circulate Locally

Creating comprehensive digital records that track a product's complete history through multiple lifecycles, repairs, and material changes.

In Chapter 4, we explored how traditional tracking systems needed to evolve to manage materials through multiple transformations. Sophisticated digital systems can create "material memory" that enables more effective recovery and value creation.

The fictional example shows digital product memory through the advanced tracking systems: Each batch of recovered material carries a complete digital history of its composition, transformations, and quality verifications. When processing titanium for medical applications, for example, their system maintained detailed records of every parameter. This tracking became essential for building trust with manufacturers and regulatory bodies.

Leading organizations today demonstrate similar capabilities. Circularise's blockchain-based system creates digital passports for materials flowing through supply chains, enabling transparent tracking through multiple transformations. Similarly, Sourcemap's digital tracing technology helps organizations track materials from original sources through recovery and reuse.

Finding Your Level

To assess your organization, you'll need input from multiple perspectives across your value chain. Schedule focused conversations with key stakeholders with the goal of understanding both the current state of repair in your organization and the barriers to advancing this capability.

Plan to speak with representatives from five key stakeholder groups. For each group, you'll see specific questions designed to uncover how this capability is valued and implemented across your organization. Take notes during these conversations—the patterns that emerge will help you identify your organization's current level and next steps.

After gathering responses to these questions, look for patterns:

- If most answers focus on basic material tracking with limited digital integration, you're likely at Level 1
- If you see digital tracking tools but limited analytics or prediction, you're probably at Level 2
- If material tracking consistently informs decisions but isn't yet driving innovation, you're at Level 3
- If digital material memory actively drives strategy and operations, you've reached Level 4

FOR TECHNOLOGY TEAMS

1 How do we digitally track materials through recovery processes?
2 What systems capture material transformation data?
3 How do we maintain digital records of material properties?
4 What prevents better material traceability?
5 How do we integrate different material tracking systems?

FOR OPERATIONS TEAMS

1 How do we capture material composition data?

2 What digital tools support material tracking?

3 How do we document material transformations?

4 What traceability gaps exist in our processes?

5 How do we verify material history data?

FOR QUALITY TEAMS

1 How do we digitally verify material properties?

2 What systems validate material transformations?

3 How do we maintain material quality records?

4 What role does data play in material certification?

5 How do we ensure material tracking accuracy?

FOR SUPPLY CHAIN PARTNERS

1 How do we share material data across partners?

2 What digital systems track material exchanges?

3 How do we verify shared material data?

4 What prevents better material traceability?

5 How do we coordinate material tracking?

FOR ANALYTICS TEAMS

1 How do we analyze material tracking data?

2 What insights do we derive from material histories?

3 How do we predict material performance?

4 What prevents better use of material data?

5 How do we improve material tracking analytics?

Level 1 (Beginning)

Organizations at this level track materials primarily through basic digital records—similar to how cities initially tracked waste before urban mining emerged. Like the early days before Maya's network, these organizations maintain simple databases of material movements without detailed composition or transformation data. Material tracking focuses on quantity rather than quality or history.

Key characteristics:

- Basic digital records of material movements
- Limited tracking of material properties
- Manual data collection and verification
- Minimal integration between tracking systems
- Few analytical capabilities

NEXT STEPS FOR LEVEL 1

Review your assessment results with your technology and operations teams. The goal is to create a shared understanding of your current tracking capabilities and align digital transformation opportunities.

Consider these targeted actions:

- Implement basic digital material tracking system
- Start collecting material composition data
- Create standardized material property documentation
- Map current material tracking gaps
- Engage technology team to evaluate tracking tools

Level 2 (Developing)

Organizations at this level mirror the earliest days in the fictional example, when Maya first began digitally tracking recovered materials. Like her initial tracking systems, they've implemented digital tools but haven't fully integrated them across operations. These organizations struggle with consistent digital documentation but recognize its importance.

Key characteristics:

- Digital tracking systems implemented
- Basic material property documentation
- Some automated data collection
- Limited analytics capabilities
- Partial system integration

NEXT STEPS FOR LEVEL 2

Focus on systematically integrating digital tracking across operations, build connections between different systems, and create formal processes for maintaining digital material memory.

Consider these targeted actions:

- Develop a comprehensive material tracking dashboard
- Implement automated data collection tools
- Create a digital material passport system
- Launch material tracking specialist training
- Establish digital verification processes

Level 3 (Advanced)

Organizations at this level operate like the maturing network in the fictional example, with digital material tracking fully integrated across operations. Just as the network expanded to track materials across London, these organizations maintain comprehensive digital records of material properties and transformations. Like Maya's system of AI-powered analysis, they actively use tracking data to optimize operations.

Key characteristics:

- Integrated digital tracking across operations
- Comprehensive material property documentation
- Automated data collection and verification
- Advanced analytics capabilities
- Connected tracking systems

NEXT STEPS FOR LEVEL 3

Work on expanding digital tracking influence. Create formal programs for advancing tracking capabilities, develop predictive analytics, and begin sharing tracking insights across partners.

Consider these targeted actions:

- Establish a predictive analytics program
- Create automated verification systems
- Develop strategy for scaling tracking
- Implement comprehensive digital passports
- Set organization-wide tracking metrics

Level 4 (Leading)

Organizations at this level have achieved what the network in the fictional example accomplished—transforming digital material memory into a competitive advantage. Like the sophisticated tracking system, they've developed advanced capabilities for documenting and analyzing material journeys. Similar to how the success in the fictional example led manufacturers to trust urban-mined materials, these organizations influence their industry's approach to digital traceability.

Key characteristics:

- Digital tracking drives strategy
- Advanced predictive capabilities
- Industry-leading verification systems
- Full supply chain integration
- Continuous tracking innovation

NEXT STEPS FOR LEVEL 4

Focus on leading industry transformation toward digital material tracking. Share knowledge to build tracking ecosystems and develop new capabilities based on digital material memory.

Consider these targeted actions:

- Create an open platform for sharing tracking data
- Develop industry-standard digital passports
- Launch tracking-based business models
- Establish digital tracking innovation centers
- Lead development of tracking standards

Predictive Recovery Intelligence to Circulate Locally

Using AI and analytics to determine optimal repair strategies and material reuse opportunities based on product condition and market needs.

In Chapter 4, we explored how traditional recovery approaches needed to expand beyond manual sorting to handle complexity at scale. Intelligent systems combining AI-powered analysis, advanced spectroscopy, and machine learning can optimize material recovery operations.

The fictional example shows examples of sophisticated processing facilities. When their system discovered that recovered materials from one industry could meet specifications for another, it showed how intelligent systems can create value opportunities that humans might miss.

STEINERT's AI-powered sorting systems use advanced sensor fusion and machine learning to identify and separate materials with high precision. Their UniSort PR EVO 5.0 uses an Intelligent Object Identifier, an AI-supported detection system that improves sorting stability and results. Similarly, ZenRobotics combines AI and robotics to sort complex waste streams, continuously learning and improving recovery rates. Their ZenRobotics 4.0 system features AI that enables robots to identify over 500 waste categories, significantly reducing commissioning times.

Finding Your Level

To assess your organization, you'll need input from multiple perspectives across your value chain. Schedule focused conversations with key stakeholders with the goal of understanding both the current state of repair in your organization and the barriers to advancing this capability.

Plan to speak with representatives from five key stakeholder groups. For each group, you'll see specific questions designed to uncover how this capability is valued and implemented across your organization. Take notes during these conversations—the patterns that emerge will help you identify your organization's current level and next steps.

After gathering responses to these questions, look for patterns:

- If most answers focus on basic analysis with limited prediction, you're likely at Level 1
- If you see some predictive tools but limited integration, you're probably at Level 2
- If predictive analytics consistently inform decisions but aren't yet driving innovation, you're at Level 3
- If predictive intelligence actively drives strategy and operations, you've reached Level 4

FOR DATA SCIENCE TEAMS

1 How do we predict material recovery opportunities?
2 What algorithms support recovery optimization?

3   How do we validate predictive models?

4   What prevents better predictive capabilities?

5   How do we improve model accuracy?

FOR OPERATIONS TEAMS

1   How do we use predictions in recovery planning?

2   What systems guide recovery decisions?

3   How do we measure prediction accuracy?

4   What prevents better use of predictions?

5   How do we integrate predictive insights?

FOR QUALITY TEAMS

1   How do predictions influence quality control?

2   What systems forecast quality issues?

3   How do we validate predicted outcomes?

4   What role does AI play in quality assurance?

5   How do we ensure prediction reliability?

FOR ENGINEERING TEAMS

1   How do we use predictions in process design?

2   What systems model recovery outcomes?

3   How do we optimize recovery processes?

4   What prevents better process prediction?

5   How do we improve recovery efficiency?

FOR BUSINESS TEAMS

1   How do predictions guide strategy?

2   What metrics track prediction value?

3   How do we measure prediction ROI?

4   What prevents better use of analytics?

5   How do we leverage predictive insights?

Level 1 (Beginning)

Organizations at this level use basic analytics for recovery operations, similar to how cities initially approached material sorting before AI-powered systems. Like the early days before the network in the fictional example, these organizations rely primarily on manual analysis and simple statistical tools. Recovery decisions are based more on experience than data-driven predictions.

Key characteristics:

- Basic statistical analysis
- Limited predictive capabilities
- Manual decision-making processes
- Minimal use of machine learning
- Reactive rather than predictive approach

NEXT STEPS FOR LEVEL 1

Review your assessment results with your analytics and operations teams. The goal is to create a shared understanding of your current predictive capabilities and align development opportunities.

Consider these targeted actions:

- Implement basic predictive analytics system
- Start collecting recovery performance data
- Create standardized prediction metrics
- Map current analytical gaps
- Engage the data science team to evaluate tools

Level 2 (Developing)

Organizations at this level showcase early capabilities of intelligent recovery using AI to optimize sorting. They have implemented some predictive tools but haven't fully integrated them across operations. These organizations struggle with prediction accuracy but recognize its potential.

Key characteristics:

- Basic predictive models implemented
- Some machine learning applications
- Partial automation of decisions

- Limited integration of predictions
- Growing analytical capabilities

NEXT STEPS FOR LEVEL 2

Focus on systematically integrating predictive analytics across operations. Build connections between different systems. Create formal processes for validating predictions.

Consider these targeted actions:

- Develop a comprehensive analytics dashboard
- Implement automated prediction systems
- Create a prediction validation framework
- Launch data science specialist training
- Establish prediction accuracy metrics

Level 3 (Advanced)

Organizations at this level operate like the maturing network in the fictional example, with analytics fully integrated. Just as the network used AI to optimize recovery across London, these organizations maintain sophisticated models that guide operations. Like using a system of AI-powered sorting, they actively use predictions to maximize recovery value.

Key characteristics:

- Integrated predictive analytics
- Advanced machine learning models
- Automated decision support
- Connected prediction systems
- Proactive optimization

NEXT STEPS FOR LEVEL 3

Work on expanding predictive influence. Create formal programs for advancing analytical capabilities. Develop more sophisticated models. Begin sharing insights across partners.

Consider these targeted actions:

- Establish an advanced AI program
- Create automated optimization systems

- Develop strategy for scaling analytics
- Implement comprehensive prediction framework
- Set organization-wide prediction metrics

Level 4 (Leading)

Organizations at this level have achieved what the network in the fictional example accomplished—transforming shared intelligence into a competitive advantage. Like the AI systems in the fictional example, they've developed advanced capabilities for optimizing recovery operations. Similar to how the success in the fictional example led manufacturers to trust systems-led recovery, these organizations influence their industry's approach to predictive analytics.

Key characteristics:

- Predictive intelligence drives strategy
- Advanced AI optimization
- Industry-leading analytical systems
- Full operational integration
- Continuous innovation in analytics

NEXT STEPS FOR LEVEL 4

Focus on leading industry transformation toward predictive recovery. Share knowledge to build analytical ecosystems. Develop new capabilities based on predictive intelligence.

Consider these targeted actions:

- Create an open platform for sharing predictions
- Develop industry-standard analytical models
- Launch prediction-based business models
- Establish AI innovation centers
- Lead development of prediction standards
- Create recovery optimization frameworks

Network Orchestration Platform to Circulate Locally

Building integrated systems that coordinate material flows, repairs, and reintegration across the circular ecosystem.

In Chapter 4, we explored how traditional systems optimized individual facilities rather than entire networks. Advanced platforms can coordinate complex material flows across cities while optimizing recovery operations and value creation.

The fictional example illustrates an integrated network: advanced systems coordinating collections across London, balancing processing loads between facilities, and matching recovered materials with manufacturing needs in real-time. This shows how network intelligence can maximize resource utilization while maintaining perfect traceability.

Leading organizations today show similar capabilities. AMCS Platform uses AI to optimize material flows across recycling networks, while SAP's Material Traceability solution helps organizations coordinate complex recovery operations across global networks. These platforms show how technology can enable sophisticated orchestration of urban mining operations at scale.

Finding Your Level

To assess your organization, you'll need input from multiple perspectives across your value chain. Schedule focused conversations with key stakeholders with the goal of understanding both the current state of repair in your organization and the barriers to advancing this capability.

Plan to speak with representatives from five key stakeholder groups. For each group, you'll see specific questions designed to uncover how this capability is valued and implemented across your organization. Take notes during these conversations—the patterns that emerge will help you identify your organization's current level and next steps.

After gathering responses to these questions, look for patterns:

- If most answers focus on basic material tracking with minimal partner coordination, you're likely at Level 1

- If you see digital platforms connecting some recovery operations but limited network-wide optimization, you're probably at Level 2

- If intelligent orchestration consistently enables multi-partner material flows but isn't yet creating new value streams, you're at Level 3

- If advanced orchestration platforms actively discover and enable cross-industry material opportunities across urban networks, you've reached Level 4

FOR NETWORK OPERATIONS TEAMS

1 How do we coordinate across recovery sites?

2 What systems manage network flows?

3 How do we optimize network capacity?

4 What prevents better network integration?

5 How do we improve network efficiency?

FOR TECHNOLOGY TEAMS

1 How do we connect different network systems?

2 What platforms enable network coordination?

3 How do we manage network data?

4 What technical barriers limit integration?

5 How do we ensure network reliability?

FOR LOGISTICS TEAMS

1 How do we optimize material movements?

2 What systems coordinate transportation?

3 How do we manage network capacity?

4 What prevents better flow optimization?

5 How do we improve network responsiveness?

FOR PARTNER MANAGEMENT TEAMS

1 How do we coordinate with network partners?

2 What systems manage partner integration?

3 How do we share network resources?

4 What prevents better collaboration?

5 How do we improve network alignment?

FOR PLANNING TEAMS

1 How do we optimize network resources?

2 What systems support network planning?

3 How do we forecast network needs?

4 What prevents better coordination?

5 How do we improve network strategy?

Level 1 (Beginning)

Organizations at this level coordinate operations through basic systems, similar to how cities initially managed waste collection before integrated networks. Like the early days before the network in the fictional example, these organizations manage each location independently with limited coordination. Network optimization relies primarily on manual planning and simple tools.

Key characteristics:

- Basic coordination systems
- Limited network visibility
- Manual resource allocation
- Minimal partner integration
- Reactive network management

NEXT STEPS FOR LEVEL 1

Review your assessment results with your operations and technology teams. The goal is to create a shared understanding of your current network capabilities and align integration opportunities.

Consider these targeted actions:

- Implement basic network management system
- Start tracking network flows
- Create standardized coordination metrics
- Map current network gaps
- Engage the technology team to evaluate platforms

Level 2 (Developing)

Organizations at this level look like the earliest days in the fictional example of network coordination, when they first began connecting recovery operations. Like the initial systems, they've implemented some network tools but haven't fully integrated operations; they struggle with coordination but recognize its importance.

Key characteristics:

- Basic network platforms implemented
- Some resource optimization
- Partial partner integration
- Limited flow optimization
- Growing coordination capabilities

NEXT STEPS FOR LEVEL 2

Focus on systematically integrating network operations. Build connections between different systems. Create formal processes for network optimization.
Consider these targeted actions:

- Develop comprehensive network dashboard
- Implement automated coordination tools
- Create network optimization framework
- Launch network specialist training
- Establish coordination metrics

Level 3 (Advanced)

Organizations at this level operate like the maturing network in the fictional example, with orchestration fully integrated across operations. Just as the network coordinated recovery across London, these organizations maintain sophisticated platforms that optimize network flows. Like the system of coordination in the fictional example, they actively balance resources across the network.
Key characteristics:

- Integrated network orchestration
- Advanced resource optimization
- Automated flow coordination
- Connected partner systems
- Proactive network management

NEXT STEPS FOR LEVEL 3

Work on expanding network influence. Create formal programs for advancing coordination capabilities. Develop more sophisticated optimization. Begin sharing resources across partners.

Consider these targeted actions:

- Establish advanced optimization program
- Create automated balancing systems
- Develop strategy for scaling network
- Implement comprehensive orchestration platform
- Set organization-wide network metrics

Level 4 (Leading)

Organizations at this level have transformed orchestration into a competitive advantage. Using systems for automated coordination, they have developed advanced capabilities for optimizing network operations and influence their industry's approach to coordination.

Key characteristics:

- Network orchestration drives strategy
- Advanced optimization systems
- Industry-leading coordination
- Full partner integration
- Continuous network innovation

NEXT STEPS FOR LEVEL 4

Focus on leading industry transformation toward network orchestration. Share knowledge to build coordination ecosystems. Develop new capabilities based on network integration.

Consider these targeted actions:

- Create an open platform for network coordination
- Develop industry-standard orchestration models
- Launch network-based business models
- Establish coordination innovation centers
- Lead development of network standards
- Create partner optimization frameworks

18

Standards Capabilities

Common Language for Circularity to Circulate Locally

Common frameworks allow for trust in urban mining operations. The network in the fictional example shows how standards must expand beyond traditional shared language to verify materials through multiple lifecycles. While technology tracks materials, it's robust standards—from performance metrics to digital protocols—that build confidence in recovered resources. Leading organizations recognize that three core standards capabilities create the foundation for trusted material recovery: Multi-life performance metrics, digital interoperability, and ecosystem collaboration protocols.

Multi-Life Performance Metrics to Circulate Locally

Establishing clear standards for measuring product and material performance across multiple use cycles.

In Chapter 4, we explored how traditional quality standards focused on virgin materials needed to evolve to evaluate recovered materials through multiple use cycles. However, recovered materials can meet or exceed original specifications while maintaining consistent quality across multiple transformations.

Approaches to material recovery like those in the fictional example show multi-life performance metrics through the work with manufacturers. Some recovered materials actually performed better than virgin ones, highlighting how standards must expand to recognize the unique properties of urban-mined materials.

Leading organizations today show similar capabilities in creating common standards for urban mining. The Electronic Industry Citizenship Coalition (EICC) has developed a Code of Conduct that addresses environmental concerns in electronics manufacturing, including adherence to regulations on restricted substances and proper waste management. Similarly, third-party certifications like GreenCircle help organizations like Closure Systems International verify the recycled content and performance of recovered materials, such as their PolyCycle PCR resin, across multiple applications.

Finding Your Level

To assess your organization, you'll need input from multiple perspectives across your value chain. Schedule focused conversations with key stakeholders with the goal of understanding both the current state of repair in your organization and the barriers to advancing this capability.

Plan to speak with representatives from five key stakeholder groups. For each group, you'll see specific questions designed to uncover how this capability is valued and implemented across your organization. Take notes during these conversations—the patterns that emerge will help you identify your organization's current level and next steps.

After gathering responses to these questions, look for patterns:

- If most answers focus on basic quality checks against new material standards, you're likely at Level 1
- If you see some adapted testing for recovered materials but limited standardization, you're probably at Level 2
- If performance metrics consistently track multiple lifecycles but aren't yet driving innovation, you're at Level 3
- If multi-life performance data actively drives material innovation and business strategy, you've reached Level 4

FOR QUALITY TEAMS

1 How do we measure recovered material performance?

2 What standards exist for evaluating multiple use cycles?

3 How do we validate long-term material reliability?

4 What prevents better tracking of material performance?

5 How do we compare recovered vs. virgin material quality?

FOR ENGINEERING TEAMS

1 How do we incorporate recovered material data into designs?

2 What testing protocols exist for recovered materials?

3 How do we predict long-term material behavior?

4 What barriers exist to using recovered materials?

5 How do we verify material performance consistency?

FOR OPERATIONS TEAMS

1 What metrics track material performance through recovery?

2 How do we document material transformation processes?

3 What quality controls exist for recovered materials?

4 How do we maintain consistent recovery quality?

5 What prevents greater use of recovered materials?

FOR PROCUREMENT TEAMS

1 How do we evaluate recovered material suppliers?

2 What specifications exist for recovered materials?

3 How do we verify supplier quality claims?

4 What role does performance data play in sourcing?

5 How do we compare different recovery sources?

FOR RESEARCH & DEVELOPMENT

1 How do we study long-term material behavior?

2 What tools support material performance prediction?

3 How do we validate new recovery processes?

4 What prevents better material performance tracking?

5 How do we share performance insights across teams?

Level 1 (Beginning)

Organizations at this level evaluate recovered materials using standards designed for virgin materials. Like the challenges with local recovery, these organizations lack systematic ways to measure and verify recovered material performance. Quality assessments focus on immediate properties rather than long-term performance potential.

Key characteristics:

- Virgin material standards applied to recovered materials
- Limited tracking of material transformation impacts
- Basic quality checks focused on immediate properties
- No systematic performance history documentation

NEXT STEPS FOR LEVEL 1

Review your assessment results with quality and engineering teams. Focus on developing basic frameworks for evaluating recovered materials on their own terms rather than just comparing to virgin material standards.

Consider these targeted actions:

- Document current material testing procedures
- Identify key performance attributes for recovered materials
- Start tracking basic material transformation data
- Create a pilot testing protocol for one recovered material
- Begin collecting performance history for recovered materials

Level 2 (Developing)

Organizations at this level look like the early days in the fictional example of material recovery, when they were just beginning to prove recovered material quality to manufacturers. Like the initial quality verification efforts, they've started adapting testing protocols for recovered materials but haven't fully standardized their approach. Similar to the early challenges with medical device manufacturers, these organizations struggle with consistently documenting material performance through multiple lifecycles.

Key characteristics:

- Basic recovered material testing protocols established
- Some tracking of material transformation effects
- Limited performance history documentation
- Emerging standards for recovered material evaluation

NEXT STEPS FOR LEVEL 2

Focus on systematizing your approach to measuring recovered material performance. Build connections between quality testing and material innovation. Create formal processes for tracking performance through multiple lifecycles.

Consider these targeted actions:

- Develop comprehensive material testing framework
- Implement systematic performance documentation
- Create recovered material specification database
- Launch material performance tracking program
- Establish a formal transformation verification process

Level 3 (Advanced)

Organizations at this level operate like the mature urban mining network in the fictional example, with systems for measuring and verifying material performance through multiple lifecycles. Just as the network provided detailed material histories to manufacturers, these organizations maintain comprehensive performance tracking and actively use this data to improve recovery processes.

Key characteristics:

- Comprehensive multi-life performance tracking
- Standardized material transformation documentation
- Active use of performance data in innovation
- Systematic quality verification across lifecycles

NEXT STEPS FOR LEVEL 3

Work on expanding performance tracking influence across your organization. Create formal programs for capturing performance insights. Develop networks to scale test capabilities. Begin sharing knowledge beyond your organization.

Consider these targeted actions:

- Establish a material innovation program using performance data
- Create automated performance-tracking systems
- Develop strategy for scaling testing capabilities

- Implement comprehensive performance prediction models
- Set organization-wide recovery quality metrics

Level 4 (Leading)

Organizations at this level have achieved what the network in the fictional example accomplished through their manufacturer partnerships, developing recovered material performance tracking into a key capability. Like the expanding network of specialized testing facilities, they've developed systems for predicting and verifying material performance through multiple lifecycles.

Key characteristics:

- Performance data drives material innovation
- Advanced prediction and verification systems
- Active development of testing capabilities
- Industry leadership in material standards

NEXT STEPS FOR LEVEL 4

Focus on leading industry transformation toward multi-life performance standards. Share knowledge openly to build testing ecosystems. Develop new business models based on performance verification capabilities.

Consider these targeted actions:

- Create an open platform for sharing performance data
- Develop industry-standard testing protocols
- Launch performance-based business models
- Establish material testing innovation centers
- Lead development of industry standards
- Create performance-focused supplier development programs

Digital Interoperability to Circulate Locally

Creating common data standards that enable seamless sharing of product information across the circular network.

In Chapter 4, we explored how traditional documentation approaches needed to evolve to support complex recovery networks. New systems must be able to track and verify material properties and transformations across multiple partners.

The fictional example illustrates digital interoperability through their "digital twin plus" system, where every batch of recovered material carried standardized documentation of its properties, history, and potential applications. When manufacturers from different industries could access exactly the verification data they needed while protecting proprietary information, it showed how standardized data sharing enables trust in recovered materials.

Leading organizations today show similar capabilities. GS1's EPCIS standard enables standardized sharing of material tracking data across supply chains. Similarly, the International Material Data System (IMDS) provides standardized formats for sharing material composition data across automotive supply chains, facilitating recovery and reuse.

Finding Your Level

To assess your organization, you'll need input from multiple perspectives across your value chain. Schedule focused conversations with key stakeholders with the goal of understanding both the current state of repair in your organization and the barriers to advancing this capability.

Plan to speak with representatives from five key stakeholder groups. For each group, you'll see specific questions designed to uncover how this capability is valued and implemented across your organization. Take notes during these conversations—the patterns that emerge will help you identify your organization's current level and next steps.

After gathering responses to these questions, look for patterns:

- If most answers focus on basic data collection with manual sharing, you're likely at Level 1
- If you see digital tools in use but limited standardization across systems, you're probably at Level 2
- If data sharing consistently enables collaboration but isn't yet driving innovation, you're at Level 3
- If interoperable systems actively drive network-wide optimization, you've reached Level 4

FOR TECHNOLOGY TEAMS

1 How do we share data across different systems?

2 What standards exist for data exchange?

3 How do we ensure data compatibility?

4 What prevents better system integration?

5 How do we maintain data consistency?

FOR OPERATIONS TEAMS

1 How do we track material flows digitally?

2 What systems support data sharing with partners?

3 How do we verify shared data accuracy?

4 What barriers exist to seamless data exchange?

5 How do we coordinate across different platforms?

FOR SUPPLY CHAIN PARTNERS

1 How do we exchange data with network partners?

2 What formats exist for sharing specifications?

3 How do we validate partner data?

4 What prevents better information sharing?

5 How do we maintain data security?

FOR QUALITY TEAMS

1 How do we share quality data across systems?

2 What standards govern data verification?

3 How do we track material certifications?

4 What role does shared data play in quality?

5 How do we maintain data integrity?

FOR INNOVATION TEAMS

1 How do we use shared data for improvement?

2 What tools support collaborative innovation?

3 How do we capture cross-system insights?

4 What prevents better knowledge sharing?

5 How do we scale successful solutions?

Level 1 (Beginning)

Organizations at this level manage data in isolated systems. Like the challenges that some supply chains can find with early with material tracing efforts, these organizations lack standardized ways to share and verify information. Data exchange often relies on manual processes and basic file transfers.

Key characteristics:

- Siloed systems with manual data sharing
- Limited standardization of data formats
- Basic digital tracking capabilities
- No systematic approach to interoperability

NEXT STEPS FOR LEVEL 1

Review your assessment results with technology and operations teams. Focus on developing basic frameworks for standardized data sharing rather than continuing with ad hoc approaches.

Consider these targeted actions:

- Document current data-sharing processes
- Identify key data exchange points
- Start implementing standard data formats
- Create a pilot for automated data sharing
- Begin mapping system integration needs

Level 2 (Developing)

Organizations at this level mirror the early days in the fictional example of network development, when they were just beginning to connect different facilities digitally. Like the initial data-sharing efforts, they've started implementing digital tools but haven't fully standardized their approach. Similar to the early challenges with manufacturers, these organizations struggle with consistent data exchange across partners.

Key characteristics:

- Basic digital sharing tools implemented
- Some standardization of data formats

- Limited system integration
- Emerging protocols for data exchange

NEXT STEPS FOR LEVEL 2

Focus on systematizing your approach to data sharing. Build connections between different systems. Create formal processes for maintaining data consistency across platforms.

Consider these targeted actions:

- Develop comprehensive data standards
- Implement automated sharing protocols
- Create a system integration roadmap
- Launch a cross-platform verification program
- Establish a formal data governance process

Level 3 (Advanced)

Organizations at this level operate like the mature urban mining network in the fictional example, with systems for sharing and verifying data across partners. Just as the network provided real-time material tracking to manufacturers, these organizations maintain comprehensive data exchange capabilities and actively use this connectivity to improve operations.

Key characteristics:

- Comprehensive data-sharing standards
- Automated system integration
- Active use of shared data for optimization
- Systematic verification across platforms

NEXT STEPS FOR LEVEL 3

Work on expanding interoperability across your network. Create formal programs for scaling integration capabilities, develop frameworks to accelerate partner onboarding, and begin sharing standards beyond your organization.

Consider these targeted actions:

- Establish network-wide data standards
- Create automated integration tools

- Develop strategy for scaling connectivity
- Implement predictive optimization models
- Set network-wide data quality metrics

Level 4 (Leading)

Organizations at this level have achieved what the network in the fictional example accomplished through their digital infrastructure—transforming interoperability into a competitive advantage. Like the expanding network of connected facilities, they've developed systems for sharing and utilizing data across complex partner networks.

Key characteristics:

- Interoperability drives network optimization
- Advanced integration capabilities
- Active development of sharing standards
- Industry leadership in digital collaboration

NEXT STEPS FOR LEVEL 4

Focus on leading industry transformation toward standardized data sharing. Share frameworks openly to build digital ecosystems. Develop new business models based on network connectivity.

Consider these targeted actions:

- Create open standards for industry adoption
- Develop automated onboarding tools
- Launch connectivity-based services
- Establish digital innovation centers
- Lead development of industry protocols
- Create interoperability-focused partner programs

Ecosystem Collaboration Protocols to Circulate Locally

Developing standard approaches for knowledge sharing and joint improvement across network partners.

In Chapter 4, we explored how traditional supplier relationships needed to evolve to enable effective collaboration across circular networks. A systematic approach to coordinating material recovery and verification across diverse partners is needed for this.

The fictional example shows this capability through the work with multiple industries: Standardized protocols for material testing, shared frameworks for quality verification, and common languages for describing material properties. When, for example, medical device, fashion, and electronics manufacturers can all trust the same recovered materials for different applications, it demonstrates how standardized collaboration enables local recovery at scale.

Leading organizations today show these capabilities. The Ellen MacArthur Foundation's Circular Electronics Partnership has created standardized protocols for electronics recovery across global supply chains. Similarly, the Building as Material Banks (BAMB) project has developed standardized approaches for documenting and recovering construction materials, showing how collaboration protocols can enable effective urban mining across industries.

Finding Your Level

To assess your organization, you'll need input from multiple perspectives across your value chain. Schedule focused conversations with key stakeholders with the goal of understanding both the current state of repair in your organization and the barriers to advancing this capability.

Plan to speak with representatives from five key stakeholder groups. For each group, you'll see specific questions designed to uncover how this capability is valued and implemented across your organization. Take notes during these conversations—the patterns that emerge will help you identify your organization's current level and next steps.

After gathering responses to these questions, look for patterns:

- If most answers focus on basic supplier management with limited collaboration, you're likely at Level 1
- If you see some partner coordination but limited standardization, you're probably at Level 2
- If collaboration protocols consistently enable network optimization but aren't yet driving innovation, you're at Level 3
- If ecosystem collaboration actively drives network-wide value creation, you've reached Level 4

FOR PARTNERSHIP TEAMS

1 How do we structure collaboration with partners?

2 What protocols exist for joint operations?

3 How do we align shared objectives?

4 What prevents better network coordination?

5 How do we measure collaborative success?

FOR OPERATIONS TEAMS

1 How do we coordinate activities across partners?

2 What systems support network collaboration?

3 How do we ensure consistent execution?

4 What barriers exist to partner integration?

5 How do we share operational knowledge?

FOR INNOVATION TEAMS

1 How do we collaborate on improvements?

2 What frameworks support joint development?

3 How do we scale successful innovations?

4 What prevents better knowledge sharing?

5 How do we capture network learning?

FOR QUALITY TEAMS

1 How do we align standards across partners?

2 What protocols govern shared processes?

3 How do we verify network-wide quality?

4 What role does collaboration play in improvement?

5 How do we maintain consistent standards?

FOR SUPPLY CHAIN TEAMS

1 How do we coordinate network activities?

2 What systems enable partner alignment?

3 How do we optimize across boundaries?

4 What prevents better network integration?

5 How do we share supply chain insights?

Level 1 (Beginning)

Organizations at this level manage partner relationships individually and lack standardized ways to collaborate effectively. Partner coordination often relies on informal arrangements and basic agreements.

Key characteristics:

- Individual partner management approaches
- Limited standardization of collaboration
- Basic coordination mechanisms
- No systematic network protocols

NEXT STEPS FOR LEVEL 1

Review your assessment results with partnership and operations teams. Focus on developing basic frameworks for standardized collaboration rather than continuing with ad hoc approaches.

Consider these targeted actions:

- Document current collaboration processes
- Identify key coordination points
- Start implementing standard protocols
- Create a pilot for network coordination
- Begin mapping collaboration needs

Level 2 (Developing)

Organizations at this level mirror the early days of network development, when teams just beginning to coordinate multiple recovery partners. During these initial collaboration efforts, they've started implementing basic protocols but haven't fully standardized their approach. These organizations struggle with consistent coordination across diverse partners.

Key characteristics:

- Basic collaboration protocols established
- Some standardization of joint processes

- Limited network coordination
- Emerging frameworks for partnership

NEXT STEPS FOR LEVEL 2

Focus on systematizing your approach to ecosystem collaboration. Build connections between different partners and create formal processes for maintaining consistent coordination across the network.

Consider these targeted actions:

- Develop comprehensive collaboration standards
- Implement network coordination protocols
- Create a partner integration roadmap
- Launch cross-partner learning program
- Establish formal collaboration governance

Level 3 (Advanced)

Organizations at this level operate like the mature local recovery network in the fictional example, with systems for coordinating activities across partners. These organizations maintain comprehensive protocols and actively use network insights to improve operations.

Key characteristics:

- Comprehensive collaboration standards
- Standardized network coordination
- Active use of shared learning
- Systematic improvement processes

NEXT STEPS FOR LEVEL 3

Work on expanding collaboration influence across your network. Create formal programs for scaling partnership capabilities, develop frameworks to accelerate network optimization, and begin sharing standards beyond your organization.

Consider these targeted actions:

- Establish network-wide innovation protocols
- Create automated coordination tools

- Develop strategy for scaling collaboration
- Implement network optimization models
- Set ecosystem-wide performance metrics

Level 4 (Leading)

Organizations at this level have achieved what the network in the fictional example accomplished through their partnership approach—transforming ecosystem collaboration into a competitive advantage. Like the expanding network of coordinated facilities, they've developed systems for orchestrating complex partner networks.

Key characteristics:

- Collaboration drives network innovation
- Advanced coordination capabilities
- Active development of partnership models
- Industry leadership in ecosystem protocols

NEXT STEPS FOR LEVEL 4

Focus on leading industry transformation toward standardized collaboration. Share frameworks openly to build partner ecosystems. Develop new business models based on network orchestration.

Consider these targeted actions:

- Create open standards for industry adoption
- Develop network orchestration tools
- Launch ecosystem-based services
- Establish collaboration innovation centers
- Lead development of industry protocols
- Create network-focused partner programs

19

Governance Capabilities

Ensuring Circular Success to Circulate Locally

Effective oversight ensures long-lasting urban mining operations. Governance must go beyond traditional supplier management to coordinate the complex networks of material recovery and reuse. While standards provide frameworks, it is governance capabilities—from value sharing to quality assurance—that enable long-term success. Leading organizations recognize that three core governance capabilities—value-sharing mechanisms, quality assurance, and continuous evolution—create the structure for lasting circular operations.

Value-Sharing Mechanisms to Circulate Locally

Creating frameworks that fairly distribute benefits among ecosystem partners who contribute to extending product life.

In Chapter 4, we explored how traditional value calculations needed to change to support circular operations. Organizations must use new approaches that recognize and reward multiple forms of value creation in material recovery operations.

The fictional example shows this capability through the network of partners: Manufacturers gaining access to high-quality recovered materials, collection points receiving compensation for quality sorting and processing facilities sharing in the value of their innovations. When their AI system identified an opportunity to redirect materials between industries, their governance structure ensured all contributors benefited from the increased value creation.

Leading organizations today show similar capabilities. The NextWave Plastics consortium has created the Framework for Socially Responsible Ocean-Bound Plastic Supply Chains, for sharing value across ocean plastic recovery networks and ensuring there are benefits for all participants. Similarly, TerraCycle's Loop platform uses value-sharing mechanisms to reward participants throughout their reuse and recovery systems.

Finding Your Level

To assess your organization, you'll need input from multiple perspectives across your value chain. Schedule focused conversations with key stakeholders with the goal of understanding both the current state of repair in your organization and the barriers to advancing this capability.

Plan to speak with representatives from five key stakeholder groups. For each group, you'll see specific questions designed to uncover how this capability is valued and implemented across your organization. Take notes during these conversations—the patterns that emerge will help you identify your organization's current level and next steps.

After gathering responses to these questions, look for patterns:

- If most answers focus on traditional transactional relationships, you're likely at Level 1
- If you see basic value-sharing initiatives but limited partner integration, you're probably at Level 2
- If value sharing consistently influences decisions but isn't yet driving innovation, you're at Level 3
- If collaborative value creation actively drives network strategy, you've reached Level 4

FOR OPERATIONS TEAMS

1 How do we track value creation across the network?
2 What systems support value distribution?
3 How do we measure partner contributions?
4 How do we share efficiency gains with partners?
5 What barriers prevent equitable value sharing?

FOR PARTNER MANAGEMENT TEAMS

1 How do we structure value-sharing agreements?

2 What mechanisms exist for sharing innovation benefits?

3 How do we verify partner contributions?

4 What prevents deeper value sharing relationships?

5 How do we handle value disputes with partners?

FOR FINANCE TEAMS

1 How do we account for shared value creation?

2 What metrics exist for partner value contributions?

3 How do we evaluate value-sharing models?

4 What role does value sharing play in investment decisions?

5 How do we track value distribution effectiveness?

FOR INNOVATION TEAMS

1 How do value-sharing mechanisms support innovation?

2 What incentives exist for collaborative improvement?

3 How do we distribute benefits from shared innovations?

4 What prevents greater innovation sharing?

5 How do we value partner intellectual contributions?

FOR EXECUTIVE LEADERSHIP

1 How do we distribute value across our material recovery partnerships?

2 What frameworks exist for rewarding partner innovations?

3 How do we measure shared value creation?

4 What role does value sharing play in partner retention?

5 How do we balance individual and collective benefits?

Level 1 (Beginning)

Organizations at this level view value sharing primarily through traditional supplier relationships; these organizations focus on immediate transaction value rather than long-term collaborative benefits. Partner relationships emphasize cost reduction over shared value creation.

Key characteristics:

- Traditional transactional relationships dominate
- No formal value-sharing frameworks
- Limited recognition of partner contributions
- Value creation measured individually, not collectively

NEXT STEPS FOR LEVEL 1

Review your assessment results with your leadership team. The goal is to create a shared understanding of your current state and align value-sharing opportunities.

Consider these targeted actions:

- Map value creation points across your network
- Identify the top three opportunities for shared value creation
- Create a pilot value-sharing program with one key partner
- Engage with partners to understand value-sharing challenges
- Develop basic metrics for tracking shared value creation

Level 2 (Developing)

Organizations at this level look like the local recovery mining network in the fictional example, when they first began establishing relationships with manufacturers and recovery partners They've started basic profit-sharing arrangements but haven't fully integrated collaborative value creation into their strategy. These organizations recognize the need for value sharing but struggle with quantifying and distributing benefits fairly.

Key characteristics:

- Basic value-sharing programs established
- Some profit-sharing mechanisms exist
- Limited integration of partner innovations
- Basic tracking of shared value creation
- Informal approaches to rewarding collaboration

NEXT STEPS FOR LEVEL 2

Focus on systematically integrating value sharing into your operations. Build formal frameworks for measuring and distributing value and create clear processes for recognizing and rewarding partner contributions.

Consider these targeted actions:

- Develop a value-sharing metrics dashboard
- Create a formal partner innovation rewards program
- Implement a systematic value-tracking system
- Launch collaborative improvement initiatives
- Establish clear value distribution protocols
- Create a framework for measuring partner contributions

Level 3 (Advanced)

Organizations at this level operate like the maturing urban mining network in the fictional example, with partnership collaboration fully integrated into their business model. Just as the network developed systems for coordinating value across partners, these organizations maintain comprehensive frameworks for collaborative value creation. Like the approach to connecting industries with AI-driven insights in the fictional example, they actively use data to inform resource allocation and see partner success as crucial to network growth.

Key characteristics:

- Value sharing integrated into strategy
- Comprehensive collaboration frameworks
- Active partner development programs
- Data-driven value distribution
- Clear innovation sharing protocols
- Regular value creation assessment
- Structured benefit-sharing mechanisms

NEXT STEPS FOR LEVEL 3

Work on expanding value-sharing influence across your network. Create formal programs for capturing and distributing innovation benefits and develop approaches to measuring and rewarding partner contributions.

Consider these targeted actions:

- Establish a network-wide innovation-sharing platform
- Create automated value distribution systems
- Develop strategy for scaling value sharing
- Implement comprehensive partner success metrics
- Set network-wide value-creation targets
- Launch advanced partner development programs

Level 4 (Leading)

Organizations at this level have achieved what the network in the fictional example accomplished through their manufacturer partnerships—transforming material recovery into a core competitive advantage. They've developed systems for coordinating across complex partner networks. Similar to how the success in the fictional example led manufacturers to redesign products for recovery, these organizations influence their entire industry's approach to collaborative value creation.

Key characteristics:

- Value sharing drives network strategy
- Advanced benefit distribution systems
- Active development of partner capabilities
- Industry leadership in collaborative models
- Innovation-sharing platforms
- Predictive value creation analytics
- Transparent value distribution mechanisms

NEXT STEPS FOR LEVEL 4

Focus on leading industry transformation toward collaborative value models. Share knowledge openly to build value-sharing ecosystems and develop new business models based on network value creation.

Consider these targeted actions:

- Create an open platform for sharing value creation methods
- Develop industry-standard value-sharing protocols
- Launch network-based business models

- Establish collaborative innovation centers
- Lead the development of industry value-sharing standards
- Create partner capability development programs
- Implement predictive value-creation systems
- Build cross-industry value-sharing networks

This guide helps organizations assess and advance their value-sharing mechanisms, supporting the development of urban mining networks where all partners benefit from collaborative value creation.

Quality Assurance Through Multiple Lives to Circulate Locally

Implementing governance structures that maintain consistent quality standards across multiple product lifecycles.

In Chapter 4, we explored how traditional quality systems struggled to address recovered materials. Organizations must develop governance frameworks that maintain consistent quality while adapting to the unique challenges of urban mining.

The fictional example shows this through their material certification processes: Comprehensive testing protocols, independent verification systems, and transparent documentation of every transformation. When they supplied recovered titanium for medical devices, their governance system ensured perfect traceability while maintaining rigorous quality standards through multiple transformations.

Leading organizations today demonstrate similar capabilities. The Responsible Minerals Initiative provides governance frameworks for verifying recovered materials across global supply chains. Similarly, UL's Environmental Claim Validation provides governance structures for verifying recycled content claims, ensuring trust in recovered materials.

Finding Your Level

To assess your organization, you'll need input from multiple perspectives across your value chain. Schedule focused conversations with key stakeholders with the goal of understanding both the current state of repair in your organization and the barriers to advancing this capability.

Plan to speak with representatives from five key stakeholder groups. For each group, you'll see specific questions designed to uncover how this capability is valued and implemented across your organization. Take notes during these conversations—the patterns that emerge will help you identify your organization's current level and next steps.

After gathering responses to these questions, look for patterns:

- If most answers focus on basic quality checks without lifecycle tracking, you're likely at Level 1
- If you see quality systems for recovered materials but limited integration, you're probably at Level 2
- If quality assurance spans multiple lifecycles but isn't yet driving innovation, you're at Level 3
- If quality systems actively enable new business models, you've reached Level 4

FOR QUALITY TEAMS

1 How do we verify quality across multiple material lifecycles?

2 What systems track material quality history?

3 How do we maintain quality standards for recovered materials?

4 What prevents better-quality assurance across lifecycles?

5 How do we validate long-term material performance?

FOR ENGINEERING TEAMS

1 How do we test recovered material properties?

2 What quality parameters do we track over time?

3 How do we incorporate quality history into specifications?

4 What barriers exist to quality verification?

5 How do we predict material degradation?

FOR OPERATIONS TEAMS

1 How do we maintain quality through recovery processes?

2 What systems verify material quality consistency?

3 How do we handle quality variations in recovered materials?

4 How do we document quality through transformations?

5 What prevents better quality control in recovery?

FOR CUSTOMER TEAMS

1 How do we demonstrate quality to customers?

2 What quality assurance data do customers require?

3 How do we handle quality concerns for recovered materials?

4 What prevents customer acceptance of recovered materials?

5 How do we build trust in material quality?

FOR SUPPLIER TEAMS

1 How do we verify incoming material quality?

2 What quality standards exist for recovered materials?

3 How do we track supplier quality performance?

4 What prevents better supplier quality assurance?

5 How do we share quality data with suppliers?

Level 1 (Beginning)

Organizations at this level view quality assurance primarily through single-use metrics, and focus on basic quality checks without considering multiple lifecycle performance. Quality systems emphasize immediate specifications over long-term material reliability.

Key characteristics:

- Basic quality checks only
- No lifecycle quality tracking
- Limited quality history documentation
- Quality focused on immediate use only
- Minimal recovery quality standards

NEXT STEPS FOR LEVEL 1

Review your assessment results with your leadership team. The goal is to create a shared understanding of your current state and align quality assurance opportunities.

Consider these targeted actions:

- Start tracking basic quality metrics through recovery
- Identify critical quality parameters for key materials
- Create a pilot program for quality history documentation
- Engage with customers to understand quality requirements
- Develop initial recovered material specifications

Level 2 (Developing)

Organizations at this level have established basic quality systems for recovered materials but struggle with consistent verification across multiple uses. Similar to the early challenges with material traceability, these organizations recognize the importance of quality history but lack comprehensive systems.

Key characteristics:

- Basic quality systems for recovery
- Some lifecycle quality tracking
- Limited quality prediction capabilities
- Initial quality documentation systems
- Growing focus on material reliability

NEXT STEPS FOR LEVEL 2

Focus on systematically integrating quality assurance across multiple lifecycles. Build formal frameworks for tracking material quality history. Create clear processes for verifying and documenting quality through transformations.

Consider these targeted actions:

- Develop a quality history tracking system
- Implement material testing protocols
- Create formal quality documentation procedures
- Launch quality prediction initiatives
- Establish recovery quality standards
- Build customer quality verification processes

Level 3 (Advanced)

Organizations at this level operate like the mature urban mining network in the fictional example, with quality assurance spanning multiple material lives. Just as the network developed advanced systems for verifying titanium quality for medical devices, these organizations maintain comprehensive frameworks for tracking and ensuring material quality through multiple transformations. Like the approach to quality verification in the fictional example, they actively use data to predict and maintain material performance.

Key characteristics:

- Quality systems span multiple lifecycles
- Comprehensive quality history tracking
- Active quality prediction programs
- Verification protocols
- Clear quality communication systems
- Regular performance monitoring
- Strong customer trust mechanisms

NEXT STEPS FOR LEVEL 3

Work on expanding quality influence across your network. Create formal programs for predicting and ensuring long-term material performance and develop approaches to building customer confidence.

Consider these targeted actions:

- Establish an advanced quality prediction platform
- Create automated quality-tracking systems
- Develop strategy for quality communication
- Implement comprehensive performance metrics
- Set network-wide quality standards
- Launch advanced testing programs

Level 4 (Leading)

Organizations at this level have achieved what the network in the fictional example accomplished through their medical device partnerships—transforming quality assurance into a competitive advantage. They have developed systems for verifying and maintaining quality across complex material transformations. Similar to how the success in the fictional example led manufacturers to trust recovered materials, these organizations influence their entire industry's approach to quality assurance.

Key characteristics:

- Quality drives business strategy
- Advanced prediction systems
- Active development of testing capabilities
- Industry leadership in quality standards
- Verification platforms
- Predictive performance analytics
- Transparent quality documentation

NEXT STEPS FOR LEVEL 4

Focus on leading industry transformation toward multi-lifecycle quality standards. Share knowledge openly to build quality assurance ecosystems and develop new business models based on quality verification capabilities.

Consider these targeted actions:

- Create an open platform for sharing quality methods
- Develop industry-standard testing protocols
- Launch quality-based business models
- Establish material science centers
- Lead development of industry standards
- Create capability development programs
- Implement predictive quality systems
- Build cross-industry verification networks

Continuous Evolution to Circulate Locally

Establishing processes for ongoing improvement and adaptation of circular practices based on network learning.

In Chapter 4, we explored how traditional governance structures couldn't support continuous improvement in circular networks. Organizations must create frameworks that encourage innovation while maintaining consistent quality.

The fictional example shows continuous evolution through the approach to innovation: Systematically capturing improvements in recovery techniques, sharing insights across industries, and scaling successful innovations network-wide.

Leading organizations today show similar capabilities. The Green Electronics Council's EPEAT system creates governance frameworks that encourage continuous improvement in electronics recovery. Similarly, Cradle to Cradle Certified™ provides governance structures that promote ongoing innovation in material recovery and reuse while maintaining rigorous standards.

Finding Your Level

To assess your organization, you'll need input from multiple perspectives across your value chain. Schedule focused conversations with key stakeholders with the goal of understanding both the current state of repair in your organization and the barriers to advancing this capability.

Plan to speak with representatives from five key stakeholder groups. For each group, you'll see specific questions designed to uncover how this capability is valued and implemented across your organization. Take notes during these conversations—the patterns that emerge will help you identify your organization's current level and next steps.

After gathering responses to these questions, look for patterns:

- If most answers focus on reactive improvements without systematic capture, you're likely at Level 1
- If you see improvement systems but limited network learning, you're probably at Level 2
- If continuous evolution influences operations but isn't yet transformative, you're at Level 3
- If systematic innovation actively drives network growth, you've reached Level 4

FOR INNOVATION TEAMS

1 How do we capture and scale improvements across our network?

2 What systems support continuous learning?

3 How do we validate and implement new solutions?

4 What prevents faster innovation adoption?

5 How do we measure improvement impact?

FOR OPERATIONS TEAMS

1 How do we identify improvement opportunities?

2 What processes support continuous evolution?

3 How do we share operational learnings?

4 What barriers prevent systematic improvement?

5 How do we implement network-wide changes?

FOR TECHNOLOGY TEAMS

1 How do we capture technical innovations?

2 What platforms support knowledge sharing?

3 How do we validate technical improvements?

4 What prevents faster technology evolution?

5 How do we scale technical solutions?

FOR PARTNER TEAMS

1 How do we collaborate on improvements?

2 What frameworks support shared learning?

3 How do we implement partner innovations?

4 What prevents better knowledge sharing?

5 How do we measure collaborative progress?

FOR LEADERSHIP TEAMS

1 How do we drive systematic evolution?

2 What resources support continuous improvement?

3 How do we measure innovation impact?

4 What prevents faster transformation?

5 How do we align improvement initiatives?

Level 1 (Beginning)

Organizations at this level approach improvement reactively, and make changes in response to problems rather than systematically driving evolution. Improvements remain localized without network-wide adoption.

Key characteristics:

- Reactive improvement approach
- No systematic innovation capture
- Limited knowledge sharing
- Localized process changes
- Minimal improvement tracking

NEXT STEPS FOR LEVEL 1

Review your assessment results with your leadership team. The goal is to create a shared understanding of your current state and align evolution opportunities.

Consider these targeted actions:

- Start documenting improvement opportunities
- Identify key areas for systematic evolution
- Create a pilot knowledge-sharing program
- Engage teams in improvement discussions
- Develop basic improvement metrics

Level 2 (Developing)

Organizations at this level look like the early evolution efforts in the fictional example. They've established basic improvement systems but struggle with network-wide implementation. These organizations recognize the importance of evolution but lack comprehensive frameworks.

Key characteristics:

- Basic improvement systems
- Some knowledge-sharing mechanisms
- Limited network learning
- Initial innovation tracking
- Growing focus on systematic change

NEXT STEPS FOR LEVEL 2

Focus on systematically integrating continuous evolution across your network. Build formal frameworks for capturing and sharing improvements. Create clear processes for validating and scaling innovations.

Consider these targeted actions:

- Develop a knowledge management system
- Implement improvement tracking tools
- Create formal validation procedures
- Launch network learning initiatives
- Establish innovation-sharing protocols
- Build systematic evolution frameworks

Level 3 (Advanced)

Organizations at this level operate like the maturing network in the fictional example, with systems for continuous evolution. Just as the network developed advanced methods for identifying and scaling improvements, these organizations maintain comprehensive frameworks for driving systematic innovation. Like the approach to AI-driven optimization in the fictional example, they actively use data to accelerate network evolution.

Key characteristics:

- Evolution systems span network
- Comprehensive improvement tracking
- Active knowledge sharing programs
- Validation protocols
- Clear scaling mechanisms
- Regular innovation monitoring
- Strong collaborative learning

NEXT STEPS FOR LEVEL 3

Work on expanding evolution influence across your network. Create formal programs for accelerating improvement adoption. Develop approaches to measuring and scaling impact.

Consider these targeted actions:

- Establish advanced innovation platform
- Create automated improvement tracking

- Develop strategy for rapid scaling
- Implement comprehensive impact metrics
- Set network-wide evolution targets
- Launch advanced validation programs

Level 4 (Leading)

Organizations at this level have achieved what the network in the fictional example accomplished through their cross-industry partnerships—transforming continuous evolution into a core capability. Like the expanding network of specialized facilities, they've developed systems for identifying, validating, and scaling improvements. Similar to how success in the fictional example led manufacturers to redesign products, these organizations influence their entire industry's approach to innovation.

Key characteristics:

- Evolution drives network strategy
- Advanced improvement systems
- Active development of capabilities
- Industry leadership in innovation
- Scaling platforms
- Predictive evolution analytics
- Transparent validation mechanisms

NEXT STEPS FOR LEVEL 4

Focus on leading industry transformation toward systematic evolution. Share knowledge openly to build innovation ecosystems. Develop new business models based on continuous improvement capabilities.

Consider these targeted actions:

- Create an open platform for sharing innovations
- Develop industry-standard evolution protocols
- Launch improvement-based business models
- Establish innovation centers
- Lead development of industry standards
- Create capability development programs
- Implement predictive evolution systems
- Build cross-industry learning networks

PART FIVE

The Capability to Collaborate Transparently

FICTIONAL EXAMPLE

The Transparency Revolution

Maya stood in the network operations center in Hackney Wick, studying a holographic display that showed data flows across London's circular supply chain network. Streams of information pulsed between repair hubs, manufacturing cells, and urban mining facilities—each point of light representing products being fixed, components being made, or materials being recovered.

"Status change on incoming request," announced the AI system. "St. Thomas's Hospital requires full material traceability for surgical device repair components. Historical data requirement: Six months. Confidence level required: 99.9 percent."

Maya watched as the system began tracing backward through their network. The component would be manufactured at their Park Royal facility, using materials recovered from their Croydon urban mining hub. But the hospital wanted more than a quality guarantee—they needed to know the complete journey of every atom that would go into their surgical devices.

"We're hitting a wall," Maya realized. "We've built the physical infrastructure for circular supply chains, but without radical transparency, we can't serve the industries that need us most."

Two months later, Maya was back in the operations center, but now the holographic display showed something far more complex. Layered over the physical flows was a new digital architecture—one designed to track and verify every aspect of their circular supply chain.

"Watch this," Maya said to Hana Rossi from the surgical device manufacturer. "Every batch of titanium is assigned a unique digital identifier. We track not just its physical properties, but every transformation it undergoes. Temperature, pressure, time—all verified by independent monitoring systems."

"That's the breakthrough," Maya explained. "We've created what we call 'trust layers'—standardized protocols for sharing critical information while protecting sensitive data. A hospital can trace their materials without accessing proprietary manufacturing data. A manufacturer can verify quality without exposing their process parameters."

Their system had evolved beyond simple tracking. It created a digital infrastructure that could verify and share specific data attributes while maintaining security and privacy. Every participant in the network could choose what information to share and with whom.

Three months into their transparency initiative, Maya found herself presenting to an unexpected audience—pharmaceutical companies, electronic vehicle manufacturers, even food processing plants.

"Every product, component, and material in our network carries what we call a 'digital twin plus'—so it's the physical properties and location, and it's also the complete history, verification records, and future potential," Maya explained.

The AI system had started identifying correlations between material properties and repair success rates, manufacturing yields, and product longevity. This insight was automatically shared—anonymously—across the network, helping everyone improve their operations.

Around the virtual conference table were representatives from competitors who normally wouldn't share the same room: Medical device manufacturers, aerospace companies, and electronics firms. All had been drawn together by a common need: Standardizing how their data was shared.

"The real power comes from what I call 'transparency network effects,'" Maya demonstrated. When everyone used the same protocols for sharing information, insights emerged faster, improvements spread more quickly, and trust grew stronger.

Their transparency system now connected hundreds of organizations: Manufacturers large and small, repair operations, material recovery facilities, testing laboratories, and certification bodies. Each participant contributed data to the network and gained insights in return. Most importantly, they could all trust what they were seeing.

"Latest network metrics," the AI announced. "Material traceability: 99.99 percent. Process verification: 100 percent. Cross-industry innovation sharing: Up 300 percent year over year."

The message was clear: The future of industry wasn't just about making products differently—it was about trusting differently too. And London was leading the way, one verified data point at a time.

20

People and Culture Capabilities

Collaborating Transparently

The transition to transparent, collaborative supply chains begins with people. Success requires developing trust-building leadership, creating new roles focused on transparency, and fostering continuous learning across traditional boundaries. While digital systems enable data sharing at scale, it's the human capabilities that make transparency meaningful, such as leaders championing radical openness to specialists managing trusted partnerships. Leading organizations recognize that investing in these three core capabilities creates the foundation for trusted circular networks: Transparency-focused circular leadership, new collaborative circularity roles, and continuous learning culture.

Circular Leadership to Collaborate Transparently

Developing leaders who understand value exists beyond single-use lifecycles. This encompasses training supply chain professionals to identify opportunities for material reuse, repair, and reintegration.

In Chapter 4, we explored how traditional supply chains treated data as proprietary assets to be protected. Change is possible where transparency creates value and trust across networks through verified data sharing. Where traditional leaders optimized for protecting information, radical openness could build trust while protecting sensitive data.

The fictional example shows this capability through the leadership of the hospital collaboration, where complete material traceability enabled partners to share critical data securely through "trust layers." Rather than seeing transparency requirements as risks, the team in the fictional example recognized them as opportunities to create new value through verified data sharing. When their AI system identified cross-industry applications for recovered materials, their network coordinated multiple industries from medical devices to construction, enabling manufacturers to redesign products for better recovery.

Leading organizations today show similar capabilities. TrusTrace's transparency platform helps fashion brands like Adidas share verified sustainability data across their supply networks, building trust through radical openness. Similarly, Provenance enables companies to make verifiable transparency claims, demonstrating how leadership in data sharing creates value. The Responsible Business Alliance's Responsible Minerals Initiative shows how industry collaboration through transparent data sharing can transform entire supply networks.

Finding Your Level

To assess your organization, you'll need input from multiple perspectives across your value chain. Schedule focused conversations with key stakeholders with the goal of understanding both the current state of repair in your organization and the barriers to advancing this capability.

Plan to speak with representatives from five key stakeholder groups. For each group, you'll see specific questions designed to uncover how this capability is valued and implemented across your organization. Take notes during these conversations—the patterns that emerge will help you identify your organization's current level and next steps.

After gathering responses to these questions, look for patterns:

- If most answers focus on protecting information with minimal sharing, you're likely at Level 1
- If you see some transparency initiatives but limited trust-building, you're probably at Level 2
- If verified data-sharing influences decisions but isn't yet driving strategy, you're at Level 3
- If radical transparency actively creates value across networks, you've reached Level 4

FOR SUPPLY CHAIN PARTNERS

1 How do we share information across our network?

2 What data do partners request most frequently?

3 How do we verify shared information?

4 What barriers prevent greater data sharing?

5 How do we build trust through transparency?

FOR OPERATIONS TEAMS

1 How do we capture and share operational data?

2 What systems support transparent decision-making?

3 How do we validate shared information?

4 What prevents greater transparency in our operations?

5 How do we use shared data to improve performance?

FOR SUSTAINABILITY TEAMS

1 How do we measure and share impact data?

2 What transparency commitments have we made?

3 How do we verify environmental claims?

4 What role does transparency play in our goals?

5 How do we communicate progress to stakeholders?

FOR QUALITY TEAMS

1 How do we share quality data across operations?

2 What metrics demonstrate trustworthiness?

3 How do we validate shared information?

4 What prevents greater quality transparency?

5 How do we use shared data to improve quality?

FOR EXECUTIVE LEADERSHIP

1 How does transparency factor into our business strategy?

2 What investments are we making in data-sharing capabilities?

3 How do we measure the value created through transparency?

4 What role does openness play in our stakeholder relationships?

5 How do we balance transparency with intellectual property protection?

Level 1 (Beginning)

Organizations at this level view data primarily as assets to be protected, and see information sharing as a risk rather than an opportunity. Leadership focuses on maintaining competitive advantage through secrecy rather than creating value through verified transparency.

Key characteristics:

- Data treated as proprietary by default
- Limited structured information sharing
- Minimal trust building with partners
- Traditional competitive mindset
- Protection prioritized over collaboration

Next Steps for Level 1

Review your assessment results with your leadership team. The goal is to create a shared understanding of your current state and align transparency opportunities.

Consider these targeted actions:

- Map current data-sharing practices and identify low-risk opportunities
- Create a pilot program for sharing one data type with key partner
- Develop basic verification protocols for shared information
- Begin measuring value created through transparency
- Engage partners to understand their data needs

Level 2 (Developing)

Organizations at this level look like the early days of transparency initiatives in the fictional example, when they were just beginning to demonstrate the value of shared data. Like their initial efforts with the hospital, they've started sharing some information but haven't fully integrated transparency into their strategy. These organizations struggle with balancing openness and protection but recognize transparency's potential value.

Key characteristics:

- Basic transparency initiatives established
- Some proactive data sharing occurs

- Limited integration with strategy
- Growing recognition of transparency's value

NEXT STEPS FOR LEVEL 2

Focus on systematically integrating transparency into operations. Build connections between data-sharing initiatives and value creation and create formal processes for validating and sharing information.

Consider these targeted actions:

- Develop a transparency metrics dashboard
- Include data sharing in strategic planning
- Create and implement validation standards
- Launch a transparency champion program
- Establish a process for evaluating sharing requests

Level 3 (Advanced)

Organizations at this level operate with transparency integrated as a strategic priority. Just as the fictional example's network expanded to serve multiple industries, these organizations maintain comprehensive data-sharing systems and actively seek opportunities to create value through openness. Like the "trust layers" in the fictional example, they actively use transparency to build trust while protecting sensitive information.

Key characteristics:

- Transparency integrated into corporate strategy
- Comprehensive verification frameworks
- Active trust building through data sharing
- Value metrics drive decisions
- Clear protocols for sensitive information
- Regular measurement of transparency impact

NEXT STEPS FOR LEVEL 3

Work on expanding transparency's influence across your organization. Create formal programs for capturing value from openness and develop networks to scale trust-building capabilities.

Consider these targeted actions:

- Establish a transparency innovation program
- Create automated validation systems
- Develop a strategy for scaling trust networks
- Implement comprehensive data-sharing guidelines
- Set organization-wide transparency metrics

Level 4 (Leading)

Organizations at this level have achieved what the network accomplished through their cross-industry partnerships in the fictional example—transforming transparency into a differentiator. Leading organizations develop systems for creating value through validated data sharing. Similar to how the success in the fictional example drew diverse industries together around standardized data sharing, these leading organizations influence their entire industry's approach to transparency.

Key characteristics:

- Transparency drives innovation and strategy
- Advanced trust-building systems
- Active development of sharing capabilities
- Industry leadership in openness

NEXT STEPS FOR LEVEL 4

Focus on leading industry transformation toward radical transparency. Share knowledge openly to build trust ecosystems and develop new business models based on validated data sharing.

Consider these targeted actions:

- Create an open platform for sharing practices
- Develop industry-standard validation protocols
- Launch transparency-based business models
- Establish trust-building innovation centers
- Lead development of industry standards
- Create transparency-focused partner programs

New Circular Supply Chain Roles to Collaborate Transparently

Building teams that excel at coordinating across traditionally separate domains. This involves bringing together specialists from across supply chain functions to collaborate on circular solutions.

In Chapter 4, we explored how traditional supply chain roles primarily focused on protecting competitive information. Where traditional positions managed proprietary information, new networks should create specialists in building trust through transparency.

The fictional example shows this through their network operations center, where they managed their "trust layers"—standard protocols for sharing critical information while protecting sensitive data.

Leading organizations today show similar capabilities. For example, Walmart's Responsible Sourcing Compliance Teams operate across 14 countries to train merchandising teams, profile supplier compliance, and drive industry-wide sustainability standards. Similarly, Microsoft's Zero Trust strategy showcases how organizations are developing roles that integrate security, technology, and collaborative capabilities across traditionally separate domains, supporting more transparent and resilient supply chain ecosystems.

Finding Your Level

To assess your organization, you'll need input from multiple perspectives across your value chain. Schedule focused conversations with key stakeholders with the goal of understanding both the current state of repair in your organization and the barriers to advancing this capability.

Plan to speak with representatives from five key stakeholder groups. For each group, you'll see specific questions designed to uncover how this capability is valued and implemented across your organization. Take notes during these conversations—the patterns that emerge will help you identify your organization's current level and next steps.

After gathering responses to these questions, look for patterns:

- If most roles focus on protecting information with minimal sharing responsibility, you're likely at Level 1
- If you see some transparency-focused positions but limited integration, you're probably at Level 2

- If dedicated transparency roles actively enable collaboration but aren't yet driving innovation, you're at Level 3
- If specialized positions are actively creating value through transparent data sharing, you've reached Level 4

FOR HR/TALENT TEAMS

1 How do job descriptions incorporate transparency requirements?
2 What new roles support data sharing and validation?
3 How do we train transparency-related skills?
4 What prevents creating new transparency roles?
5 How do we measure success in transparency roles?

FOR OPERATIONS LEADERSHIP

1 What roles coordinate data sharing across teams?
2 How do we staff transparency initiatives?
3 What new skills are needed for transparent operations?
4 Where do we lack transparency expertise?
5 How do roles evolve to support greater openness?

FOR TECHNOLOGY TEAMS

1 Who manages our data-sharing platforms?
2 What roles support transparent system operation?
3 How do we staff data validation needs?
4 What new positions would improve transparency?
5 How do technical roles support trust building?

FOR SUPPLY CHAIN TEAMS

1 Who coordinates transparency with partners?
2 What roles manage shared data quality?
3 How do we staff cross-organization initiatives?
4 What prevents better partner collaboration?
5 How do roles support network trust?

FOR TRAINING TEAMS

1   How do we develop transparency capabilities?

2   What skills are most needed for open operations?

3   How do we validate transparency competencies?

4   What prevents better capability building?

5   How do we share best practices across roles?

Level 1 (Beginning)

Organizations at this level maintain traditional supply chain roles with minimal focus on transparency, similar to the network in the fictional example before they began sharing data across industries. These organizations lack dedicated positions for managing transparent collaboration and roles focus on protecting rather than sharing information.

Key characteristics:

- Traditional supply chain roles dominate
- No dedicated transparency positions
- Limited cross-organizational coordination
- Minimal focus on trust-building skills

NEXT STEPS FOR LEVEL 1

Review your assessment results with your HR and operations teams. The goal is to identify where new roles could enable better transparency and collaboration.

Consider these targeted actions:

- Map current roles against transparency needs
- Identify critical transparency skill gaps
- Create a pilot position for data-sharing coordination
- Develop initial transparency training modules

Level 2 (Developing)

Organizations at this level look like the early network evolution in the fictional example, when they first recognized that "without radical transparency, we can't serve the industries that need us most." Developing organizations have established some transparency-focused roles but haven't fully integrated them across operations. These organizations struggle with defining these new positions but recognize their importance.

Key characteristics:

- Some specialist transparency roles exist
- Basic data-sharing coordination established
- Limited integration across functions
- Growing recognition of role importance

NEXT STEPS FOR LEVEL 2

Focus on systematically developing transparency roles. Create clear career paths for transparency specialists and establish formal development programs for new positions.

Consider these targeted actions:

- Develop transparency role frameworks
- Create dedicated training programs
- Establish mentorship initiatives
- Define success metrics for new roles
- Create cross-functional coordination positions

Level 3 (Advanced)

Organizations at this level operate like the maturing network in the fictional example, with transparency fully integrated across operations. Just as the network expanded to connect hundreds of organizations through standardized protocols, these organizations maintain comprehensive role structures for enabling verified collaboration. Like the operations center team in the fictional example, these advanced organizations actively develop new positions to support trust building.

Key characteristics:

- Transparency roles integrated across operations
- Comprehensive skill development programs
- Active creation of new positions
- Clear career paths established

NEXT STEPS FOR LEVEL 3

Work on expanding role influence across your organization. Create formal programs for developing new positions. Build networks to scale transparency capabilities.

Consider these targeted actions:

- Establish a role innovation program
- Create advanced development pathways
- Develop strategy for scaling capabilities
- Implement comprehensive competency frameworks
- Set organization-wide development metrics

Level 4 (Leading)

Organizations at this level have developed transparency capabilities into strategic advantages, including positions for enabling trusted collaboration. These organizations lead in developing new transparency roles.

Key characteristics:

- Roles drive transparency innovation
- Advanced capability development systems
- Active creation of industry-leading positions
- Strategic influence on role evolution

NEXT STEPS FOR LEVEL 4

Focus on leading industry transformation through role innovation. Share best practices to build capability ecosystems and develop new organizational models based on transparency.

Consider these targeted actions:

- Create an open platform for role development
- Develop industry-standard competencies
- Launch new organizational models
- Establish capability innovation centers
- Lead development of role standards
- Create transparency talent programs

Continuous Learning Culture to Collaborate Transparently

Creating an environment where teams actively share knowledge about repair techniques, material innovations, and process improvements across the circular network.

In Chapter 4, we explored how traditional organizations kept knowledge siloed within their boundaries. Breaking down these barriers enables continuous learning through verified data sharing. Where traditional operations protected insights as competitive advantages, their network created value through systematic knowledge exchange.

The fictional example shows this capability through the AI-enabled learning platform, which could identify and share patterns across industries while protecting sensitive information. Their system enabled cross-industry benefits, with the AI identifying correlations between material properties and performance metrics, automatically sharing these insights anonymously across the network to help everyone improve their operations. This systematic approach to learning through transparency accelerates innovation while maintaining trust.

Leading organizations today show similar capabilities. Tesla's "fleet learning" system shares performance insights across their entire vehicle network, continuously improving their products through shared data. Similarly, Schneider Electric's EcoStruxure platform enables learning across customer operations through secure data sharing. BASF's ChemCycling program demonstrates how transparency across value chains accelerates circular innovation through shared insights about material recovery and reuse.

Finding Your Level

To assess your organization, you'll need input from multiple perspectives across your value chain. Schedule focused conversations with key stakeholders with the goal of understanding both the current state of repair in your organization and the barriers to advancing this capability.

Plan to speak with representatives from five key stakeholder groups. For each group, you'll see specific questions designed to uncover how this capability is valued and implemented across your organization. Take notes during these conversations—the patterns that emerge will help you identify your organization's current level and next steps.

After gathering responses to these questions, look for patterns:

- If learning is primarily individual and information sharing is limited, you're likely at Level 1

- If some knowledge sharing exists but isn't systematic, you're probably at Level 2
- If transparent learning consistently influences operations but isn't yet driving innovation, you're at Level 3
- If open knowledge sharing actively drives continuous improvement, you've reached Level 4

FOR LEARNING AND DEVELOPMENT TEAMS

1 How do we enable learning across organizational boundaries?
2 What systems verify shared knowledge?
3 How do we protect IP while sharing insights?
4 What prevents better cross-organization learning?
5 How do we measure the impact of shared knowledge?

FOR OPERATIONS TEAMS

1 How do we share operational insights securely?
2 What platforms support verified learning?
3 How do we implement cross-industry best practices?
4 What barriers prevent knowledge exchange?
5 How do we validate external learning?

FOR INNOVATION TEAMS

1 How does transparency enable innovation?
2 What frameworks protect IP in shared learning?
3 How do we scale verified insights?
4 What prevents collaborative innovation?
5 How do we measure learning impact?

FOR PARTNER MANAGEMENT

1 How do we structure learning exchanges?
2 What systems verify shared insights?
3 How do we build trust in shared knowledge?
4 What prevents deeper learning collaboration?
5 How do we measure collaborative growth?

FOR NETWORK TEAMS

1 How do we enable network-wide learning?

2 What platforms support knowledge exchange?

3 How do we validate shared insights?

4 What prevents ecosystem learning?

5 How do we scale verified practices?

Level 1 (Beginning)

Organizations at this level keep learning primarily within their boundaries—similar to how companies operated before the trust network emerged in the fictional example. These organizations view knowledge as proprietary advantage rather than a source of collaborative value. Learning stays siloed, with minimal structured sharing beyond immediate teams.

Key characteristics:

- Individual learning dominates
- Limited knowledge-sharing systems
- Minimal cross-functional learning
- Information typically stays in silos

NEXT STEPS FOR LEVEL 1

Review your assessment results with your leadership team. The goal is to identify opportunities for creating more transparent learning systems.

Consider these targeted actions:

- Map current knowledge-sharing patterns
- Identify critical learning bottlenecks
- Create a pilot for cross-team learning
- Establish basic sharing platforms

Level 2 (Developing)

Organizations at this level look like the early learning initiatives in the fictional example, when the network first began sharing verified insights across operations. Like the initial trust layers, they've started some knowledge exchange but haven't fully developed verification systems. These organizations struggle with balancing openness and protection but recognize the value of shared learning.

Key characteristics:

- Some knowledge sharing occurs
- Basic learning systems established
- Limited cross-organizational learning
- Growing recognition of sharing value

NEXT STEPS FOR LEVEL 2

Focus on systematically developing learning capabilities. Create clear processes for knowledge sharing and establish formal systems for spreading insights.

Consider these targeted actions:

- Develop a learning metrics dashboard
- Create knowledge-sharing platforms
- Establish cross-functional learning teams
- Define success metrics for learning
- Create improvement-sharing processes

Level 3 (Advanced)

Organizations at this level operate like the mature transparency network in the fictional example, with verified learning fully integrated across operations. These organizations maintain sophisticated systems for exchanging validated knowledge. Like the trust layers in the fictional example, they actively enable learning while protecting sensitive information.

Key characteristics:

- Learning integrated across operations
- Comprehensive knowledge-sharing systems
- Active improvement identification
- Clear processes for spreading insights

NEXT STEPS FOR LEVEL 3

Work on expanding learning influence across your organization. Create formal programs for capturing improvements and build networks to scale knowledge sharing.

Consider these targeted actions:

- Establish an innovation capture program
- Create advanced learning platforms
- Develop strategy for scaling insights
- Implement comprehensive sharing frameworks
- Set organization-wide learning metrics

Level 4 (Leading)

Organizations at this level have achieved what the network accomplished in the fictional example—developing transparent learning into a critical capability. They've developed sophisticated systems for creating value through verified knowledge sharing and lead in developing new approaches to collaborative learning.

Key characteristics:

- Learning drives continuous innovation
- Advanced knowledge-sharing systems
- Active creation of learning networks
- Strategic influence on industry practices

NEXT STEPS FOR LEVEL 4

Focus on leading industry transformation through learning innovation. Share best practices to build knowledge ecosystems and develop new models based on transparent learning.

Consider these targeted actions:

- Create an open platform for insight sharing
- Develop industry-standard learning practices
- Launch new collaborative models
- Establish learning innovation centers
- Lead development of sharing standards
- Create cross-industry learning networks

21

Process Capabilities

Orchestrating Circular Flows to Collaborate Transparently

Transparent collaboration requires reimagining core processes. Success comes from creating visible value streams, implementing smart recovery protocols, and orchestrating resources across partner networks. While technology enables tracking and verification, it's the underlying processes that make transparency actionable—from material flow documentation to validated recovery procedures. Leading organizations understand that developing these three process capabilities enables trusted circular operations at scale: Transparent value streams, verified recovery protocols, and coordinated resource optimization.

The Circular Value Stream to Collaborate Transparently

Expanding traditional value stream mapping to capture circular opportunities, including repair loops, material recovery, and reintegration points.

In Chapter 4, we explored how circular value streams function more like water cycles than linear flows. Transparent loops of material and value creation across multiple industries can be created.

The fictional example shows this capability through their digital infrastructure that traced materials from urban mining through manufacturing and into medical devices. When St. Thomas's Hospital required complete material traceability, the system could verify every transformation in their titanium's journey, creating trust through transparency. This visibility can connect industries that traditionally operated in isolation.

Leading organizations show similar capabilities. For example, Adidas LOOP designs shoes for full recyclability, with processes for collecting used products and remanufacturing new shoes from original materials. Similarly, Globechain's B2B marketplace connects organizations to list and repurpose unused assets across industries, tracking material flows and creating circular value streams across sectors.

Finding Your Level

To assess your organization, you'll need input from multiple perspectives across your value chain. Schedule focused conversations with key stakeholders with the goal of understanding both the current state of repair in your organization and the barriers to advancing this capability.

Plan to speak with representatives from five key stakeholder groups. For each group, you'll see specific questions designed to uncover how this capability is valued and implemented across your organization. Take notes during these conversation—the patterns that emerge will help you identify your organization's current level and next steps.

After gathering responses to these questions, look for patterns:

- If most answers focus on basic linear tracking with limited visibility, you're likely at Level 1
- If you see some circular tracking but limited integration across flows, you're probably at Level 2
- If transparent value streams influence decisions but aren't yet driving strategy, you're at Level 3
- If transparent circular flows actively drive innovation and operations, you've reached Level 4

FOR OPERATIONS TEAMS

1 How do we map and visualize our circular value streams?
2 What systems track material flows through multiple transformations?
3 How do we share value stream data with partners?
4 What prevents greater transparency in our operations?
5 How do we verify material transformations across our network?

FOR SUPPLY CHAIN TEAMS

1 How do we coordinate material flows with partners?
2 What data do we share across our value stream?

3 How do we track materials through multiple lifecycles?

4 What barriers prevent transparent material tracking?

5 How do we optimize circular flows across partners?

FOR TECHNOLOGY TEAMS

1 What platforms support our value stream tracking?

2 How do we ensure data transparency and security?

3 What analytics capabilities support flow optimization?

4 How do we integrate partner data into our systems?

5 What prevents better value stream visibility?

FOR SUSTAINABILITY TEAMS

1 How do we measure circular impact across value streams?

2 What metrics track material circulation?

3 How do we verify environmental claims?

4 What role does transparency play in our goals?

5 How do we communicate value stream performance?

FOR EXECUTIVE LEADERSHIP

1 How do we track value creation across multiple product lifecycles?

2 What investments are we making in transparent value stream capabilities?

3 How do we measure value creation in circular flows?

4 What role does transparency play in our value stream strategy?

5 How do we balance immediate tracking needs with long-term transparency?

Level 1 (Beginning)

Organizations at this level view value streams primarily as linear flows—similar to how traditional supply chains tracked simple transactions before the transparency network in the fictional example. Like early linear operations, these organizations track basic material movements but struggle to see or optimize circular opportunities. Value stream mapping focuses on immediate transactions rather than multiple transformations.

Key characteristics:

- Value streams viewed as linear flows
- Limited visibility beyond immediate transactions
- Basic material tracking without circulation focus
- Minimal sharing of flow data with partners

NEXT STEPS FOR LEVEL 1

Review your assessment results with your leadership team. The goal is to create a shared understanding of your current state and align transparency opportunities.

Consider these targeted actions:

- Map one product's complete lifecycle including potential circular flows
- Begin tracking material transformations beyond first use
- Identify key points where transparency could enable circularity
- Engage with partners to understand their data needs

Level 2 (Developing)

Organizations at this level look like the early transparency efforts in the fictional example, when they first began tracking repairs and material flows. Like the initial network, they've started documenting circular possibilities but haven't fully integrated transparent tracking across operations. These organizations struggle with sharing flow data but recognize its potential value.

Key characteristics:

- Basic circular flow tracking established
- Some transparency across immediate partners
- Limited integration of multi-lifecycle data
- Initial sharing of material transformation data

NEXT STEPS FOR LEVEL 2

Focus on systematically expanding value stream visibility. Build connections between different circular flows and create formal processes for tracking and sharing transformation data.

Consider these targeted actions:

- Develop a circular value stream dashboard
- Implement material transformation tracking

- Create standardized data-sharing protocols
- Launch a value stream mapping initiative
- Establish a process for verifying circular flows

Level 3 (Advanced)

Organizations at this level operate like the maturing transparency network in the fictional example, with circular value streams actively tracked and optimized. These organizations maintain comprehensive visibility across multiple transformations. Like the system of verified tracking in the fictional example, they actively use flow data to influence decisions and see transparency as a value creator.

Key characteristics:

- Transparency integrated into value stream strategy
- Comprehensive circular flow tracking
- Active optimization of material transformations
- Flow data influences operational decisions

NEXT STEPS FOR LEVEL 3

Work on expanding transparency across your network. Create formal programs for optimizing circular flows, develop capabilities to scale transparent operations and begin influencing industry practices.

Consider these targeted actions:

- Establish a value stream innovation program
- Create automated transformation tracking
- Develop a strategy for scaling transparent operations
- Implement comprehensive flow optimization tools
- Set organization-wide transparency metrics

Level 4 (Leading)

Organizations at this level have achieved what the network accomplished in the fictional example through their medical device partnerships—to develop transparency as a key capability and comparative advantage for trust building. Like the expanding network of verified flows in the fictional example, they've developed systems for tracking and optimizing material transformations. Similar to how the success led manufacturers to demand traceability in the fictional example, these organizations influence their entire industry's approach to transparency.

Key characteristics:

- Transparency drives value stream innovation
- Advanced flow tracking and prediction systems
- Active development of circular optimization
- Industry leadership in transparent operations

NEXT STEPS FOR LEVEL 4

Focus on leading industry transformation toward transparent circular flows. Share knowledge openly to build trust ecosystems and develop new business models based on verified tracking capabilities.

Consider these targeted actions:

- Create an open platform for sharing flow data
- Develop industry-standard tracking protocols
- Launch transparency-based business models
- Establish circular optimization centers
- Lead development of industry standards
- Create transparency-focused partner programs

Smart Recovery Protocols to Collaborate Transparently

Standardizing how teams assess, repair, and reintegrate materials and products, ensuring consistent quality across multiple lifecycles.

In Chapter 4, we explored how traditional recovery approaches needed processes to scale effectively.

The fictional example shows this capability through the material recovery operations, where standardized data protocols enabled pharmaceutical, aerospace, and electronics manufacturers to verify their exacting requirements were met. Their "trust layers" allowed sharing of critical validation data while protecting proprietary information, enabling recovery operations across multiple industries.

Leading organizations show similar capabilities. Dell's Closed-Loop Recycling program uses standardized assessment methods for recovered plastics, ensuring consistent quality as materials are reprocessed and reintegrated into new products. Similarly, Patagonia's Worn Wear initiative transparently tracks garments through repair, breakdown, and remanufacturing processes. Both companies have established clear protocols that allow stakeholders to verify the quality and origin of recovered materials, increasing trust in their circular economy efforts.

Finding Your Level

To assess your organization, you'll need input from multiple perspectives across your value chain. Schedule focused conversations with key stakeholders with the goal of understanding both the current state of repair in your organization and the barriers to advancing this capability.

Plan to speak with representatives from five key stakeholder groups. For each group, you'll see specific questions designed to uncover how this capability is valued and implemented across your organization. Take notes during these conversations – the patterns that emerge will help you identify your organization's current level and next steps.

After gathering responses to these questions, look for patterns:

- If most answers focus on basic repair procedures with limited documentation, you're likely at Level 1
- If you see documented recovery processes but limited verification, you're probably at Level 2
- If transparent recovery protocols influence decisions but aren't yet driving strategy, you're at Level 3
- If verified recovery processes actively drive innovation and trust, you've reached Level 4

FOR EXECUTIVE LEADERSHIP

1 How do recovery capabilities factor into our business strategy?
2 What investments are we making in transparent recovery processes?
3 How do we measure recovery protocol effectiveness?
4 What role does verification play in our recovery strategy?
5 How do we balance quality requirements with transparency needs?

FOR RECOVERY OPERATIONS TEAMS

1 How do we document and verify recovery procedures?

2 What systems support recovery process tracking?

3 How do we share recovery data with partners?

4 What prevents greater transparency in recovery?

5 How do we validate recovery protocol effectiveness?

FOR QUALITY TEAMS

1 How do we verify recovery process outcomes?

2 What standards guide our recovery protocols?

3 How do we maintain consistent quality across recovery operations?

4 What prevents better recovery verification?

5 How do we document recovery quality assurance?

FOR TECHNOLOGY TEAMS

1 What platforms support recovery protocol management?

2 How do we ensure recovery data transparency?

3 What analytics capabilities support recovery optimization?

4 How do we integrate recovery data across systems?

5 What prevents better recovery process visibility?

FOR PARTNER ORGANIZATIONS

1 How do we share recovery protocol information?

2 What verification standards exist across partners?

3 How do we collaborate on recovery improvements?

4 What barriers prevent transparent recovery sharing?

5 How do we maintain consistent recovery quality?

Level 1 (Beginning)

Organizations at this level view recovery primarily as basic repair—similar to how traditional operations approached maintenance before the transparent network in the fictional example. Like early repair operations, these organizations follow simple procedures without systematic documentation or verification. Recovery processes aren't standardized or shared across partners.

Key characteristics:

- Recovery viewed as basic repair
- Limited documentation of procedures
- Minimal verification of outcomes
- No systematic sharing of recovery data

NEXT STEPS FOR LEVEL 1

Review your assessment results with your leadership team. The goal is to create a shared understanding of your current state and align recovery transparency opportunities.

Consider these targeted actions:

- Document core recovery procedures
- Begin tracking recovery outcomes
- Identify key points where verification is crucial
- Engage with partners to understand their recovery needs

Level 2 (Developing)

Organizations at this level look like the early recovery efforts in the fictional example, when they first began standardizing repair procedures. Like the initial protocols, developing organizations have started documenting processes but haven't fully integrated verification systems. These organizations struggle with proving recovery quality but recognize its importance.

Key characteristics:

- Basic recovery protocols documented
- Some verification of outcomes
- Limited sharing of recovery data
- Initial quality standards established

NEXT STEPS FOR LEVEL 2

Focus on systematically verifying recovery processes. Build connections between different recovery operations and create formal systems for documenting and sharing outcomes.

Consider these targeted actions:

- Develop recovery protocol database
- Implement outcome verification system
- Create standardized documentation methods
- Launch recovery quality program
- Establish process for validating results

Level 3 (Advanced)

Organizations at this level operate like the maturing recovery network in the fictional example, with verified protocols driving operations. Just as the network expanded to handle critical medical components, these organizations maintain comprehensive documentation and verification across all recovery processes. Like the system of trust layers in the fictional example, they actively use recovery data to build confidence and enable collaboration.

Key characteristics:

- Verification integrated into recovery strategy
- Comprehensive protocol documentation
- Active quality assurance systems
- Recovery data drives improvement

NEXT STEPS FOR LEVEL 3

Work on expanding verification across your network. Create formal programs for optimizing recovery processes, develop capabilities to scale transparent operations, and begin influencing industry practices.

Consider these targeted actions:

- Establish a recovery innovation program
- Create automated verification systems
- Develop strategy for scaling protocols
- Implement comprehensive quality tools
- Set organization-wide recovery metrics

Level 4 (Leading)

Organizations at this level have built verified recovery into a capability. Like the expanding network of trusted processes in the fictional example, they've developed systems for documenting and verifying every recovery operation. Similar to how the success in the fictional example led manufacturers to trust local repair, these organizations influence their entire industry's approach to recovery.

Key characteristics:

- Verification drives recovery innovation
- Advanced protocol documentation systems
- Active development of quality standards
- Industry leadership in recovery trust

NEXT STEPS FOR LEVEL 4

Focus on leading industry transformation toward verified recovery. Share knowledge openly to build trust ecosystems and develop new business models based on proven capabilities.

Consider these targeted actions:

- Create an open platform for sharing protocols
- Develop industry-standard verification methods
- Launch recovery-based business models
- Establish protocol innovation centers
- Lead development of industry standards
- Create verification-focused partner programs

Resource Optimization to Collaborate Transparently

Developing processes that maximize the use of existing materials through sharing, repair, and alternative sourcing.

In Chapter 4, we explored how circular operations require resource coordination across networks. Where traditional systems optimize within organizational boundaries, new networks create value through transparent resource sharing across industries.

The fictional example shows this capability through their system that shares complete history, verification records, and future potential across different industries, enabling network-wide improvements.

The transparent data infrastructure in the fictional example enabled AI systems to optimize resource flows across the network while maintaining trust through verified tracking and documentation.

Leading organizations show similar capabilities. Microsoft's Circular Centers give an example of resource optimization through transparent collaboration. These centers focus on reusing and recycling cloud computing hardware, processing decommissioned servers and components to maximize resource recovery. By sorting materials for optimal reuse or repurposing, Microsoft has achieved an impressive 83 percent reuse rate within just two years of opening its first center in Amsterdam in 2020.[1] Similarly, Caterpillar's global remanufacturing network uses tracking for core returns and remanufactured components, sharing detailed resource allocation data across its operations. By using predictive analytics, Caterpillar optimizes inventory and production planning, resulting in an up to 85 percent reduction in energy use compared to manufacturing new parts.[2]

Finding Your Level

To assess your organization, you'll need input from multiple perspectives across your value chain. Schedule focused conversations with key stakeholders with the goal of understanding both the current state of repair in your organization and the barriers to advancing this capability.

Plan to speak with representatives from five key stakeholder groups. For each group, you'll see specific questions designed to uncover how this capability is valued and implemented across your organization. Take notes during these conversations—the patterns that emerge will help you identify your organization's current level and next steps.

After gathering responses to these questions, look for patterns:

- If most answers focus on internal resource management with limited coordination, you're likely at Level 1
- If you see some network optimization but limited data sharing, you're probably at Level 2
- If transparent resource coordination influences decisions but isn't yet driving strategy, you're at Level 3
- If network-wide optimization actively drives innovation and efficiency, you've reached Level 4

FOR EXECUTIVE LEADERSHIP

1 How does resource optimization factor into our network strategy?

2 What investments are we making in coordination capabilities?

3 How do we measure network-wide efficiency?

4 What role does transparency play in resource decisions?

5 How do we balance local optimization with network benefits?

FOR OPERATIONS TEAMS

1 How do we coordinate resources across partners?

2 What systems support network optimization?

3 How do we share resource availability data?

4 What prevents better network coordination?

5 How do we verify resource utilization?

FOR NETWORK PARTNERS

1 How do we share resource information?

2 What coordination mechanisms exist?

3 How do we optimize across organizations?

4 What barriers prevent better resource sharing?

5 How do we maintain efficient allocation?

FOR TECHNOLOGY TEAMS

1 What platforms support network optimization?

2 How do we ensure data visibility and security?

3 What analytics enable resource coordination?

4 How do we integrate partner systems?

5 What prevents better network visibility?

FOR PLANNING TEAMS

1 How do we optimize across the network?

2 What metrics track resource efficiency?

3 How do we coordinate capacity?

4 What role does shared data play?

5 How do we predict resource needs?

Level 1 (Beginning)

Organizations at this level view resource optimization primarily within their own boundaries—similar to how traditional operations managed resources before the transparent network in the fictional example. Like early efficiency efforts, these organizations focus on local optimization without considering network-wide opportunities. Resource coordination is limited to immediate partners.

Key characteristics:

- Resources managed internally
- Limited network coordination
- Basic efficiency metrics
- Minimal sharing of resource data

NEXT STEPS FOR LEVEL 1

Review your assessment results with your leadership team. The goal is to create a shared understanding of your current state and align network optimization opportunities.

Consider these targeted actions:

- Map resource flows across immediate partners
- Begin tracking network-wide utilization
- Identify key points for coordination
- Engage partners in optimization discussions

Level 2 (Developing)

Organizations at this level look like early coordination efforts in the fictional example, when they first began optimizing across repair locations. Like the initial network, they've started sharing resource data but haven't fully integrated network-wide optimization. Similar to the early challenges with data transparency in the fictional example, these organizations struggle with coordination but recognize its potential value.

Key characteristics:

- Basic network coordination established
- Some sharing of resource data
- Limited cross-organization optimization
- Initial efficiency metrics defined

NEXT STEPS FOR LEVEL 2

Focus on systematically expanding network optimization. Build connections between different resource pools and create formal processes for coordination and sharing.

Consider these targeted actions:

- Develop a network efficiency dashboard
- Implement resource-sharing protocols
- Create standardized coordination methods
- Launch a network optimization program
- Establish a process for tracking benefits

Level 3 (Advanced)

Organizations at this level operate like the maturing network in the fictional example, with transparent coordination driving operations. Just as the network expanded to balance loads across facilities, these organizations maintain comprehensive visibility and optimization across their network. Like the system of AI-driven coordination in the fictional example, they actively use shared data to improve efficiency.

Key characteristics:

- Coordination integrated into strategy
- Comprehensive resource visibility
- Active network optimization
- Shared data drives decisions

NEXT STEPS FOR LEVEL 3

Work on expanding optimization across your network. Create formal programs for improving coordination, develop capabilities to scale efficient operations, and begin influencing industry practices.

Consider these targeted actions:

- Establish a network innovation program
- Create automated optimization systems
- Develop strategy for scaling coordination
- Implement comprehensive efficiency tools
- Set network-wide optimization metrics

Level 4 (Leading)

Organizations at this level have achieved what the network accomplished in the fictional example through their cross-industry partnerships—transforming transparent coordination into a core competitive advantage. Like the expanding network of optimized flows in the fictional example, they've developed systems for balancing resources across diverse partners. Similar to how the success led manufacturers to join their network, these leading organizations influence their entire industry's approach to resource optimization.

Key characteristics:

- Coordination drives network innovation
- Advanced optimization systems
- Active development of sharing protocols
- Industry leadership in efficiency

NEXT STEPS FOR LEVEL 4

Focus on leading industry transformation toward network optimization. Share knowledge openly to build efficient ecosystems and develop new business models based on coordination capabilities.

Consider these targeted actions:

- Create an open platform for sharing best practices
- Develop industry-standard coordination methods
- Launch optimization-based business models
- Establish network innovation centers
- Lead development of industry standards
- Create coordination-focused partner programs

Notes

1 Association for Supply Chain Management (2023) Microsoft computes a winning strategy for supply chain sustainability, www.ascm.org/ascm-insights/microsoft-computes-a-winning-strategy-for-supply-chain-sustainability/ (archived at https://perma.cc/ABF5-KZGF)

2 Caterpillar (n.d.) 3 cost-saving maintenance strategies, www.cat.com/en_US/articles/solutions/oil-gas/3-cost-saving-maintenance-strategies.html (archived at https://perma.cc/CT2R-BP8W)

22

Technology Capabilities

Digital Enablement to Collaborate Transparently

Digital infrastructure can accelerate transparent collaboration for circular supply chains. Technology can evolve to create trusted product memories, enable predictive recovery intelligence, and orchestrate complex partner networks. While processes and people drive operations, it's the technological capabilities that make transparency scalable—from digital twins tracking material journeys to AI systems optimizing recovery. Leading organizations recognize that these three capabilities form the technical foundation for trusted circular systems: Digital product memory, predictive analytics, and network orchestration platforms.

Digital Product Memory to Collaborate Transparently

Creating comprehensive digital records that track a product's complete history through multiple lifecycles, repairs, and material changes.

In Chapter 4, we explored how traditional tracking systems needed to grow to manage products through multiple lifecycles. For example, "digital twin plus" systems maintain complete, verified histories of every product and material. Where traditional systems track basic location data, new networks can create trusted digital records of every transformation.

The fictional example shows this capability through the handling of components, where each item carried a complete digital history—from material origin through recovery processes to final validation. Their system not only tracked what happened, but verified each step through independent monitoring systems, creating trust through transparency.

Leading organizations show similar capabilities. IBM's Food Trust platform creates verified digital records of food products from farm to consumer, demonstrating how digital tracking builds trust in complex supply chains. Intel's Transparent Supply Chain program uses digital passports to verify component authenticity through multiple supply chain tiers, showing how transparent tracking can ensure product integrity.

Finding Your Level

To assess your organization, you'll need input from multiple perspectives across your value chain. Schedule focused conversations with key stakeholders with the goal of understanding both the current state of repair in your organization and the barriers to advancing this capability.

Plan to speak with representatives from five key stakeholder groups. For each group, you'll see specific questions designed to uncover how this capability is valued and implemented across your organization. Take notes during these conversations—the patterns that emerge will help you identify your organization's current level and next steps.

After gathering responses to these questions, look for patterns:

- If most answers focus on basic product tracking and minimal data sharing, you're likely at Level 1
- If you see digital tracking systems but limited integration or verification, you're probably at Level 2
- If digital product data actively enables collaboration but isn't yet driving innovation, you're at Level 3
- If comprehensive digital product histories are creating new value across networks, you've reached Level 4

FOR ENGINEERING TEAMS

1 How do we capture and verify product transformation data?
2 What systems track products through multiple lifecycles?
3 How do we share product data with external partners?
4 What prevents more comprehensive product tracking?
5 How do we validate data accuracy across the network?

FOR OPERATIONS TEAMS

1   What digital tools support product traceability?

2   How do we document product changes and modifications?

3   What verification processes exist for shared data?

4   How do we coordinate tracking across facilities?

5   What barriers prevent better product transparency?

FOR TECHNOLOGY TEAMS

1   What platforms manage our product digital twins?

2   How do we ensure data security and accessibility?

3   What capabilities exist for external data sharing?

4   How do we integrate data from multiple sources?

5   What prevents more automated product tracking?

FOR QUALITY TEAMS

1   How do we verify product history data?

2   What metrics track product integrity over time?

3   How do we validate data from external sources?

4   What role does transparency play in quality assurance?

5   How do we maintain data consistency across partners?

FOR EXECUTIVE LEADERSHIP

1   How does product data transparency factor into our business strategy?

2   What investments are we making in digital tracking infrastructure?

3   How do we measure value created through data sharing?

4   What role does product transparency play in stakeholder trust?

5   How do we balance data openness with intellectual property protection?

Level 1 (Beginning)

Organizations at this level maintain basic product records with minimal sharing, similar to how the network began with simple repair documentation in the fictional example. These organizations track basic location and maintenance data but lack the digital infrastructure for comprehensive product histories.

Key characteristics:

- Basic product tracking focused on location and status
- Limited digital documentation of changes or modifications
- Minimal data sharing with external partners
- No formal verification of shared information

NEXT STEPS FOR LEVEL 1

Review your assessment results with your leadership team. The goal is to create a shared understanding of your current state and align digital tracking opportunities.

Consider these targeted actions:

- Begin systematically documenting product changes and modifications
- Identify critical product data needed by key stakeholders
- Create basic digital records for high-value products
- Implement a standard process for validating shared data

Level 2 (Developing)

Organizations at this level look like the early transparency efforts in the fictional example, when the network first began tracking component histories. Like the initial digital tracking system in the fictional example, they've established basic digital documentation but haven't yet created comprehensive product memories. These organizations can verify some product data but struggle to provide complete traceability.

Key characteristics:

- Digital tracking systems established for key products
- Basic verification of critical product data
- Limited integration between tracking systems
- Product histories focused on internal operations

NEXT STEPS FOR LEVEL 2

Focus on expanding your digital tracking capabilities while building verification systems. Create connections between different data sources and begin standardizing how product information is captured and shared.

Consider these targeted actions:

- Implement digital twin technology for critical products
- Develop standard protocols for data verification
- Create integration between tracking systems
- Establish a process for external data sharing
- Build basic analytics capabilities for product data

Level 3 (Advanced)

Organizations at this level have comprehensive digital tracking that enables trusted collaboration, operating like the mature transparency network in the fictional example. Just as the network expanded to serve multiple industries, these organizations maintain verified product histories that partners can trust. Like the system of "trust layers," they actively use digital product data to enable collaboration while protecting sensitive information.
Key characteristics:

- Comprehensive digital product histories maintained
- Verified data sharing with external partners
- Integrated tracking across operations
- Product data actively enables collaboration

NEXT STEPS FOR LEVEL 3

Work on expanding your digital product memory capabilities across your network. Create systems for capturing innovation opportunities from shared data and begin using product histories to drive strategic decisions.
Consider these targeted actions:

- Implement predictive analytics using product histories
- Create automated verification systems
- Develop cross-industry data-sharing protocols
- Launch a digital product passport program
- Set organization-wide transparency metrics

Level 4 (Leading)

Organizations at this level show that digital product memory is a strategic advantage. Like the "digital twin plus" system, they've developed capabilities for tracking and verifying every aspect of a product's life. Similar to how the success led to cross-industry innovation in the fictional example, these organizations use comprehensive product histories to create new value across networks.

Key characteristics:

- Digital product histories drive innovation and strategy
- Advanced verification and analytics capabilities
- Active development of new value from shared data
- Industry leadership in product transparency

NEXT STEPS FOR LEVEL 4

Focus on leading industry transformation toward transparent product tracking. Share knowledge to build trust across networks and develop new business models based on verified product histories.

Consider these targeted actions:

- Create open standards for product tracking
- Develop industry-wide verification protocols
- Launch transparency-based business models
- Establish innovation programs based on shared data
- Lead development of industry traceability standards
- Create ecosystem-wide transparency initiatives

Predictive Recovery Intelligence to Collaborate Transparently

Using AI and analytics to determine optimal repair strategies and material reuse opportunities based on product condition and market needs.

In Chapter 4, we explored how traditional recovery approaches needed to evolve beyond individual expertise, such as AI systems that can analyze verified data across industries to optimize recovery operations. Where traditional systems work with limited information, trusted data from multiple sources can predict and improve outcomes.

The fictional example shows this capability through the AI's ability to identify patterns across medical, aerospace, and electronics manufacturing, discovering improvements that would be impossible to spot without transparent data sharing. Their system could predict material performance and optimize recovery processes by learning from verified data across the entire network.

Leading organizations demonstrate similar capabilities. Siemens' MindSphere platform analyzes shared operational data to predict maintenance needs across industrial equipment, showing how transparent data enables predictive intelligence. Similarly, Nokia's AVA system uses shared network data to predict and prevent equipment failures, demonstrating how trusted data sharing improves recovery operations.

Finding Your Level

To assess your organization, you'll need input from multiple perspectives across your value chain. Schedule focused conversations with key stakeholders with the goal of understanding both the current state of repair in your organization and the barriers to advancing this capability.

Plan to speak with representatives from five key stakeholder groups. For each group, you'll see specific questions designed to uncover how this capability is valued and implemented across your organization. Take notes during these conversations—the patterns that emerge will help you identify your organization's current level and next steps.

After gathering responses to these questions, look for patterns:

- If most answers focus on reactive recovery with minimal prediction, you're likely at Level 1
- If you see basic analytics but limited integration across operations, you're probably at Level 2
- If predictive capabilities actively guide recovery but aren't yet driving innovation, you're at Level 3
- If advanced AI is optimizing recovery across networks, you've reached Level 4

FOR ENGINEERING TEAMS

1 How do we predict potential recovery opportunities?

2 What systems analyze recovery performance?

3 How do we share recovery insights across operations?

4 What prevents better recovery prediction?

5 How do we validate predictive models?

FOR OPERATIONS TEAMS

1 What predictive tools guide recovery decisions?

2 How do we track recovery success rates?

3 What data drives recovery optimization?

4 How do we coordinate recovery across facilities?

5 What barriers prevent better prediction?

FOR ANALYTICS TEAMS

1 What platforms support recovery prediction?

2 How do we ensure model accuracy?

3 What data sources inform our predictions?

4 How do we integrate external data?

5 What prevents more analysis?

FOR RECOVERY TEAMS

1 How do predictions influence recovery processes?

2 What metrics guide recovery decisions?

3 How do we validate prediction accuracy?

4 What role does shared data play in recovery?

5 How do we maintain prediction quality?

FOR EXECUTIVE LEADERSHIP

1 How does predictive analysis inform our recovery strategy?

2 What investments are we making in recovery intelligence?

3 How do we measure the value of predictive capabilities?

4 What role does shared data play in recovery planning?

5 How do we balance prediction accuracy with data access?

Level 1 (Beginning)

Organizations at this level operate reactively with minimal prediction, similar to how the network began with basic repair tracking in the fictional example. Like the early days of their recovery operations, these organizations respond to failures rather than predicting and preventing them.

Key characteristics:

- Reactive approach to recovery operations
- Limited use of historical data
- Minimal predictive capabilities
- No systematic learning from recovery data

NEXT STEPS FOR LEVEL 1

Review your assessment results with your leadership team. The goal is to create a shared understanding of your current state and align predictive opportunities.

Consider these targeted actions:

- Begin collecting structured recovery data
- Identify key recovery metrics to track
- Create a basic recovery performance dashboard
- Implement a standard process for data collection

Level 2 (Developing)

Organizations at this level look like the early efforts in the fictional example, when the network first began analyzing repair patterns. Like the initial system in the fictional example, they've established basic tracking capabilities but haven't yet created comprehensive recovery intelligence. These organizations can predict some failures but struggle to provide consistent optimization.

Key characteristics:

- Basic predictive models established
- Some use of historical data for planning
- Limited integration of data sources
- Predictions focused on common failures

NEXT STEPS FOR LEVEL 2

Focus on expanding your predictive capabilities while building data integration. Create connections between different recovery operations and begin standardizing how insights are captured and shared.

Consider these targeted actions:

- Implement machine learning for key processes
- Develop standard data collection protocols
- Create integration between prediction systems
- Establish a process for sharing insights
- Build basic optimization capabilities

Level 3 (Advanced)

Organizations at this level operate with analytics enabling proactive recovery. Just as the fictional example's network expanded to serve multiple industries, these organizations maintain predictive models that partners can rely on. They actively use shared data to optimize recovery while protecting sensitive information.

Key characteristics:

- Comprehensive predictive models deployed
- Active optimization of recovery operations
- Integrated data analysis across network
- Predictions actively guide decisions

NEXT STEPS FOR LEVEL 3

Work on expanding your predictive capabilities across your network. Create systems for capturing innovation opportunities from shared insights and begin using predictions to drive strategic decisions.

Consider these targeted actions:

- Implement advanced AI for recovery optimization
- Create automated learning systems
- Develop cross-industry prediction models
- Launch a predictive maintenance program
- Set network-wide optimization metrics

LEVEL 4 (LEADING)

Organizations at this level have developed recovery intelligence into an important capability, and have developed capabilities for predicting and optimizing across networks. These organizations use predictive intelligence to create new value across industries.

Key characteristics:

- AI-driven recovery optimization at scale
- Advanced learning and prediction capabilities
- Active development of new recovery insights
- Industry leadership in predictive analytics

NEXT STEPS FOR LEVEL 4

Focus on leading industry transformation toward predictive recovery. Share knowledge to build learning networks and develop new business models based on predictive capabilities.

Consider these targeted actions:

- Create open standards for recovery analytics
- Develop industry-wide prediction protocols
- Launch AI-based optimization services
- Establish innovation programs based on shared learning
- Lead development of industry prediction standards
- Create ecosystem-wide optimization initiatives

Network Orchestration Platform to Collaborate Transparently

Building integrated systems that coordinate material flows, repairs, and reintegration across the circular ecosystem.

In Chapter 4, we explored how traditional systems struggled to optimize across organizational boundaries. Where traditional platforms managed simple handoffs, improved systems orchestrate multi-party collaborations through verified data sharing.

The fictional example shows this through the ability to orchestrate material flows across a network of manufacturers, with the system tracking and verifying every batch through a "digital twin plus" that includes complete history and verification records.

Their platform could optimize complex networks of recovery and reuse while maintaining trust through transparent tracking and verification.

Leading organizations show similar capabilities. Eastman's molecular recycling facilities utilize advanced technology to break down hard-to-recycle plastics into their molecular building blocks, allowing for infinite recycling and resource recovery. This process promotes collaboration across industries while ensuring traceability of materials. Similarly, Transparency-One connects global supply chains, allowing companies to monitor and analyze suppliers and components in real-time, which helps with responsible sourcing and better decision-making throughout the supply chain.

Finding Your Level

To assess your organization, you'll need input from multiple perspectives across your value chain. Schedule focused conversations with key stakeholders with the goal of understanding both the current state of repair in your organization and the barriers to advancing this capability.

Plan to speak with representatives from five key stakeholder groups. For each group, you'll see specific questions designed to uncover how this capability is valued and implemented across your organization. Take notes during these conversations – the patterns that emerge will help you identify your organization's current level and next steps.

After gathering responses to these questions, look for patterns:

- If most answers focus on basic coordination with minimal integration, you're likely at Level 1
- If you see digital platforms but limited network optimization, you're probably at Level 2
- If network orchestration actively enables collaboration but isn't yet driving innovation, you're at Level 3
- If advanced platforms are optimizing value across networks, you've reached Level 4

FOR PLATFORM TEAMS

1 How do we coordinate network activities?
2 What systems manage partner interactions?
3 How do we optimize network flows?
4 What prevents better network integration?
5 How do we validate platform performance?

FOR OPERATIONS TEAMS

1 What platforms support network coordination?

2 How do we manage multi-party processes?

3 What capabilities exist for network optimization?

4 How do we coordinate with partners?

5 What barriers prevent better orchestration?

FOR TECHNOLOGY TEAMS

1 What infrastructure supports our network?

2 How do we ensure platform security?

3 What integration capabilities exist?

4 How do we manage network data?

5 What prevents more automated coordination?

FOR PARTNER MANAGEMENT TEAMS

1 How do platforms enable collaboration?

2 What metrics track network performance?

3 How do we validate partner interactions?

4 What role does transparency play in coordination?

5 How do we maintain network integrity?

FOR EXECUTIVE LEADERSHIP

1 How does network coordination factor into our strategy?

2 What investments are we making in orchestration platforms?

3 How do we measure network effectiveness?

4 What role does shared infrastructure play in partnerships?

5 How do we balance control with collaboration?

Level 1 (Beginning)

Organizations at this level maintain basic network connections with minimal coordination, similar to how the network began with simple repair tracking in the fictional example. Like the early days of their orchestration journey, these organizations manage basic partner interactions but lack the infrastructure for network optimization.

Key characteristics:

- Basic partner coordination systems
- Limited digital integration
- Minimal network optimization
- No formal orchestration platform

NEXT STEPS FOR LEVEL 1

Review your assessment results with your leadership team. The goal is to create a shared understanding of your current state and align network orchestration opportunities.

Consider these targeted actions:

- Begin mapping network interactions
- Identify key coordination points
- Create a basic partner dashboard
- Implement standard communication protocols

Level 2 (Developing)

Organizations at this level look like the early orchestration efforts in the fictional example, when the network first began coordinating across facilities. Like the initial platform, they've established basic digital coordination but haven't yet created comprehensive network optimization. These organizations can manage simple flows but struggle with complex network orchestration.

Key characteristics:

- Digital platforms established for key processes
- Basic network visualization capabilities
- Limited optimization across partners
- Coordination focused on direct relationships

NEXT STEPS FOR LEVEL 2

Focus on expanding your platform capabilities while building network integration. Create connections between different operations and begin standardizing how activities are coordinated and optimized.

Consider these targeted actions:

- Implement network modeling tools
- Develop standard coordination protocols
- Create integration between platforms
- Establish a process for network optimization
- Build basic analytics for network performance

Level 3 (Advanced)

Organizations at this level operate like the mature network in the fictional example, with standardized protocols enabling complex coordination. Just as the network expanded to connect hundreds of organizations through trust layers and shared protocols, these organizations maintain platforms that partners can rely on. They actively optimize network flows while protecting participant interests.

Key characteristics:

- Comprehensive network orchestration deployed
- Active optimization across partners
- Integrated coordination across operations
- Platform actively enables innovation

NEXT STEPS FOR LEVEL 3

Work on expanding your orchestration capabilities across your network. Create systems for capturing innovation opportunities from network interactions and begin using platform insights to drive strategic decisions.

Consider these targeted actions:

- Implement advanced network optimization
- Create automated coordination systems
- Develop cross-industry orchestration models
- Launch a network innovation program
- Set ecosystem-wide performance metrics

Level 4 (Leading)

Organizations at this level show that network orchestration can be a competitive advantage, and have developed capabilities for optimizing complex networks. Similar to how success led to continuous improvement in the fictional example, these organizations use platform capabilities to create new value across ecosystems.

Key characteristics:

- AI-driven network optimization at scale
- Advanced orchestration capabilities
- Active development of network value
- Industry leadership in platform innovation

NEXT STEPS FOR LEVEL 4
Focus on leading industry transformation toward intelligent orchestration. Share platform knowledge to build ecosystem capabilities and develop new business models based on network optimization.

Consider these targeted actions:

- Create open standards for network orchestration
- Develop industry-wide coordination protocols
- Launch platform-based services
- Establish innovation programs based on network insights
- Lead development of industry orchestration standards
- Create ecosystem-wide optimization initiatives

23

Standards Capabilities

*Common Language for Circularity
to Collaborate Transparently*

Common frameworks can accelerate trusted collaboration across circular networks. Success requires developing shared approaches to measuring multi-life performance, enabling digital interoperability, and structuring ecosystem collaboration. While technology enables tracking, it's standardized methods that create mutual understanding—from verified quality protocols to data-sharing frameworks. Leading organizations recognize that these three capabilities establish the shared language needed for transparent circular operations: Multi-life performance metrics, digital interoperability standards, and ecosystem collaboration protocols.

Multi-Life Performance Metrics to Collaborate Transparently

Establishing clear standards for measuring product and material performance across multiple use cycles.

In Chapter 4, we explored how traditional standards focused on new production needed to expand. Where traditional metrics focused on single-use specifications, their network created trusted standards for continuous material circulation.

The fictional example shows this capability through the work with medical device manufacturers, where they developed verification protocols that multiple industries could trust. Their "trust layers" created standardized ways to measure performance while protecting proprietary information, enabling materials to flow confidently among applications.

Leading organizations show similar capabilities. The Ellen MacArthur Foundation's Circulytics provides standardized metrics for measuring circular performance across industries, showing how shared measurement enables trust in circular systems. ISO 59020's circular economy standards establish common frameworks for measuring product circularity, demonstrating how standardized metrics accelerate circular adoption.

Finding Your Level

To assess your organization, you'll need input from multiple perspectives across your value chain. Schedule focused conversations with key stakeholders with the goal of understanding both the current state of repair in your organization and the barriers to advancing this capability.

Plan to speak with representatives from five key stakeholder groups. For each group, you'll see specific questions designed to uncover how this capability is valued and implemented across your organization. Take notes during these conversations—the patterns that emerge will help you identify your organization's current level and next steps.

After gathering responses to these questions, look for patterns:

- If most answers focus on single-use performance metrics and basic quality measures, you're likely at Level 1
- If you see some tracking across multiple uses but limited standardization, you're probably at Level 2
- If performance metrics consistently track multiple lifecycles but aren't yet driving innovation, you're at Level 3
- If multi-life metrics actively drive design and strategy decisions, you've reached Level 4

FOR QUALITY TEAMS

1 How do we measure performance beyond first use?
2 What metrics track product degradation over time?
3 How do we verify performance after repair or remanufacturing?
4 What standards guide our multi-life quality assessment?
5 How do we ensure consistent measurement across lifecycles?

FOR ENGINEERING TEAMS

1 How do we incorporate lifecycle data into specifications?
2 What tools support multi-life performance tracking?

3 How do we validate performance after material recovery?

4 What prevents better lifecycle performance measurement?

5 How do we standardize testing across multiple uses?

FOR OPERATIONS TEAMS

1 How do we track performance through repair cycles?

2 What metrics guide remanufacturing decisions?

3 How do we measure recovered material quality?

4 What performance data influences production choices?

5 How do we maintain quality standards across cycles?

FOR SUPPLY CHAIN TEAMS

1 How do we verify supplier performance claims?

2 What metrics track material quality through recovery?

3 How do we measure circular supply chain effectiveness?

4 What prevents better performance tracking?

5 How do we share performance data across partners?

FOR CUSTOMER SERVICE TEAMS

1 How do we track product performance in the field?

2 What metrics indicate need for repair/replacement?

3 How do we measure customer satisfaction across multiple uses?

4 What performance data influences service decisions?

5 How do we capture lifecycle performance feedback?

Level 1 (Beginning)

Organizations at this level focus primarily on first-use performance metrics, similar to quality teams who struggle to evaluate refurbished product. They typically measure against new production standards only, with limited ability to assess performance through multiple lifecycles.

Key characteristics:

- Performance metrics focused on new production
- Limited tracking of product lifecycle performance

- Quality standards based on single-use scenarios
- Basic performance data collection

NEXT STEPS FOR LEVEL 1

Start tracking basic performance metrics beyond first use. Identify key indicators for multiple lifecycle performance and consider testing out new approaches with partners.
  Consider these targeted actions:

- Create a pilot program for measuring repaired product quality
- Engage with repair teams to understand performance needs
- Begin documenting performance through repair cycles

Level 2 (Developing)

Organizations at this level have begun tracking performance across multiple uses but lack standardized approaches. Like early circular operations, they recognize the need for lifecycle metrics but struggle with consistent measurement methods.
  Key characteristics:

- Some multi-life performance tracking established
- Basic repair quality measurements in place
- Limited standardization of lifecycle metrics
- Emerging focus on circular performance indicators

NEXT STEPS FOR LEVEL 2

Develop standardized multi-life testing protocols and create performance metrics dashboard for repair operations.
  Consider these targeted actions:

- Establish baseline measurements for material recovery
- Launch a pilot program for lifecycle performance tracking
- Begin correlating performance data across multiple uses

Level 3 (Advanced)

Organizations at this level maintain comprehensive performance metrics across multiple lifecycles, similar to how the team developed sophisticated correlations in the fictional example. They actively track and verify performance through multiple uses, with standardized measurement approaches.

Key characteristics:

- Standardized multi-life performance metrics established
- Comprehensive lifecycle quality tracking
- Performance data actively influences decisions
- Integrated measurement across repair and remanufacturing
- Clear protocols for verifying recovered material quality

Next Steps for Level 3

Establish predictive performance modeling capabilities, create cross-industry performance standards, and develop automated performance tracking systems.

Consider these targeted actions:

- Implement comprehensive lifecycle testing protocols
- Set performance-based circular economy targets
- Build partner network for shared performance metrics

Level 4 (Leading)

Organizations at this level have transformed multi-life performance metrics into a competitive advantage. They drive industry standards for circular performance measurement and actively shape how products are evaluated across multiple lifecycles.

Key characteristics:

- Performance metrics drive circular innovation
- Advanced lifecycle quality prediction systems
- Industry-leading measurement standards
- Performance data enables new business models
- Continuous improvement through lifecycle insights

NEXT STEPS FOR LEVEL 4

Lead development of industry performance standards. Create open platforms for sharing performance data and develop new circular metrics for industry adoption.

Consider these targeted actions:

- Establish innovation centers for measurement methods
- Launch performance-based circular business models
- Build industry coalitions for standardization
- Create supplier development programs based on lifecycle metrics

Digital Interoperability to Collaborate Transparently

Creating common data standards that enable seamless sharing of product information across the circular network.

In Chapter 4, we explored how traditional data systems struggled to support complex recovery networks. Where traditional systems created data silos, their network established common languages for sharing critical information while protecting sensitive data.

The fictional example shows this capability through the ability to share verified data between pharmaceutical, aerospace, and electronics manufacturers, each accessing exactly what they needed through standardized interfaces. Their digital infrastructure created trust through consistent, verified data sharing that multiple industries could rely on.

Leading organizations show similar capabilities. For example, GS1's EPCIS 2.0 standard enables trusted supply chain visibility across industries, showing how shared protocols enable transparent collaboration. The International Data Spaces Association's standards for secure data sharing demonstrate how standardized protocols enable trusted information exchange in circular networks.

Finding Your Level

To assess your organization, you'll need input from multiple perspectives across your value chain. Schedule focused conversations with key stakeholders with the goal of understanding both the current state of repair in your organization and the barriers to advancing this capability.

Plan to speak with representatives from five key stakeholder groups. For each group, you'll see specific questions designed to uncover how this capability is valued and implemented across your organization. Take notes during these conversations—the patterns that emerge will help you identify your organization's current level and next steps.

After gathering responses to these questions, look for patterns:

- If most answers focus on internal data systems with minimal sharing, you're likely at Level 1
- If you see some data exchange but limited standardization, you're probably at Level 2
- If standardized data sharing exists but isn't yet driving innovation, you're at Level 3
- If interoperability actively enables new value creation, you've reached Level 4

FOR IT TEAMS

1 How do we enable data exchange between systems?

2 What standards guide our data architecture?

3 How do we manage data security in sharing?

4 What prevents better system integration?

5 How do we validate data quality across systems?

FOR OPERATIONS TEAMS

1 How do we share data with partners?

2 What systems track circular material flows?

3 How do we manage product data through lifecycles?

4 What data barriers exist in partner collaboration?

5 How do we ensure consistent data across operations?

FOR ENGINEERING TEAMS

1 How do we share product specifications?

2 What tools support digital collaboration?

3 How do we track design changes across systems?

4 What prevents better data integration?

5 How do we maintain data accuracy across platforms?

FOR SUPPLY CHAIN TEAMS

1 How do we exchange data with suppliers?

2 What standards guide partner data sharing?

3 How do we track materials across networks?

4 What data synchronization challenges exist?

5 How do we verify shared data quality?

FOR QUALITY TEAMS

1 How do we share quality data across systems?

2 What standards ensure consistent measurement?

3 How do we validate data from partners?

4 What prevents better-quality data sharing?

5 How do we maintain data integrity across platforms?

Level 1 (Beginning)

Organizations at this level maintain primarily internal data systems with limited external sharing, similar to early supply chains before the transparency network in the fictional example. They typically struggle with data silos and inconsistent formats across systems.

Key characteristics:

- Limited data sharing beyond organization
- Inconsistent data formats and standards
- Manual data transfer between systems
- Basic digital tracking capabilities

NEXT STEPS FOR LEVEL 1

Map current data flows and systems to get a better understanding of flows and identify key data sharing needs from internal and external partners.

Consider these targeted actions:

- Create a pilot for standardized data exchange
- Begin documenting data standards
- Evaluate secure sharing platforms

Level 2 (Developing)

Organizations at this level have established some data exchange capabilities but lack comprehensive standards. Like the early repair documentation efforts in the fictional example, they recognize the need for better data sharing but struggle with consistent approaches.

Key characteristics:

- Basic data sharing established
- Some standardization of formats
- Limited partner data integration
- Emerging focus on interoperability

NEXT STEPS FOR LEVEL 2

Develop standardized data protocols using industry standards or collaborations and create data quality verification systems.

Consider these targeted actions:

- Establish a baseline for partner data exchange
- Launch a pilot for automated sharing
- Begin implementing common data standards

Level 3 (Advanced)

Organizations at this level maintain comprehensive data-sharing standards, similar to the "trust layers" that enabled secure information exchange in the fictional example. They actively share data across networks while protecting sensitive information.

Key characteristics:

- Standardized data exchange protocols
- Comprehensive sharing frameworks
- Active partner data integration
- Secure information exchange systems
- Clear protocols for data validation

NEXT STEPS FOR LEVEL 3

Establish predictive data analytics, create cross-industry sharing standards, and develop automated validation systems.

Consider these targeted actions:

- Implement comprehensive data governance
- Set interoperability performance targets
- Build partner network for data exchange

Level 4 (Leading)

Organizations at this level have transformed digital interoperability into strategic advantage, similar to how the network enabled complex material flows in the fictional example. They drive industry standards for data sharing and actively shape how information moves across circular networks.

Key characteristics:

- Interoperability drives innovation
- Advanced data exchange systems
- Industry-leading sharing standards
- Data enables new business models
- Continuous improvement through shared insights

NEXT STEPS FOR LEVEL 4

Lead development of industry data standards, create open platforms for secure sharing, and develop new interoperability frameworks.

Consider these targeted actions:

- Establish innovation centers for data exchange
- Launch data-driven circular business models
- Build industry coalitions for standardization
- Create supplier development programs based on data sharing

Ecosystem Collaboration Protocols to Collaborate Transparently

Developing standard approaches for knowledge sharing and joint improvement across network partners.

In Chapter 4, we explored how traditional supplier relationships needed to expand for circular operations. Where traditional relationships limited information sharing, circular networks create frameworks for trusted partnership across industries.

The fictional example shows this capability through the ability to coordinate complex material flows, with clear protocols for what information to share and how to verify it. Their framework enabled collaboration while protecting each participant's sensitive data.

Leading organizations demonstrate similar capabilities. The Sustainable Apparel Coalition's Higg Index creates standardized protocols for sharing environmental impact data, showing how structured collaboration enables industry transformation. The World Business Council for Sustainable Development's circular metrics demonstrate how shared protocols enable trusted partnership across value chains.

Finding Your Level

To assess your organization, you'll need input from multiple perspectives across your value chain. Schedule focused conversations with key stakeholders with the goal of understanding both the current state of repair in your organization and the barriers to advancing this capability.

Plan to speak with representatives from five key stakeholder groups. For each group, you'll see specific questions designed to uncover how this capability is valued and implemented across your organization. Take notes during these conversations—the patterns that emerge will help you identify your organization's current level and next steps.

After gathering responses to these questions, look for patterns:

- If most answers focus on traditional supplier relationships with minimal collaboration, you're likely at Level 1
- If you see some ecosystem engagement but limited structure, you're probably at Level 2
- If standardized collaboration exists but isn't yet driving innovation, you're at Level 3
- If ecosystem collaboration actively creates new value, you've reached Level 4

FOR PARTNERSHIP TEAMS

1 How do we structure collaboration agreements?

2 What frameworks guide partner engagement?

3 How do we manage shared initiatives?

4 What prevents deeper collaboration?

5 How do we measure partnership success?

FOR OPERATIONS TEAMS

1 How do we coordinate with ecosystem partners?
2 What protocols guide shared operations?
3 How do we manage collective resources?
4 What barriers exist to collaboration?
5 How do we ensure consistent practices?

FOR INNOVATION TEAMS

1 How do we share developments with partners?
2 What frameworks protect intellectual property?
3 How do we collaborate on improvements?
4 What prevents collaborative innovation?
5 How do we scale shared solutions?

FOR SUPPLY CHAIN TEAMS

1 How do we integrate partner operations?
2 What standards guide network collaboration?
3 How do we manage shared resources?
4 What coordination challenges exist?
5 How do we optimize network performance?

FOR SUSTAINABILITY TEAMS

1 How do we align circular objectives?
2 What frameworks measure collective impact?
3 How do we share environmental data?
4 What prevents better collaboration?
5 How do we scale circular initiatives?

Level 1 (Beginning)

Organizations at this level maintain traditional supplier relationships with limited collaboration, similar to linear supply chains before the network in the fictional example. They typically focus on transaction-based relationships rather than ecosystem engagement.

Key characteristics:

- Traditional supplier relationships
- Limited partner collaboration
- Transaction-focused engagement
- Basic coordination mechanisms

NEXT STEPS FOR LEVEL 1
Map current partner relationships to understand current trust levels and identify collaboration opportunities.
Consider these targeted actions:

- Create a pilot ecosystem initiative
- Begin documenting shared practices
- Evaluate collaboration platforms

Level 2 (Developing)

Organizations at this level have established some ecosystem engagement but lack comprehensive frameworks. Like the early repair network in the fictional example, they recognize the value of collaboration but struggle with structured approaches.
Key characteristics:

- Basic ecosystem engagement established
- Some collaborative initiatives
- Limited standardization of practices
- Emerging focus on shared value

NEXT STEPS FOR LEVEL 2
Develop or join collaboration frameworks within and across industries and create a shared metrics system.
Consider these targeted actions:

- Establish a baseline for ecosystem initiatives
- Launch a pilot for structured engagement
- Begin implementing common standards

Level 3 (Advanced)

Organizations at this level maintain comprehensive collaboration frameworks, similar to how the network enabled complex coordination between industries in the fictional example. They actively manage ecosystem relationships while protecting partner interests.

Key characteristics:

- Standardized collaboration protocols
- Comprehensive partnership frameworks
- Active ecosystem management
- Shared resource optimization
- Clear value-sharing mechanisms

NEXT STEPS FOR LEVEL 3

Establish ecosystem innovation programs, create cross-industry collaboration standards, and develop automated coordination systems.

Consider these targeted actions:

- Implement comprehensive governance
- Set ecosystem performance targets
- Build a partner network for shared learning

Level 4 (Leading)

Organizations at this level have transformed ecosystem collaboration into strategic advantage, similar to how the network enabled new forms of value creation across industries in the fictional example. They drive industry standards for collaboration and actively shape how partners work together in circular networks.

Key characteristics:

- Collaboration drives innovation
- Advanced ecosystem orchestration
- Industry-leading partnership models
- Ecosystem enables new business models
- Continuous improvement through collective learning

NEXT STEPS FOR LEVEL 4

Lead development of industry collaboration standards, create open platforms for ecosystem engagement, and develop new partnership frameworks.
Consider these targeted actions:

- Establish innovation centers for collaboration
- Launch ecosystem-based business models
- Build industry coalitions for standardization
- Create supplier development programs based on ecosystem engagement

24

Governance Capabilities

Ensuring Circular Success to Collaborate Transparently

Trusted collaboration in circular networks requires robust governance structures. Frameworks are very important for sharing value fairly, ensuring quality across multiple lives, and enabling continuous evolution. While technology and standards enable tracking, it's governance mechanisms that maintain trust—from value distribution protocols to quality assurance systems. Leading organizations recognize that these three capabilities create the foundation for sustained circular collaboration: Value-sharing mechanisms, multi-life quality governance, and continuous evolution frameworks.

Value-Sharing Mechanisms to Collaborate Transparently

Creating frameworks that fairly distribute benefits among ecosystem partners who contribute to extending product life.

In Chapter 4, we explored how traditional value calculations needed to change for circular operations. Where traditional models focused on point-to-point transactions, circular networks create mechanisms for valuing transparency and trust.

The fictional example shows this capability through the approach to cross-industry innovation, where insights discovered through shared data can benefit multiple partners. When their AI identified correlations and insights that could benefit different manufacturers, these were automatically shared anonymously across the network, helping everyone improve their operations. Leading organizations demonstrate similar capabilities. The Ocean Plastic Leadership Network creates frameworks for sharing value from transparent plastic recovery, showing how governance enables collaborative circular systems. ReMade Institute's circular plastics program establishes mechanisms for distributing value from shared data and innovation, demonstrating how transparency governance accelerates circular adoption.

Finding Your Level

To assess your organization, you'll need input from multiple perspectives across your value chain. Schedule focused conversations with key stakeholders with the goal of understanding both the current state of repair in your organization and the barriers to advancing this capability.

Plan to speak with representatives from five key stakeholder groups. For each group, you'll see specific questions designed to uncover how this capability is valued and implemented across your organization. Take notes during these conversations—the patterns that emerge will help you identify your organization's current level and next steps.

After gathering responses to these questions, look for patterns:

- If most answers focus on traditional transactional relationships with limited data sharing, you're likely at Level 1
- If you see some value-sharing initiatives but limited formal governance, you're probably at Level 2
- If value sharing consistently influences decisions but isn't yet driving strategy, you're at Level 3
- If transparent value sharing actively drives ecosystem innovation, you've reached Level 4

FOR LEGAL/COMPLIANCE TEAMS

1 What governance structures support value sharing across partners?
2 How do we protect participant interests in collaborative projects?
3 What frameworks exist for managing shared IP?
4 How do we structure data-sharing agreements?
5 What prevents greater transparency with partners?

FOR OPERATIONS TEAMS

1 How do we capture value from shared operational insights?
2 What mechanisms exist for implementing cross-partner improvements?

3 How do we verify and validate shared data?

4 What systems support fair value distribution?

5 How do we measure collaborative benefits?

FOR INNOVATION TEAMS

1 How do we govern shared innovation processes?

2 What frameworks exist for collaborative development?

3 How do we distribute value from joint innovations?

4 What prevents greater innovation sharing?

5 How do we protect IP while enabling collaboration?

FOR PARTNERSHIP TEAMS

1 How do we structure value-sharing agreements?

2 What metrics track collaborative value creation?

3 How do we ensure fair benefit distribution?

4 What governance enables transparent collaboration?

5 How do we build trust through value sharing?

FOR EXECUTIVE LEADERSHIP

1 How do we measure and distribute value from shared data and insights?

2 What frameworks exist for rewarding collaborative innovation?

3 How do we balance individual IP protection with network benefits?

4 What role does transparency play in our partnership strategy?

5 How do we evaluate returns from collaborative initiatives?

Level 1 (Beginning)

Organizations at this level approach value sharing through traditional transactional relationships. They see limited value in data sharing and lack formal governance structures for collaborative value creation.

Key characteristics:

- Traditional supplier relationships with minimal data sharing
- No formal frameworks for collaborative value creation

- Limited transparency in partner interactions
- Value measured purely in transactional terms

NEXT STEPS FOR LEVEL 1

Review your assessment results with your leadership team. The goal is to create a shared understanding of your current state and align transparency opportunities.

Consider these targeted actions:

- Map potential value-creation opportunities from data sharing
- Identify a pilot collaborative project with trusted partner
- Create a basic framework for measuring shared benefits
- Develop initial data-sharing protocols
- Build a business case for transparency initiatives

Level 2 (Developing)

Organizations at this level mirror the early transparency efforts in the fictional example, when they were just beginning to demonstrate the value of shared data. Like the initial work with medical device manufacturers, they've started basic collaborative initiatives but lack comprehensive governance frameworks.

Key characteristics:

- Basic value-sharing initiatives established
- Some collaborative projects underway
- Initial frameworks for data sharing
- Limited mechanisms for distributing benefits

Next Steps for Level 2

Focus on developing formal governance structures for value sharing. Build frameworks for measuring and distributing collaborative benefits and create clear protocols for data sharing and value capture.

Consider these targeted actions:

- Develop a comprehensive value-sharing framework
- Create a formal collaborative innovation process

- Establish clear data-sharing protocols
- Implement a shared benefit-tracking system
- Build a partner engagement program

Level 3 (Advanced)

Organizations at this level operate like the mature transparency network in the fictional example, with value sharing fully integrated into their governance framework. Just as the network in the fictional example created "trust layers" that enabled sophisticated collaboration across industries, these organizations maintain comprehensive frameworks for measuring and distributing value from shared data and insights.

Key characteristics:

- Value sharing integrated into partnership strategy
- Comprehensive governance frameworks established
- Active collaborative innovation programs
- Sophisticated benefit distribution mechanisms

NEXT STEPS FOR LEVEL 3

Work on expanding value-sharing influence across your ecosystem. Create formal programs for capturing and distributing collaborative innovations and develop frameworks to scale transparent partnerships.

Consider these targeted actions:

- Establish innovation-sharing program with dedicated resources
- Create automated value-tracking systems
- Develop strategy for scaling collaborative networks
- Implement comprehensive value distribution guidelines
- Set network-wide transparency metrics
- Launch cross-industry innovation initiatives

Level 4 (Leading)

Organizations at this level have developed transparent collaboration into a critical capability, achieving what the network accomplished through their cross-industry partnerships in the fictional example. Like their expanding network that enabled innovations to flow between industries, they've developed sophisticated governance systems for capturing and sharing value across complex ecosystems.

Key characteristics:

- Value sharing drives ecosystem strategy
- Advanced frameworks for collaborative innovation
- Network-wide benefit distribution systems
- Industry leadership in transparent collaboration

NEXT STEPS FOR LEVEL 4

Focus on leading industry transformation toward transparent value sharing models. Share governance frameworks openly to build collaborative ecosystems and develop new business models based on network value creation.

Consider these targeted actions:

- Create an open platform for sharing governance frameworks
- Develop industry-standard value distribution protocols
- Launch ecosystem-based business models
- Establish transparency innovation centers
- Lead development of industry collaboration standards
- Create partner development programs focused on transparency
- Build mechanisms for scaling network benefits
- Implement predictive value-sharing analytics

Quality Assurance Through Multiple Lives to Collaborate Transparently

Implementing governance structures that maintain consistent quality standards across multiple product lifecycles.

In Chapter 4, we explored how traditional quality systems struggled with circular operations. Where traditional systems focused on point-in-time verification, circular networks create continuous quality assurance through transparent documentation.

The fictional example shows this capability through the work with medical device manufacturers, where transparent quality verification enabled critical components to enter circular flows. Their governance framework ensured consistent quality while protecting proprietary information, creating trust through verified documentation.

Leading organizations show similar capabilities. UL's Circularity Facts Program provides a governance framework that quantifies and assesses a company's circular economy efforts. This promotes transparency in sustainability initiatives and material flows. Another example is from the Healthcare Plastics Recycling Council (HPRC), which has established protocols that maintain quality standards in recycling processes for healthcare plastics, ensuring safety and sustainability throughout multiple material cycles.

Finding Your Level

To assess your organization, you'll need input from multiple perspectives across your value chain. Schedule focused conversations with key stakeholders with the goal of understanding both the current state of repair in your organization and the barriers to advancing this capability.

Plan to speak with representatives from five key stakeholder groups. For each group, you'll see specific questions designed to uncover how this capability is valued and implemented across your organization. Take notes during these conversations—the patterns that emerge will help you identify your organization's current level and next steps.

After gathering responses to these questions, look for patterns:

- If most answers focus on traditional quality control with limited lifecycle tracking, you're likely at Level 1

- If you see quality tracking across multiple uses but limited verification, you're probably at Level 2

- If quality governance consistently spans lifecycles but isn't yet driving innovation, you're at Level 3

- If transparent quality assurance actively enables circular operations, you've reached Level 4

FOR QUALITY TEAMS

1 How do we verify quality across multiple product lives?

2 What systems track product performance through multiple uses?

3 How do we maintain quality standards across partner networks?

4 What prevents better quality verification across lifecycles?

5 How do we document quality through transformations?

FOR ENGINEERING TEAMS

1 How do we validate product performance across multiple uses?

2 What frameworks exist for lifecycle quality assessment?

3 How do we verify recovered material quality?

4 What testing protocols span multiple lives?

5 How do we track quality degradation over time?

FOR OPERATIONS TEAMS

1 How do we maintain quality through recovery processes?

2 What systems verify remanufactured product quality?

3 How do we document quality across transformations?

4 What prevents better lifecycle quality tracking?

5 How do we ensure consistent recovery quality?

FOR COMPLIANCE TEAMS

1 How do we certify quality across multiple uses?

2 What frameworks verify regulatory compliance through recovery?

3 How do we maintain documentation across lifecycles?

4 What prevents better compliance verification?

5 How do we validate recovered product safety?

FOR PARTNER TEAMS

1 How do we align quality standards across networks?

2 What systems verify partner quality compliance?

3 How do we share quality data securely?

4 What prevents better-quality collaboration?

5 How do we build trust in recovered products?

Level 1 (Beginning)

Organizations at this level approach quality assurance through traditional single-life perspectives, without considering that multi-life performance can equal or outperform through high-quality repairs. Like the early days before the transparency system, these organizations struggle to verify quality beyond first use and lack frameworks for lifecycle quality governance.

Key characteristics:

- Traditional quality control focused on new production
- No formal tracking across multiple lives
- Limited verification of recovered materials
- Quality systems designed for single use

NEXT STEPS FOR LEVEL 1

Review your assessment results with your leadership team. The goal is to create a shared understanding of your current state and align lifecycle quality opportunities.

Consider these targeted actions:

- Map quality verification needs across product lifecycles
- Create a pilot for tracking quality through one recovery cycle
- Develop initial multi-life testing protocols
- Build basic recovered material quality standards
- Establish a framework for documenting product history

Level 2 (Developing)

Organizations at this level mirror the early quality verification efforts in the fictional example, when they were just beginning to prove recovered materials could meet medical device standards. Like the initial work establishing trust layers, they've started tracking quality across multiple uses but lack comprehensive governance frameworks.

Key characteristics:

- Basic lifecycle quality tracking established
- Some verification of recovered materials
- Initial frameworks for multi-use quality standards
- Limited quality documentation across transformations

NEXT STEPS FOR LEVEL 2

Focus on developing formal governance structures for lifecycle quality assurance. Build frameworks for verifying and documenting quality through multiple transformations and create clear protocols for quality validation.

Consider these targeted actions:

- Develop a comprehensive lifecycle quality framework
- Create a formal recovery validation process
- Establish clear documentation protocols
- Implement a quality tracking system
- Build a partner quality verification program
- Launch a recovered material testing program

Level 3 (Advanced)

Organizations at this level operate like the mature quality assurance network in the fictional example, with multi-life verification fully integrated into their governance framework. Just as the network enabled medical device manufacturers to trust recovered materials, these organizations maintain comprehensive frameworks for ensuring quality across multiple lifecycles.

Key characteristics:

- Quality verification spans multiple lives
- Comprehensive governance frameworks established
- Active quality tracking across transformations
- Sophisticated verification mechanisms

NEXT STEPS FOR LEVEL 3

Work on expanding quality influence across your ecosystem. Create formal programs for verifying quality through multiple transformations and develop frameworks to scale quality assurance.

Consider these targeted actions:

- Establish a quality innovation program with dedicated resources
- Create automated verification systems
- Develop a strategy for scaling quality networks
- Implement comprehensive testing guidelines
- Set network-wide quality metrics
- Launch cross-industry quality standards

Level 4 (Leading)

Organizations at this level show that quality verification is an important enabler of circular operations, achieving what the network accomplished through their multi-industry partnerships in the fictional example. Like the expanding network that enabled medical device repair with full material traceability and high confidence levels, they've developed sophisticated governance systems for ensuring quality across complex circular flows.

Key characteristics:

- Quality governance drives circular strategy
- Advanced frameworks for lifecycle verification
- Network-wide quality assurance systems
- Industry leadership in circular quality standards

NEXT STEPS FOR LEVEL 4

Focus on leading industry transformation toward circular quality models. Share governance frameworks openly to build verification ecosystems and develop new approaches to lifecycle quality assurance.

Consider these targeted actions:

- Create an open platform for sharing quality frameworks
- Develop industry-standard verification protocols
- Launch circular quality business models
- Establish verification innovation centers
- Lead development of recovery standards
- Create partner development programs focused on quality
- Build predictive quality analytics
- Implement cross-industry verification systems

Continuous Evolution to Collaborate Transparently

Establishing processes for ongoing improvement and adaptation of circular practices based on network learning.

In Chapter 4, we explored how traditional governance structures couldn't support ongoing improvement in circular networks. Where traditional structures focus on maintaining current operations, circular networks create governance for continuous improvement through shared learning.

The fictional example shows this capability through the AI's ability to identify and implement cross-industry improvements, with clear protocols for sharing innovations while protecting intellectual property. Their governance structure enabled the network to continuously evolve while maintaining trust through transparent verification.

Leading organizations show similar capabilities. The Carbon Trust's circular economy governance frameworks enable continuous improvement through transparent impact measurement, showing how structured evolution drives circular progress. The Sustainable Packaging Coalition's innovation program demonstrates how governance can accelerate circular development through shared learning and verified impact.

Finding Your Level

To assess your organization, you'll need input from multiple perspectives across your value chain. Schedule focused conversations with key stakeholders with the goal of understanding both the current state of repair in your organization and the barriers to advancing this capability.

Plan to speak with representatives from five key stakeholder groups. For each group, you'll see specific questions designed to uncover how this capability is valued and implemented across your organization. Take notes during these conversations—the patterns that emerge will help you identify your organization's current level and next steps.

After gathering responses to these questions, look for patterns:

- If most answers focus on internal improvements with limited sharing, you're likely at Level 1
- If you see some collaborative learning but limited systematic evolution, you're probably at Level 2
- If shared learning consistently drives improvement but isn't yet transformative, you're at Level 3
- If network-wide evolution actively drives circular innovation, you've reached Level 4

FOR INNOVATION TEAMS

1 How do we capture and scale improvements across networks?

2 What frameworks exist for shared learning?

3 How do we govern collaborative innovation?

4 What prevents faster evolution of capabilities?

5 How do we protect IP while enabling improvement?

FOR OPERATIONS TEAMS

1 How do we implement network-wide improvements?

2 What systems support continuous evolution?

3 How do we validate and scale new approaches?

4 What prevents better knowledge sharing?

5 How do we measure evolutionary success?

FOR TECHNOLOGY TEAMS

1 How do we enable network-wide learning?

2 What platforms support shared improvement?

3 How do we scale validated innovations?

4 What prevents faster capability development?

5 How do we track evolutionary progress?

FOR PARTNERSHIP TEAMS

1 How do we structure improvement sharing?

2 What frameworks govern collaborative evolution?

3 How do we build network learning capability?

4 What prevents better partner development?

5 How do we measure shared progress?

FOR STRATEGY TEAMS

1 How does network learning inform strategy?

2 What governance enables rapid evolution?

3 How do we balance stability and change?

4 What prevents faster transformation?

5 How do we lead industry evolution?

Level 1 (Beginning)

Organizations at this level approach evolution through traditional internal improvement processes, similar to how repair centers initially operated independently in the network in the fictional example. Like the early days before the AI system enabled shared learning, these organizations struggle to evolve beyond their own experience.

Key characteristics:

- Internal focus on improvement
- Limited network learning capability
- No formal evolution frameworks
- Improvements remain localized

NEXT STEPS FOR LEVEL 1

Review your assessment results with your leadership team. The goal is to create a shared understanding of your current state and align evolutionary opportunities.

Consider these targeted actions:

- Map potential network learning opportunities
- Create a pilot for sharing improvements with partners
- Develop initial knowledge-sharing protocols
- Build a basic improvement tracking system
- Establish a framework for collaborative learning

Level 2 (Developing)

Organizations at this level mirror the early network development in the fictional example, when improvements began flowing between repair centers. Like the initial work with cross-industry learning, they've started sharing improvements but lack comprehensive evolution frameworks.

Key characteristics:

- Basic improvement sharing established
- Some collaborative learning occurring
- Initial frameworks for network evolution
- Limited scaling of innovations

Focus on developing formal governance structures for continuous evolution. Build frameworks for capturing and scaling improvements across networks and create clear protocols for shared learning.

Consider these targeted actions:

- Develop a comprehensive evolution framework
- Create a formal improvement-sharing process
- Establish clear learning protocols
- Implement network improvement tracking
- Build a partner development program
- Launch a collaborative innovation system

Level 3 (Advanced)

Organizations at this level operate like the mature network in the fictional example, where AI-driven insights enabled continuous improvement across industries. These organizations maintain comprehensive frameworks for capturing and scaling innovations while protecting participant interests.

Key characteristics:

- Evolution integrated into network strategy
- Comprehensive governance frameworks established
- Active shared learning programs
- Sophisticated improvement scaling mechanisms

NEXT STEPS FOR LEVEL 3
Work on expanding evolutionary influence across your ecosystem. Create formal programs for scaling improvements and develop frameworks to accelerate network learning.

Consider these targeted actions:

- Establish innovation-scaling program with dedicated resources
- Create automated learning systems
- Develop strategy for accelerating evolution
- Implement comprehensive improvement guidelines
- Set network-wide learning metrics
- Launch cross-industry innovation programs

Level 4 (Leading)

Organizations at this level transform continuous evolution into a core network capability, achieving what the network accomplished through their AI-driven improvement system in the fictional example. Like the expanding network that enabled innovations to flow between industries, they've developed sophisticated systems for accelerating circular evolution.

Key characteristics:

- Evolution drives network strategy
- Advanced frameworks for scaling improvement
- Network-wide learning systems
- Industry leadership in circular innovation

NEXT STEPS FOR LEVEL 4

Focus on leading industry transformation through rapid evolution. Share governance frameworks openly to build learning ecosystems and develop new approaches to accelerating improvement.

Consider these targeted actions:

- Create an open platform for sharing evolutionary frameworks
- Develop industry-standard learning protocols
- Launch network-based innovation models
- Establish evolution accelerator centers
- Lead development of improvement standards
- Create partner acceleration programs
- Build predictive evolution analytics
- Implement cross-industry learning systems

PART SIX

Conclusion

25

Next Steps

Getting Started: Where Are You Today?

The journey to circular supply chains begins with understanding your current position. Throughout this book, we've explored 15 capabilities across people, process, technology, standards, and governance—from the network in the fictional example demonstrating how transparent collaboration creates trust, to real companies showing how digital product memories enable material tracking across lifecycles. Now it's time to bring these together to help you identify where to focus first.

Think of this assessment as taking a snapshot of your organization's circular capabilities—not to judge, but to understand. Just as the fictional example began with simple repair tracking before evolving into sophisticated material flows, your starting point creates the foundation for future transformation. Some capabilities will be more developed than others, and that's exactly as it should be.

Understanding Your Current State

Before diving into specific metrics, let's consider how circular thinking shows up in your organization today. Are circular principles part of strategic discussions, or do they remain confined to sustainability initiatives? Do your teams view materials as single-use resources or potential assets for multiple lifecycles? How do partners engage with your circular ambitions—as compliance requirements or opportunities for shared value creation?

These questions help frame the more detailed assessment that follows. Remember that no organization starts with perfect capabilities across all dimensions. The key is identifying where you have strong foundations to build upon and where focused development will create the most value.

We've explored these 15 capabilities many times together, and here's a summary of the levels so you can have another look at where your organization is today.

Rate your organization's current state in:

Circular Leadership

- Level 1: We view sustainability mainly as compliance
- Level 2: We have some circular initiatives but they're not strategic
- Level 3: Circular thinking influences most decisions
- Level 4: Circular principles drive our strategy and innovation

New Supply Chain Roles

- Level 1: Traditional supply chain roles dominate
- Level 2: Some specialized circular roles exist
- Level 3: Comprehensive circular roles established
- Level 4: Roles actively drive circular transformation

Continuous Learning

- Level 1: Learning happens individually with limited sharing
- Level 2: Basic knowledge sharing exists
- Level 3: Systematic learning across operations
- Level 4: Learning drives continuous innovation

Rate your organization's approach to:

Circular Value Streams

- Level 1: Linear, one-way material flows
- Level 2: Some circular flows identified
- Level 3: Active circular flow optimization
- Level 4: Value streams maximize circular potential

Smart Recovery

- Level 1: Basic repair and maintenance only
- Level 2: Some recovery processes standardized

- Level 3: Comprehensive recovery systems
- Level 4: AI-driven recovery optimization

Resource Optimization

- Level 1: Resources managed locally
- Level 2: Basic resource sharing exists
- Level 3: Network-wide resource optimization
- Level 4: Predictive resource orchestration

TECHNOLOGY CAPABILITIES
Evaluate your systems for:

Digital Product Memory

- Level 1: Basic product tracking only
- Level 2: Some lifecycle data captured
- Level 3: Comprehensive digital histories
- Level 4: Full digital twin capabilities

Predictive Recovery

- Level 1: Reactive maintenance approach
- Level 2: Basic predictive capabilities
- Level 3: Advanced prediction systems
- Level 4: AI-optimized recovery

Network Orchestration

- Level 1: Manual coordination dominates
- Level 2: Basic digital coordination
- Level 3: Integrated network platforms
- Level 4: Autonomous network optimization

STANDARDS CAPABILITIES
Assess your approach to:

Multi-Life Performance

- Level 1: Single-use specifications only
- Level 2: Some multi-use standards

- Level 3: Comprehensive lifecycle standards
- Level 4: Industry-leading circular standards

Digital Interoperability

- Level 1: Limited data sharing
- Level 2: Basic data exchange protocols
- Level 3: Standardized data sharing
- Level 4: Advanced network integration

Ecosystem Collaboration

- Level 1: Transactional relationships
- Level 2: Some partner collaboration
- Level 3: Active ecosystem engagement
- Level 4: Leading industry partnerships

GOVERNANCE CAPABILITIES
Evaluate your frameworks for:

Value Sharing

- Level 1: Traditional contract models
- Level 2: Basic value sharing exists
- Level 3: Comprehensive sharing frameworks
- Level 4: Advanced ecosystem value creation

Quality Assurance

- Level 1: Basic quality control only
- Level 2: Some lifecycle quality tracking
- Level 3: Multi-life quality systems
- Level 4: Leading quality frameworks

Continuous Evolution

- Level 1: Ad-hoc improvements
- Level 2: Basic improvement processes
- Level 3: Systematic evolution
- Level 4: Industry-leading innovation

Making Sense of Your Results

The patterns in your assessment tell an important story about your organization's circular journey. Areas where you consistently score at Level 1 aren't just gaps—they're opportunities to lay new foundations for circular operations. Level 2 capabilities show where you've begun the transition but haven't yet created systematic approaches. Level 3 areas demonstrate mature capabilities that can support broader transformation. Level 4 capabilities represent centers of excellence that can help pull the entire organization forward.

Consider the fictional example again—the company didn't start with sophisticated AI systems and verified material tracking. They began by documenting repair procedures, building trust through transparency, and gradually expanding their capabilities. Their early focus on creating value through simple improvements gave them credibility and resources to tackle larger transformations.

The key isn't perfecting every capability simultaneously. Instead, look for the intersections where strengthening one capability amplifies others. For example, improving digital product tracking often enhances both quality assurance and partner collaboration. Similarly, developing new circular roles frequently accelerates process improvement and innovation.

Let your assessment guide you toward these high-leverage opportunities. Which capabilities, if developed together, would create the most value for your organization? Where do you have strong foundations that could support broader transformation? What critical gaps might hold back otherwise promising initiatives?

Remember that this assessment isn't just a one-time exercise. Successful organizations regularly evaluate their capabilities, celebrating progress while identifying new opportunities for development. Use this as a living tool that evolves with your organization's circular journey.

Building Your Core Team

The transition to circular supply chains begins with people. Just as the network in the fictional example grew from a small team of repair specialists into a sophisticated collaborative ecosystem, your journey starts with bringing together the right mix of expertise, vision, and practical capabilities.

The Art of Team Composition

Think of building your circular team like assembling an orchestra. You need different instruments and skills, but what matters most is how they work together to create something greater than the sum of their parts. Your technical experts bring deep knowledge of systems and materials, like first violins laying down the melody. Operations specialists contribute practical know-how of getting things done, providing the rhythm and tempo. Business innovators add creative exploration of possibilities, like jazz improvisations that open new directions. Sustainability experts help ensure everything aligns with broader environmental and social goals, conducting the entire ensemble toward shared purpose.

The most successful teams we've seen don't necessarily start large. They begin with a small core group that combines critical perspectives. Consider how Philips Healthcare built their circular medical imaging program. They started with a team that brought together technical expertise in medical devices, operational experience in service and maintenance, and business innovation skills in developing new models. This combination allowed them to see opportunities others missed while maintaining the rigorous standards their industry demands.

Beyond the Core Team

However, circular transformation can't succeed in isolation. Like the fictional example's network that connected repair technicians with manufacturers and hospitals, your initiative needs strong links across the organization. Rather than creating a separate circular economy department, consider how to embed circular thinking throughout existing teams.

One effective approach we've seen is the "hub and spoke" model. A small core team acts as a central coordinating point, while a network of champions embedded in different functions helps drive change from within. This structure combines dedicated focus with broad organizational reach. Interface used this approach to great effect in their Mission Zero initiative, with sustainability champions in every facility helping to identify and implement circular opportunities.

The Power of Cross-Pollination

Some of the most powerful innovations emerge when different perspectives collide. When the team in the fictional example discovered that quality techniques from aerospace could improve medical device manufacturing, it came from having people who could bridge between industries and functions. Your team needs these "translators" who can help different parts of the organization see new possibilities in existing capabilities.

Regular cross-functional working sessions become crucial forums for this kind of innovation. These aren't meant to be update meetings. They are opportunities for different perspectives to combine in unexpected ways. For example, it may be that a medical device manufacturer will make breakthrough progress in circular design when their service technicians start joining product development reviews. This brings real-world repair experience into the design process.

Growing Your Team's Capabilities

Just as the network in the fictional example continuously evolved their capabilities, your team needs ongoing development, but this doesn't always mean formal training programs. Some of the most effective capability building happens through carefully structured projects that stretch people's skills while providing support for learning.

Consider starting with focused pilot projects that allow team members to develop new capabilities in a controlled environment. Look for opportunities where existing skills can be applied to circular challenges while building new expertise. Valeo began their circular journey by having their quality team apply their analytical skills to understanding product return patterns—building circular knowledge while leveraging proven capabilities.

Valeo's approach demonstrates how companies can leverage their teams' existing capabilities while building new circular economy knowledge. For instance, their remanufacturing process, which has been in place for over 40 years, allows their design and manufacturing experts to apply their skills to circular initiatives, such as disassembling, inspecting, cleaning, and testing used vehicle parts for remanufacture.[1]

Creating Your Circle of Stakeholders

Successful circular initiatives ripple outward through organizations like waves in a pond. At the center, executive sponsors provide the initial energy and direction. Their commitment creates momentum that spreads through functional leaders, engages front-line teams, and ultimately reaches external partners. Understanding how to work with each of these groups turns potential resistance into forward motion.

Consider how Ellen MacArthur first built support for circular economy initiatives. Her experience sailing solo around the world gave her a powerful metaphor for finite resources that resonated with executive—but she didn't stop there. She worked systematically to engage stakeholders at every level, creating a broad coalition that would become the Ellen MacArthur Foundation.

The Art of Executive Engagement

Executive support needs to be more than just verbal approval. It requires genuine understanding of how circular initiatives advance strategic objectives. The most successful organizations we've seen connect circular projects directly to existing priorities—whether that's cost reduction, risk management, or growth opportunities.

Take Renault's remanufacturing program. They gained executive support by demonstrating how local remanufacturing could reduce supply chain risks while improving margins. The initiative aligned perfectly with both operational and financial objectives, giving executives concrete reasons to champion the program. This wasn't only about sustainability; it was a new way to build business value.

Empowering Functional Leaders

Functional leaders often feel caught between competing priorities. The key is helping them see how circular initiatives can enhance rather than compete with their existing objectives. When Philips Healthcare began their circular transformation, they showed how improved product recovery data could help service teams reduce maintenance costs while supporting sustainability goals.

An effective approach is to involve functional leaders early in planning circular initiatives. The team at Philips Healthcare embedded circular economy principles into their strategy, developing a set of "circular KPIs" as part of a broader set of sustainability targets. They created a formal structure to ensure progress on their circular transformation journey, involving leaders across different functions. This approach allowed Philips to balance departmental needs while driving toward their circular economy goals, such as generating 25 percent of sales from circular products, services, and solutions by 2025.[2]

Engaging Front-Line Teams

The people closest to daily operations often have the deepest insights into circular opportunities. Just as the network in the fictional example grew stronger through insights from repair technicians, your initiative needs active engagement from front-line teams. This engagement has to be more than suggestion boxes—it needs to be a genuine dialogue about challenges and opportunities.

Consider how Vestas approached their wind turbine maintenance program. They created regular forums where field technicians could share insights directly with senior leaders. Many of their breakthrough innovations in predictive maintenance came from technicians who recognized emerging failure patterns. By giving front-line teams both voice and resources to implement improvements, they accelerated their circular transformation.

Building Partner Ecosystems

No organization can become circular alone. Even the highly capable network in the fictional example depended on collaboration with manufacturers, hospitals, and other partners. The art lies in creating partnerships that balance structure with flexibility—enough governance to ensure quality and fair value sharing, but enough freedom to enable innovation.

ASML began their reuse program working closely with a few key semiconductor customers. These early partnerships helped them develop the processes and trust mechanisms that would later support their global reuse network, achieving 94 percent active systems after 30 years.[3] They learned that successful partner ecosystems grow through demonstrated mutual benefit.

When Teams Face Headwinds

Every team encounters challenges, and it's how they respond that determines success. One common issue is scope creep—the temptation to tackle too many initiatives at once. Organizations can overcome this by adopting "focused flexibility"—maintaining clear priorities while remaining open to unexpected opportunities.

Another frequent challenge is the "not invented here" syndrome, where different parts of the organization resist adopting practices from elsewhere. The network in the fictional example overcame this by creating clear protocols for validating and sharing innovations, making adoption about improvement rather than criticism. Similar approaches have helped many organizations break down silos while maintaining high standards.

The key is viewing challenges as opportunities for strengthening your team rather than obstacles to progress. Each successfully navigated challenge builds capabilities that accelerate your circular transformation.

Cost-Effective Starting Points

The journey to circular supply chains often starts smaller than you might expect. While the end vision may seem transformative, the first steps can be remarkably practical. Just as the network in the fictional example began with simple repair documentation before evolving into AI-driven material optimization, successful organizations find ways to create value quickly while building toward larger ambitions.

Start With What You Already Know

Some of the most valuable circular opportunities are hiding in plain sight. Before investing in new systems or capabilities, look carefully at your existing operations. What materials currently leave your facilities as waste? Which products generate the most service calls? Where do quality issues typically arise? The answers often reveal immediate opportunities for value creation.

Consider how Authentise began their manufacturing execution journey. They started by simply tracking production parameters in their digital system. This basic data collection revealed patterns that would eventually lead to their comprehensive digital product passport program. They didn't begin with sophisticated blockchain technology—they began by understanding their core processes.

Building on Digital Foundations

Most organizations already have more digital capabilities than they realize. The same systems that track inventory, monitor quality, or manage maintenance can often be adapted to support circular initiatives. Before investing in new technology, explore how existing systems might help map material flows or document product transformations.

Fast Radius provides an excellent example. Their initial steps toward distributed manufacturing didn't require new tracking systems. Instead, they began using their existing production management platform to document which components were most frequently requested. This data helped them identify opportunities for local manufacturing while building the business case for more sophisticated digital coordination.

The Art of the Pilot Project

Selecting the right pilot project is like choosing where to plant a garden—the conditions need to be right for growth. The most successful pilots we've seen share certain characteristics. They're visible enough to demonstrate value but contained enough to manage risk. They engage key stakeholders without requiring universal buy-in. Most importantly, they create learning that supports broader transformation.

Take TerraCycle's Loop platform experience. They began with a small-scale reusable packaging program in Paris, working with a single retail partner. This focused approach allowed them to refine their processes and demonstrate value before expanding. Today their platform operates globally, but those early pilots provided essential learning about everything from logistics to consumer engagement.

The Power of Partner Selection

Your first circular initiatives don't need to encompass your entire supply chain. Start with partners who share your vision and have complementary capabilities. The key is finding opportunities where collaboration creates mutual benefit while building trust for larger initiatives.

Consider how ZenRobotics developed their waste sorting program. They began working with a small group of recycling facilities that already had strong material identification capabilities. These partners provided valuable insights about sorting accuracy while benefiting from new revenue streams through improved recovery rates.

Creating Momentum Through Success

The most effective circular initiatives build momentum through demonstrated success. Each small win provides resources and credibility for larger transformation. The key is being intentional about how you sequence initiatives to build capabilities while delivering value.

One automotive supplier began their circular journey by focusing on high-value materials that were relatively easy to recover. The revenue from these initial material recovery efforts funded more sophisticated sorting technology, which enabled them to handle more complex material streams. Each success created both financial and organizational capacity for bigger challenges.

Remember that circular transformation isn't about perfection—it's about progress. Start where you can create measurable value while building capabilities for larger change. Focus on opportunities that leverage existing strengths while developing new ones. Most importantly, remember that every successful circular supply chain started with a single step toward better material use.

Common Pitfalls and How to Avoid Them

Every transformation journey has its challenges, and circular supply chains are no exception. Having studied organizations across industries making this transition, we've observed patterns in both the obstacles they encounter and the strategies successful organizations use to overcome them.

The Perfection Trap

One of the most common pitfalls we see is waiting for perfect conditions before starting. Organizations sometimes believe they need complete data, perfect systems, or universal buy-in before beginning their circular journey. Yet the most successful transformations often start with imperfect but practical steps.

Consider how BASF approached their ChemCycling program. They didn't wait until they could track every molecule or predict every reaction. They began with a focused effort on specific plastic waste streams where they already had processing expertise. Their initial processes weren't perfect, but they created immediate value while building capabilities for expansion.

The Scale Illusion

Another frequent challenge is attempting to scale too quickly. Inspired by circular economy visions, organizations sometimes try to transform everything at once. This typically leads to overwhelmed teams, strained resources, and frustrated stakeholders.

The network in the fictional example offers an instructive contrast. They built their capabilities systematically, starting with basic repair tracking in one location before expanding to more sophisticated operations across London. Each expansion came after they'd proven success at a smaller scale. This measured approach allowed them to learn and adjust while maintaining quality and stakeholder confidence.

The Technology Temptation

It's easy to believe that the right technology will solve all circular challenges. While digital systems are important enablers, we've seen organizations invest in sophisticated platforms before developing the underlying processes and capabilities needed to use them effectively.

Tomra's success with sensor-based sorting came not from technology alone, but from careful development of processes and people. They began with basic material identification and sorting before investing in advanced AI-powered systems. This foundation-first approach ensured their technical investments supported rather than substituted for core capabilities.

The Isolation Risk

Some organizations try to build circular capabilities in isolation, either within a sustainability department or a single facility. While this might seem easier to manage, it often leads to solutions that can't scale or gain broader organizational support.

Like Arrival's micro-factories, they integrate design, production, and quality in a coordinated system. Their electric vehicle manufacturing works because it connects digital design, local production, and quality assurance in an integrated approach. This integration took longer to establish but created more sustainable results

The Metrics Misalignment

Traditional performance metrics can inadvertently work against circular initiatives. For example, purchasing teams measured on unit cost might resist paying more for repairable components, even when total lifecycle costs are lower.

When Umicore developed their precious metals recovery program, they adjusted their partner incentives to reward material recovery along with processing volume. This alignment of metrics with circular goals was crucial to program success.

Creating Your Roadmap

The path to circular supply chains is more like navigating by stars than following a printed map. While the destination might be clear, the exact route often reveals itself as you move forward. The most successful organizations combine clear direction with flexible navigation, allowing them to adapt while maintaining progress toward their goals.

Setting Your North Star

Before diving into detailed plans, successful organizations establish a clear vision of what they're trying to achieve. This isn't about buzzwords or vague aspirations—it's about tangible outcomes that create value for your organization and stakeholders.

Consider how Nokia approached their equipment recovery program. Their vision of maximizing component reuse gave clear direction while allowing multiple paths forward. Each decision, from repair protocols to testing procedures, could be evaluated against this ultimate goal.

Understanding Your Starting Point

Just as the network in the fictional example began by thoroughly understanding their current repair operations, your journey starts with honest assessment of your existing capabilities. Where do you already create circular value? What capabilities could be adapted for circular initiatives? Which stakeholders are already engaged in sustainability efforts?

Materialise's journey into manufacturing standards began with careful analysis of their production operations. They discovered they already had many of the capabilities needed for lifecycle performance measurement— from quality verification to material testing protocols.

Choosing Your First Mountains

While the ultimate goal might be transformative, the journey happens one step at a time. The art lies in choosing first initiatives that create immediate value while building capabilities for larger change. These "first mountains" should be challenging enough to matter but achievable enough to build confidence.

Take DMG Mori's approach to their open innovation centers. They began with high-value machining processes where they already had optimization expertise. This focused start allowed them to prove the business case while developing the collaboration and knowledge-sharing capabilities they'd need for expansion.

Building Your Base Camps

Major transformations need stable foundations. Just as mountaineers establish base camps for major climbs, successful circular initiatives need reliable support systems. These might be dedicated teams, proven processes, or trusted partner relationships that provide platforms for bigger changes.

Apple's recycling program shows how this works in practice. They began by establishing collection partnerships with key retailers before investing in their innovative recycling technologies. These partnerships provided stable material flows that justified more sophisticated recovery capabilities. Each base camp supported moves to higher levels of circular performance.

Planning Your Route

While the exact path might adjust, successful organizations maintain clear markers for progress. These aren't just calendar dates—they're capability milestones that indicate readiness for next steps. Think of them as waypoints that help confirm you're moving in the right direction.

The most effective roadmaps we've seen balance three horizons:

- Immediate actions that create momentum
- Medium-term initiatives that build capabilities
- Long-term transformations that reshape operations

Each horizon informs the others. Immediate successes provide resources for medium-term changes. Capability building enables larger transformations. Long-term vision guides near-term choices.

Next Steps Checklist

At this point, you might be wondering, "What should I do tomorrow morning?" While every organization's journey is unique, successful circular transformations often begin with similar concrete actions. Like the team in the fictional example starting their first repair hub, your initial steps create the foundation for everything that follows.

Your First 30 Days

Begin where discovery meets action. Start by gathering insights while taking small but meaningful steps forward. This isn't about dramatic changes—it's about building understanding while demonstrating commitment.

Spend time with your operations teams watching material flows. Which resources enter your facilities? What leaves as waste? Where do quality issues typically arise? These observations often reveal immediate opportunities for circular value creation. SABIC, a leading chemical manufacturer, has demonstrated this approach by developing a comprehensive plan to achieve carbon neutrality goals, which includes careful analysis of their production processes.

SABIC's strategy involves a multi-billion-dollar investment plan focused on reducing direct and indirect emissions by 20 percent compared to a 2018 baseline. Through this process, they are mapping their material flows and identifying areas for improvement, such as energy efficiency enhancements, renewable electricity adoption, and implementation of carbon capture, utilization, and storage infrastructure.[4]

Schedule conversations with key stakeholders. Ask customers about their sustainability challenges. Talk to suppliers about circular opportunities they see. Meet with repair teams to understand common failure patterns. These discussions not only provide insights but begin building the network of relationships you'll need for larger transformation.

Your First Quarter

With initial insights gathered, focus on proving what's possible. Choose one meaningful opportunity—perhaps a valuable material stream or common repair challenge—and demonstrate how circular thinking creates value. Arburg's journey with industrial machines began with understanding repair patterns in a single product line.

Build your core team during this period. Look for people who combine technical expertise with collaborative mindsets. Some of your best circular champions may already be experimenting with better ways to use resources or extend product life. Find them, support them, and connect them with others who share their vision.

Document everything during this period—what works, what doesn't, and what you learn along the way. These insights become invaluable as you scale. Markforged's success with adaptive manufacturing came from careful documentation of their first pilot projects in materials recovery.

Your First Year

As initial projects demonstrate success, focus on building systematic capabilities while maintaining momentum. Develop clear protocols for things that work. Create regular forums for sharing insights across teams. Begin engaging partners in longer-term planning.

This is when many organizations start seeing unexpected opportunities emerge. As teams gain confidence with circular principles, they often discover possibilities that weren't visible at the start. One automotive supplier's material recovery project led to innovations in product design that created whole new business opportunities.

The Journey Begins

The transition to circular supply chains represents one of the most significant transformations in industrial history. It requires rethinking not just how we make and move products and materials, but how we create and measure value. Yet as we've seen throughout this book, this transformation doesn't have to happen all at once. It begins with practical steps grounded in current realities while building toward larger possibilities.

Remember that every circular supply chain—from the network in the fictional example to Circularise's blockchain-based material tracking system—started with similar first steps. They began by seeing existing resources differently, engaging others in new possibilities, and systematically building capabilities that enabled larger change.

Your journey starts now, with the understanding you already have the capabilities present in your organization. The key is taking the first step. Don't wait for perfect conditions or complete solutions—take thoughtful action that creates immediate value while building toward your circular vision. The future of supply chains is circular, and your next step helps create that future.

The opportunity is to create supply chains that are more resilient, more innovative, and more capable of meeting the challenges of our time. The capabilities explored in this book provide a foundation for this transformation. The rest depends on people like you, taking the insights and tools provided here and applying them to create positive change in your own operations.

The journey to circular supply chains is one of continuous discovery and improvement. Each step teaches us something new about what's possible. I hope this book helps you take your next steps with confidence, knowing that while the path may not always be easy, the destination is worth the journey.

Notes

1   Valeo (2024) Circular economy in the automotive industry, www.valeo.com/en/preserving-natural-resources/ (archived at https://perma.cc/U8PJ-U8CG)
2   Ellen MacArthur Foundation (2021) Pioneering circularity in the healthcare industry: Royal Philips, www.ellenmacarthurfoundation.org/circular-examples/pioneering-circularity-in-the-healthcare-industry-royal-philips (archived at https://perma.cc/6L24-V2N4)
3   ASML (n.d.) Designing for circularity, www.asml.com/en/news/stories/2022/designing-for-circularity (archived at https://perma.cc/NS62-26UE)
4   World Economic Forum (2023) How the chemical industry can usher in a circular economy, www.weforum.org/stories/2023/03/chemicals-industry-low-carbon-economy/ (archived at https://perma.cc/3M8D-BPST)

INDEX

3D Hubs 181
3M 51–52

Abbott Laboratories 137
Additive Industries 171
Adidas 326
    LOOP 341–42
advertising, impact of 7–8
Amazon 10
AMCS Platform 282
AMFG 188
Apple
    Daisy (robot) 34
    recycling program 56, 421
    refurbishment 31
Arburg 62, 422
Arrival 154, 419
artificial intelligence (AI) 40, 48, 50, 96, 416
    AI-powered diagnostic systems 67,
        97, 85
    CoDAI (Collaborative Data & Artificial
        Intelligence) 266
    myVW Virtual Assistant 90
    see also predictive recovery; resource
        optimization
ASML 36–37
    partnerships 415
    roles in 44
    smart recovery 85
Asnæs Power Station 33
assessment, for your organization 407–11
augmented reality (AR) 40, 50, 153
    AR-guided repairs 50, 65, 67, 85, 102
    intelligent recovery 50, 102
Aurubis 255
Authentise 188, 416

BASF 245, 336, 418
Benyus, Janine 20–21, 22, 31
Beveridge Report 6
Beyond Zero 23
biofacturing 31
blockchain 272, 416, 423
Blue Economy initiative 21
BMW 32
    Automotive Service Technician Education
        Program 67

Boliden 261
Bosch 52
British welfare state, the 6
Building as Material Banks (BAMB)
        project 298
"Building the Circular Supply Chain" 19
Bulova 8
business case, for circular transformation 41

Carbon 226
Carbon Trust 400
Carpenter Technology 176
Caterpillar 27, 79–80
    augmented reality, use of 50, 102
    resource optimization 352
CHEP 30
circular leadership 43
    assessment 408
    collaboration, transparent 325–30
        advanced organizations 329–30
        beginning organizations 328
        developing organizations 328–29
        leading organizations 330
        real-world examples 326
        stakeholder questions 326–27
    in-market manufacture 153–58
        advanced organizations 157–58
        beginning organizations 155–56
        developing organizations
            156–57
        leading organizations 158
        real-world examples 154
        stakeholder questions 154–55
    local circulation 239–44
        advanced organizations 243
        beginning organizations 241–42
        developing organizations 242–43
        leading organizations 243–44
        real-world examples 240
        stakeholder questions 240–41
    repair at scale 61–67
        advanced organizations 65–66
        beginning organizations 64
        developing organizations 64–65
        leading organizations 66–67
        real-world examples 62
        stakeholder questions 62–63

circular value streams 46
  assessment 408
  collaboration, transparent 341–46
    advanced organizations 345
    beginning organizations 343–44
    developing organizations 344–45
    leading organizations 345–46
    real-world examples 341–42
    stakeholder questions 342–43
  in-market manufacture 170–75
    advanced organizations 174–75
    beginning organizations 172–73
    developing organizations 173–74
    leading organizations 175
    real-world examples 171
    stakeholder questions 171–72
  local circulation 255–60
    advanced organizations 259
    beginning organizations 257–58
    developing organizations 258–59
    leading organizations 259–60
    real-world examples 255–56
    stakeholder questions 256–57
  repair at scale 79–84
    advanced organizations 83
    beginning organizations 81–82
    developing organizations 82–83
    leading organizations 84
    real-world examples 79–80
    stakeholder questions 80–81
Circularise 272, 423
Closure Systems 288
"cobots" 12
coffee cups, disposable 3, 28
COMPOSITION Collaborative
    Ecosystem 214
consumer credit 7
container shipping 10
Continental 43
continuous evolution 56
  assessment 410
  collaboration, transparent 399–404
    advanced organizations 403
    beginning organizations 402
    developing organizations
      402–03
    leading organizations 404
    real-world examples 400
    stakeholder questions 400–01
  in-market manufacture 231–36
    advanced organizations 234–35
    beginning organizations 233
    developing organizations 234
    leading organizations 235–36
    real-world examples 231
    stakeholder questions 232–33

  local circulation 314–19
    advanced organizations 318–19
    beginning organizations 317
    developing organizations
      317–18
    leading organizations 319
    real-world examples 315
    stakeholder questions 315–16
  repair at scale 142–47
    advanced organizations 145–46
    beginning organizations 144
    developing organizations 145
    leading organizations 146–47
    real-world examples 142
    stakeholder questions 143–44
continuous learning 44–45
  assessment 408
  collaboration, transparent 336–40
    advanced organizations 339–40
    beginning organizations 338
    developing organizations 338–39
    leading organizations 340
    real-world examples 336
    stakeholder questions 337–38
  in-market manufacture 164–69
    advanced organizations 167–68
    beginning organizations 166–67
    developing organizations 167
    leading organizations 168–69
    real-world examples 164
    stakeholder questions 165–66
  local circulation 249–54
    advanced organizations 253
    beginning organizations 251–52
    developing organizations 252–53
    leading organizations 254
    real-world examples 250
    stakeholder questions 250–52
  repair at scale 72–78
    advanced organizations 76–77
    beginning organizations 75
    developing organizations 75–76
    leading organizations 77–78
    real-world examples 73
    stakeholder questions 74–75
COVID-19 pandemic 3, 12, 13
Cradle to Cradle certification system
    18–19, 315
"Cradle to Cradle: Remaking the Way We
    Make Things" 18
Crest 30
Cummins 48

Dell 346–47
Dentsu 8
Desktop Metal 204

digital interoperability 52–53
  assessment 410
  collaboration, transparent 379–83
    advanced organizations 383
    beginning organizations 381
    developing organizations 381–82
    leading organizations 384
    real-world examples 379
    stakeholder questions 380–81
  in-market manufacture 208–14
    advanced organizations 212–13
    beginning organizations 211
    developing organizations 211–12
    leading organizations 213–14
    real-world examples 209
    stakeholder questions 210–11
  local circulation 292–97
    advanced organizations 296–97
    beginning organizations 295
    developing organizations 295–96
    leading organizations 297
    real-world examples 293
    stakeholder questions 293–94
  repair at scale 119–24
    advanced organizations 122–23
    beginning organizations 121
    developing organizations 122
    leading organizations 123–24
    real-world examples 119
    stakeholder questions 120–21
digital passports 39, 40, 272, 359, 416
digital product memory 49
  assessment 409
  collaboration, transparent 358–63
    advanced organizations 362
    beginning organizations 360–61
    developing organizations 361–62
    leading organizations 362–63
    real-world examples 359
    stakeholder questions 359–60
  in-market manufacture 187–92
    advanced organizations 191
    beginning organizations 189–90
    developing organizations 190–91
    leading organizations 191–92
    real-world examples 188
    stakeholder questions 188–89
  local circulation 271–76
    advanced organizations 275
    beginning organizations 273–74
    developing organizations 274–75
    leading organizations 276
    real-world examples 272
    stakeholder questions 272–73
  repair at scale 96–102
    advanced organizations 100–01
    beginning organizations 99

developing organizations 99–100
    leading organizations 101–02
    real-world examples 97
    stakeholder questions 98–99
digital transformation 10–11
"digital twins" 358
  Digital Twin Orchestrator role 40
  "digital twin plus" systems 358
  ISO 23247 series 209
distributed repair networks 39
DMG Mori 164, 421
DoCoMo 11
"Doughnut Economics" 20

Eastman 369
e-commerce, growth of 10–11, 12
ecosystem collaboration 53
  assessment 410
  collaboration, transparent 383–88
    advanced organizations 387
    beginning organizations 385–86
    developing organizations 386
    leading organizations 387–88
    real-world examples 384
    stakeholder questions 384–85
  in-market manufacture 214–19
    advanced organizations 217–18
    beginning organizations 216–17
    developing organizations 217
    leading organizations 218–19
    real-world examples 214
    stakeholder questions 215–16
  local circulation 297–302
    advanced organizations 301–02
    beginning organizations 300
    developing organizations 300–01
    leading organizations 302
    real-world examples 298
    stakeholder questions 299–300
  repair at scale 124–29
    advanced organizations 128
    beginning organizations 126–27
    developing organizations 127–28
    leading organizations 128–29
    real-world examples 124
    stakeholder questions 125–26
Electronic Industry Citizenship Coalition
  (EICC) 288
electronics, in the supply chain 11
Ellen MacArthur Foundation 19, 30, 414
  Circular Electronics Partnership 298
  Circulytics 374–75
EOS 171
EPCIS standard 293
  EPCIS 2.0 379
EPEAT system 315
Ericsson 46

EU Circular Economy Action Plan 12
EY 221

Fairphone 13, 39, 44
Fast Radius 159, 417
Federal Communications Commission
        (FCC) 7
Fictiv 197
first 30 days, your 422
first quarter, your 422–23
first year, your 423
Ford Willow Run factory 7
Formlabs 226
Framework for Socially Responsible Ocean-
        Bound Plastic Supply Chains 304

GE Healthcare 45
global financial crisis, 2008 11
Globechain 342
"going to Gemba" 45
governance capabilities 54–56
    see also continuous evolution; quality
        assurance; value sharing
Great Recession, the 11
Green Electronics Council 315
GreenCircle 288
Grundfos 42
GS1 293, 379
Gyproc 33

Häagen-Dazs 30
Healthcare Plastics Recycling Council
        (HPRC) 395
Helen of Troy 27
Herman Miller 18
Higg Index 384
Hitachi Construction Machinery 46–47
HP 56
HPE 49
"hub and spoke" model 412
Hubs 197
Hyundai Robotics 12
    Food Trust platform 359

iFixit 39, 119
i-mode 11
Industrial Internet of Things (IIoT) 214, 266
industrial symbiosis 12–13, 33
Inkbit 192
Intel 359
Interface
    energy use 34
    Mission Zero initiative 13, 412
    Net-Works program 23, 124
    ReEntry program 23, 31, 240

International Data Spaces Association 379
International Material Data System
        (IMDS) 293
Internet of Things (IoT) 40
iPhone 11, 34
ISO 23247 series 209
ISO 59020 375

Jabil 164
"Jobs for Tomorrow: The Potential for
        Substituting Manpower for
        Energy" 18
John Deere 47, 221
Just-in-Time manufacturing 10

Lamers 36
Lenovo 50
light bulbs, planned obsolescence of 5–6, 28
Local Motors 154
Loop platform 30, 31, 304, 417
L'Oréal 8

MacArthur, Ellen 19, 22, 414
Markforged 176, 423
Materialise 204, 420
material use, hierarchy of 31
McDonough, William and Braungart,
        Michael 18–19, 22
metrics, for circularity 40
Michelin 29, 53
Microsoft
    Circular Centers 352
    digital interoperability 53
    Zero Trust strategy 331
Mobile Oil 34
Modern Meadow 31
"Moonlight Project" 9
Morinaga Milk Caramel 8
MTConnect standards 209
multi-life performance 51–52
    assessment 409–10
    collaboration, transparent 374–79
        advanced organizations 377–78
        beginning organizations 376–77
        developing organizations 377
        leading organizations 378–79
        real-world examples 374–75
        stakeholder questions 375–76
    in-market manufacture 203–08
        advanced organizations 207–08
        beginning organizations 205–06
        developing organizations 206–07
        leading organizations 208
        real-world examples 204
        stakeholder questions 204–05

local circulation 287–92
    advanced organizations 291–92
    beginning organizations 289–90
    developing organizations 290–91
    leading organizations 292
    real-world examples 288
    stakeholder questions 288–89
repair at scale 113–19
    advanced organizations 117–18
    beginning organizations 116
    developing organizations 116–17
    leading organizations 118–19
    real-world examples 114
    stakeholder questions 114–15

network orchestration 48, 50–51
    assessment 409
    collaboration, transparent 368–73
        advanced organizations 372
        beginning organizations 370–71
        developing organizations 371–72
        leading organizations 372–73
        real-world examples 369
        stakeholder questions 369–70
    in-market manufacture 197–201
        advanced organizations 200–01
        beginning organizations 199–200
        developing organizations 200
        leading organizations 201–02
        real-world examples 197
        stakeholder questions 198–99
    local circulation 281–86
        advanced organizations 285–86
        beginning organizations 284
        developing organizations 284–85
        leading organizations 286
        real-world examples 282
        stakeholder questions 283–84
    repair at scale 107–12
        advanced organizations 111
        beginning organizations 109–10
        developing organizations 110–11
        leading organizations 112
        real-world examples 107
        stakeholder questions 108–09
New Deal, the 6
NextWave Plastics 304
Nike 9
Nokia 420
    AVA system 364
"not invented here" syndrome 415–16
Novo Nordisk 33

Ocean Plastic Leadership Network 389–90
oil crisis, the 8–9

OPC UA Companion Specifications 209
OPEC oil embargo 9
Oqton 192

P&G 221
packaging, reusable 30
partnerships 415, 417
Patagonia 22, 119, 347
Pauli, Gunter 21, 22
people capabilities 42–45
    see also circular leadership; continuous
        learning; supply chain roles, new
Philips 39
    lighting division 24
    Philips Healthcare
        "circular KPIs" 414
        governance 54
        "innovation hubs" 73
        roles in 44
        team composition 412
        value streams 80
Phoebus cartel 5, 6, 13, 28, 61
pilot projects 413, 417
pitfalls, avoiding 418–20
"planned obsolescence" 5, 28, 61
predictive recovery 49–50
    assessment 409
    collaboration, transparent 363–68
        advanced organizations 367
        beginning organizations 365–66
        developing organizations 366–67
        leading organizations 367–68
        real-world examples 364
        stakeholder questions 364–65
    in-market manufacture 192–97
        advanced organizations 195–96
        beginning organizations 194–95
        developing organizations 195
        leading organizations 196–97
        real-world examples 192
        stakeholder questions 193–94
    local circulation 276–81
        advanced organizations 280–81
        beginning organizations 279
        developing organizations 279–80
        leading organizations 281
        real-world examples 277
        stakeholder questions 277–78
    repair at scale 102–07
        advanced organizations 105–06
        beginning organizations 104–05
        developing organizations 105
        leading organizations 106–07
        real-world examples 102
        stakeholder questions 103–04

process capabilities 45–48
    see also circular value streams; resource
        optimization; smart recovery
Protolabs 159
Provenance 326
Publicis 8

quality assurance 55
    assessment 410
    collaboration, transparent 394–99
        advanced organizations 398
        beginning organizations 397
        developing organizations 397–98
        leading organizations 399
        real-world examples 395
        stakeholder questions 395–96
    in-market manufacture 225–30
        advanced organizations 229–30
        beginning organizations 228
        developing organizations 228–29
        leading organizations 230
        real-world examples 226
        stakeholder questions 227–28
    local circulation 309–14
        advanced organizations 313
        beginning organizations 311–12
        developing organizations 312
        leading organizations 313–14
        real-world examples 309
        stakeholder questions 310–11
    repair at scale 136–41
        advanced organizations 140–41
        beginning organizations 139
        developing organizations 139–40
        leading organizations 141
        real-world examples 137
        stakeholder questions 137–38

Raworth, Kate 20, 22
Reagan, Ronald 9
Reday-Mulvey, Genevieve 18
Redwood Materials 255–56
ReMade Institute 390
Remondis 266
Renault 23–24, 32, 414
Rent the Runway 30
resource optimization 47–48
    assessment 409
    collaboration, transparent 351–56
        advanced organizations 355–56
        beginning organizations 354
        developing organizations 354–55
        leading organizations 356
        real-world examples 352

        stakeholder questions 353–54
    in-market manufacture 181–86
        advanced organizations 184–85
        beginning organizations 183–84
        developing organizations 184
        leading organizations 185–86
        real-world examples 181
        stakeholder questions 182–83
    local circulation 265–70
        advanced organizations 269–70
        beginning organizations 268
        developing organizations 268–69
        leading organizations 270
        real-world examples 266
        stakeholder questions 267–68
    repair at scale 90–95
        advanced organizations 93–94
        beginning organizations 92
        developing organizations 92–93
        leading organizations 94–95
        real-world examples 90
        stakeholder questions 91–92
Responsible Business Alliance 326
Responsible Minerals Initiative 309, 326
roadmap to 2035, the 40–41
roadmap, your 420–21
Rolls-Royce
    digital product lifecycle management
        49, 97
    governance 55
    servitization 29

Saatchi & Saatchi 8
SABIC 422
Saint-Gobain 35
Samsung 142
SAP 52, 282
Schneider Electric 336
Sears 10
secondary markets, building 35–36
servitization 29
Seventh Generation 27
sharing economy, the 29–30
Shaw Industries 18–19
Shinkansen bullet train 21
Siemens
    augmented reality, use of 85
    "digital twins" 97
    Mechatronic Systems Certification
        Program 67
    MindSphere platform 364
    network intelligence, use of 107
    quality assurance 55
Signify 24

Sims Metal Management 250
SKF 51, 114
smart recovery 46–47
    assessment 408–09
    collaboration, transparent 346–51
        advanced organizations 350
        beginning organizations 348–49
        developing organizations 349–50
        leading organizations 350–51
        real-world examples 346–47
        stakeholder questions 347–48
    in-market manufacture 176–81
        advanced organizations 179–80
        beginning organizations 178
        developing organizations 178–79
        leading organizations 180–81
        real-world examples 176
        stakeholder questions 177–78
    local circulation 260–65
        advanced organizations 264–65
        beginning organizations 263
        developing organizations 263–64
        leading organizations 265
        real-world examples 261
        stakeholder questions 261–62
    repair at scale 84–89
        advanced organizations 88–89
        beginning organizations 87
        developing organizations 87–88
        leading organizations 89
        real-world examples 85
        stakeholder questions 85–86
Sourcemap 272
Stahel, Walter 17–18, 22, 29
standards capabilities 51–53
    see also digital interoperability;
        ecosystem collaboration; multi-life
        performance
state income multiplier effect 6
Statoil 33
STEINERT 277
stock market crash, 1929 6
Stratasys 231
Stryker 55
Suez 266
supply chain roles, new 40, 44
    assessment 408
    collaboration, transparent 331–35
        advanced organizations 334–35
        beginning organizations 333
        developing organizations 333–34
        leading organizations 335
        real-world examples 331
        stakeholder questions 332–33
    in-market manufacture 159–64
        advanced organizations 162–63

        beginning organizations 161–62
        developing organizations 162
        leading organizations 163–64
        real-world examples 159
        stakeholder questions 160–61
    local circulation 244–49
        advanced organizations 248
        beginning organizations 247
        developing organizations 247–48
        leading organizations 249
        real-world examples 245
        stakeholder questions 245–46
    repair at scale 67–72
        advanced organizations 71
        beginning organizations 69–70
        developing organizations 70–71
        leading organizations 72
        real-world examples 67
        stakeholder questions 68–69
Sustainable Apparel Coalition 384
Sustainable Packaging Coalition 400

"take-make-waste" 30, 239
team, building your 411–16
    capability building 413
    cross-functional working 413
    "focused flexibility" 415–16
    functional leaders 414
    "hub and spoke" model 412
    stakeholders, engaging 413–14
technology capabilities 48–51
    see also digital product memory; network
        orchestration; predictive recovery
TerraCycle 30, 304, 417
Tesla 336
Thatcher, Margaret 8, 9
three principles, of the circular economy 27
Tide 30
Tokyo Electric alliance 6
Tomra 261, 419
Toyota
    network intelligence, use of 50–51, 107
    resource optimization 90
    Share program 73
    Toyota Production System 10, 124
    water use 34
trade barriers, breaking down of 9
TransparencyOne 369
TrusTrace 326

Uber 29
UL Solutions
    Circularity Facts Program 395
    Environmental Claim Validation 309
Umicore 244, 419–20
Unilever 13

Universal Data Exchange initiative 214
"Use Less, Use Better, Use Forever" 27

value sharing 54–55
  assessment 410
  collaboration, transparent 389–94
    advanced organizations 393
    beginning organizations 391–92
    developing organizations 392–93
    leading organizations 393–94
    real-world examples 389–90
    stakeholder questions 390–91
  in-market manufacture 220–25
    advanced organizations 224
    beginning organizations 222–23
    developing organizations 223–24
    leading organizations 225
    real-world examples 221
    stakeholder questions 221–22
  local circulation 303–09
    advanced organizations 307–08
    beginning organizations 305–06
    developing organizations 306–07
    leading organizations 308–09
    real-world examples 304
    stakeholder questions 304–05
  repair at scale 131–36
    advanced organizations 135
    beginning organizations 133–34
    developing organizations 134
    leading organizations 135–36
    real-world examples 131
    stakeholder questions
      132–33
Velo3D 231
Veolia 250
Verkaufsstelle Vereinigter
    Glühlampenfabriken 5–6
Vestas 49–50, 102, 415
Vitsœ 62
Volkswagen 90
Volvo 47

Walmart 9–10, 331
warranties 64
"waste as resource" 33–34
WeWork 29
Whirlpool 53
World Business Council for Sustainable
    Development 384
World Trade Organization 10
World War II, impact of 7

Xerox 43
Xometry 181

YKK Group 4

ZenRobotics 277, 417
Zero Emissions Research and Initiatives
    (ZERI) network 21
Zipcar 29

Looking for another book?

Explore our award-winning books from global business experts in Logistics, Supply Chain and Operations

Scan the code to browse

www.koganpage.com/logistics

More from Kogan Page

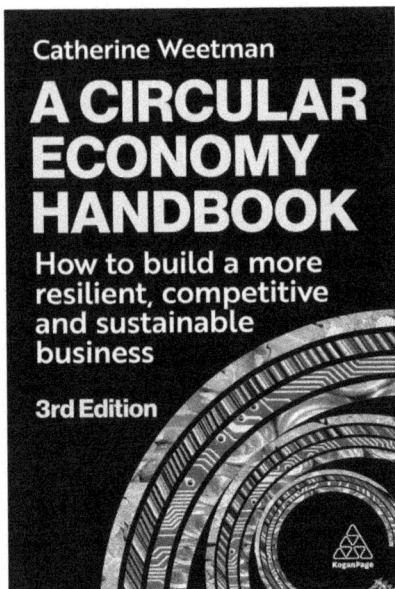

Catherine Weetman

A CIRCULAR ECONOMY HANDBOOK

How to build a more resilient, competitive and sustainable business

3rd Edition

ISBN: 9781398622982

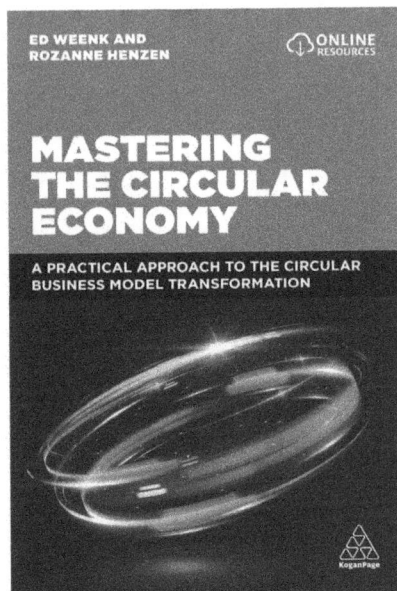

ED WEENK AND ROZANNE HENZEN

ONLINE RESOURCES

MASTERING THE CIRCULAR ECONOMY

A PRACTICAL APPROACH TO THE CIRCULAR BUSINESS MODEL TRANSFORMATION

ISBN: 9781398602748

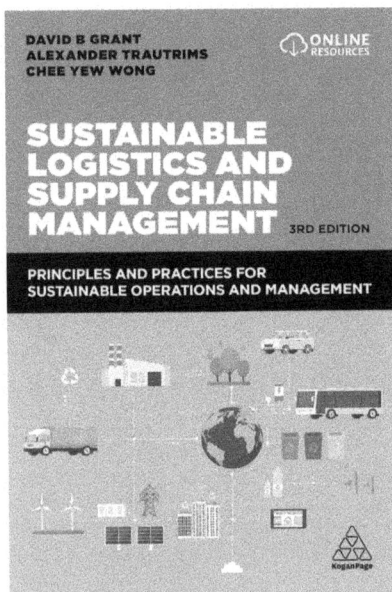

DAVID B GRANT
ALEXANDER TRAUTRIMS
CHEE YEW WONG

ONLINE RESOURCES

SUSTAINABLE LOGISTICS AND SUPPLY CHAIN MANAGEMENT 3RD EDITION

PRINCIPLES AND PRACTICES FOR SUSTAINABLE OPERATIONS AND MANAGEMENT

ISBN: 9781398604438

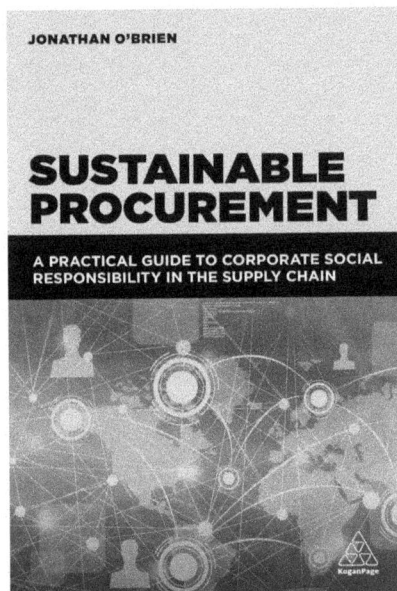

JONATHAN O'BRIEN

SUSTAINABLE PROCUREMENT

A PRACTICAL GUIDE TO CORPORATE SOCIAL RESPONSIBILITY IN THE SUPPLY CHAIN

ISBN: 9781398604681

www.koganpage.com

From 4 December 2025 the EU Responsible Person (GPSR) is:
eucomply oÜ, Pärnu mnt. 139b – 14, 11317 Tallinn, Estonia
www.eucompliancepartner.com

www.ingramcontent.com/pod-product-compliance
Lightning Source LLC
Chambersburg PA
CBHW040913210326
41597CB00030B/5064

9 781398 620674